THE EMPIRE BUILDERS

THE EMPIRE BUILDERS

Inside the Harvard Business School

• • •

J. PAUL MARK

William Morrow and Company, Inc., New York

Library of Congress Cataloging-in-Publication Data

Mark, J. Paul.
    The empire builders.
    Includes index.
    1. Harvard University. Graduate School of Business
School of Business Administration. I. Title.
HF1134.H4.M37   1987   650'.07'117444   87-13064
ISBN 0-688-06962-2

Printed in the United States of America

First Edition

1 2 3 4 5 6 7 8 9 10

BOOK DESIGN BY BARBARA MARKS

PREFACE

Harvard Business School, because it is the richest, most influential, and most prestigious business school in the world, is the subject of much debate, a fact to which the school has not reconciled itself. When the institution comes in for any criticism, the knee-jerk response from the administration is: Here is yet another example of Harvard-bashing.

To hear the school tell it, Harvard Business School is a place where all professors lead happy, scholarly lives, where no one is ever fired or demoted, and where there is but one goal—excellence in academics. The school goes to extreme lengths to avoid the appearance of public controversy, and to control everything that is written about itself. This is a book that the school would prefer not be written. I offer no apologies. I feel compelled to point out only that criticism is often constructive.

You will meet a range of people both inside and outside the school. Whether they constitute a representative sample is impossible for me to say. This book is based on my experiences as a staff member, and on research I did on the school while I was there and after I left. Since the people and events are seen through my eyes, some degree of bias is unavoidable.

By design, this book does not dwell on the intimate aspects of the lives of the people profiled. This does not mean that they have none of the problems that plague others. They do. The concern here is with the business lives of the men and women who educate America's business elite.

CONTENTS

Contents

The
Competitive
Advantage

• • •

Michael Porter stood before his Business Policy I class of eighty-five first-year MBA students and withdrew a football from a crimson athletic kit bag bearing the Harvard logo.

"OK, John," he said tossing the football to a student sitting in the first row. "You're the NFL's quarterback. What's your strategy to beat the USFL?"

The student caught the ball and the class clapped in a mock cheer as Porter turned to take his seat on the edge of a table to start the session.

Porter's plan for the NFL vs. USFL case discussion followed a pattern identical to that in all his other Business

Policy classes. It began with him choosing one student to "open" or lead off for five minutes (in this case the young man to whom Porter tossed the football), and then the class continuing in a lively debate involving nearly every one of the eighty-five students who were present. The NFL case, however, differed from most others in one important respect. Unlike his classes on such topics as the chainsaw industry or the disposable-diaper industry, the NFL case practically scintillated. Where else could students talk about Commissioner Pete Rozelle's legal battles against the United States Football League and get academic credit for it in the process? It was one of the highlights of the semester, and the class jocks came alive in force to present their ideas for solving Rozelle's problems.

"They've got to show that the USFL is just using the lawsuit as a weapon to make money for the owners, instead of trying to build a real football league," said one beefy MBA student. "Their charge that the NFL is a monopoly is . . . is totally trumped up."

Students began laughing at the sarcastic reference to Donald Trump, owner of the New Jersey Generals franchise of the USFL, who was one of the major participants in the lawsuit against the NFL. Porter raised his hand to quiet the class and scowled.

"This isn't a game. This is reality, and if the USFL wins this suit your Sunday afternoon football matches will be as watered down as the beer they serve at the stadium. Now does anyone have any *good* ideas about how to deal with this situation?"

Six hands shot up and Porter pointed to one of them. "Alan, where's the NFL's strategy leading, and where is it vulnerable?"

Porter's student began laying out his analysis of the previous five years of NFL history as he interpreted it from the case study written by Michael Porter, a case that was restricted for use to Porter's Business Policy course.

At the time, none of the students in the class knew that

their professor had anything more than just a passing interest in their analysis of his NFL vs. USFL case study. They believed that Porter had written it to spice up an otherwise bland course. No one knew that Porter's real agenda in writing and teaching the case was to use his students' responses to help him in formulating his own strategy. He was being paid to deliver creative solutions to National Football League executives who had hired him and his consulting firm, Monitor Company. Porter was the coach putting his students through his own drill to see if he could learn any valuable pointers from their fumbles, punts, and touchdown passes.

If the United States Football League hadn't found out that Porter was employed by the National Football League, and hadn't forced Porter and his partner, Mark Fuller, a 1978 Harvard JD/MBA graduate, to testify on their involvement in the antitrust suit, the information might never have been made public that Porter was intentionally using his students to help him in his personal consulting practice. Nevertheless, many of the students who were in the classes never saw the account written by *The New York Times* on May 27, 1986, about Porter's involvement with the National Football League, nor did they see the *Time* magazine coverage of the same story four months later when it was raised in connection with the teaching of business ethics at the school.

Some at HBS argued that it would have made no difference to the students if Porter had mentioned at the beginning of the class that the National Football League paid him to set strategy, and that he intended to use the students' best responses within the body of his report. In fact, they said, he might actually have gotten even better responses had he done so, particularly if he had offered free football tickets to the students with the best strategic analyses.

Porter tried to downplay his involvement in helping the National Football League set strategy, which resulted in a token $1 damage award for the USFL in the summer of

1986. He told *The New York Times* that "I just happened to get invited to give a speech, which I did, and did a moderate amount of tailoring of it to the football industry." What he failed to mention was that the "laundry list" of possible strategies he presented to the NFL executives came mostly from his students, and that the two-session case study he wrote on the NFL vs. USFL became one of the more important industry "modules" in his strategy course. He conceded that "my teaching and consulting are very closely entwined."

Those professors who knew Michael Porter at all had reason to believe that his statement to *The New York Times*, to the effect that his outside consulting activities occupied just 20 percent of his time, was an underestimate. Porter's Monitor Company employed more than one hundred professionals, mostly his former MBA students, and his work on company business often kept him away from his office at HBS for prolonged stretches of time.

Porter's consulting company was the envy of a lot of his colleagues, and the story in the *Times* only increased their jealousy, rather than make them angry at him for using the case-study method for his personal gain and getting caught at it. *Time* magazine, in its September 8, 1986, cover story on Harvard University's 350th anniversary, went so far as to call it an "ethical embarrassment," which distressed Porter and overshadowed the festivities of that year's celebration.

What *The New York Times* and *Time* accused Porter of was a common practice throughout the school, and would probably never have been publicized at all if his work had been with an unglamorous, noncontroversial company, rather than the National Football League. Porter bitterly complained to some of his colleagues that he was unfairly singled out. "There's nothing at all unethical about what I do for companies, unless you call making money for them unethical," he said. Porter felt that he was much more discreet than most professors at the school when it came to using students for ideas in business ventures.

One associate professor of marketing, for example, started a new health-food company that manufactured vitamins, organic products, and protein powder for body builders, and he unabashedly asked his students for information and leads about companies that sold through house parties, such as Tupperware and Mary Kay Cosmetics, which was the method he had decided the company would use to market its products. That was something Porter would never do, although he saw nothing morally or ethically wrong with his colleague doing it. Professors often felt that their consulting and outside business interests gave them material for sharing real business situations with their students, many of whom were eager to know whether their professors could perform as well as teach.

HBS dean John McArthur, too, wondered what all the fuss was about. "It's a tempest in a teapot," he told a faculty meeting. "The issue will blow over when they get tired of telling each other the same stories." The school's public relations firm, Hill and Knowlton, was instructed to continue publicizing the positive stories coming from the school, including the teaching of entrepreneurial studies, the mandatory use of personal computers in the MBA curriculum, and the sponsoring of seminars on international competitiveness.

Porter took care of himself. He dodged sensitive questions from the *Times* reporter about his consulting company and the NFL trial, and moved the topic of conversation to his research on Japanese competition. The May 29, 1986, article concluded with a summary of Porter's research, and his analysis of America's trade imbalance: "Just because the dollar goes down and interest rates fall, we are not going to solve the underlying problem [of competing with the Japanese]." This artful misdirection prompted Professor Joseph Bower, whose office was directly across from Porter's in Morgan Hall, to say to him, "You certainly charmed the fangs off the snake."

PART I

NOTABLES OF HARVARD BUSINESS SCHOOL

. . .

CHAPTER 1

The Organization

• • •

The year 1988 will mark the eightieth anniversary of the founding of Harvard Business School in Harvard Yard, and the sixtieth anniversary of the building of the school's campus at Soldiers Field, across the Charles River from the main Harvard campus. Only two token links remain between Harvard Business School and the university, reminders that the schools were once physically joined.

The first is an oval conference table from the Harvard president's office, which became a part of the business-school dean's permanent collection of office furniture. The second is a bell from Harvard Yard, which was placed in the bell tower of Baker Library at the very center of campus. The bell, hidden from view, is seldom rung, but the bell tower is a prominent feature of the campus. Indeed, for a long time, it was the only bell tower at Harvard that was entirely gold-leafed. David Kuechle, a professor at Harvard's Graduate School of Education, and a graduate of Harvard Business School, once commented on this unique feature by saying simply, "It is no accident that the bell tower at Harvard Business School is gold."

Other graduate schools at Harvard exist mainly to educate; the business school's mission is to educate and to make money. In many ways the school has become its own model of business efficiency. It makes and accumulates money by investing in long-term research and development and by courting America's largest and most powerful corporations.

Financially, its success has grown with succeeding generations, and has rapidly outstripped all other graduate schools at Harvard except the medical school. The law school, by comparison, which had more students enrolled in degree programs than the business school in 1986, had net income that year of $30 million, a third of the business school's. Only the medical school, with its large endowments that support medical research, had higher net income ($120 million).

What Harvard Business School does organizationally today is not materially different from what other graduate schools of business do, except that HBS does it better and at a higher level. Other schools send faculty out to do research in corporate America; HBS invented a method for systematically getting inside companies for long periods of time. Other schools have executive-training programs to instruct midcareer managers; HBS runs a dozen specialized programs, which then give participants the benefits of being Harvard alumni. Other schools have newsletters and clubs to communicate with their graduates; HBS spends millions of dollars to organize and sponsor alumni associations whose purpose is to raise more money for HBS.

There are many people who say that Harvard Business

School is the top business school in the world, and it is by almost any objective method of determining such rankings. The school's alumni occupy more positions of power in corporations worldwide than any other, the school spends more on business research than any other, the school's business library is larger than any other, the school's endowment is larger than any other, and so on.

Some may ask whether the quality of instruction is materially better, or whether the school's faculty members are as dedicated or talented as their counterparts at other schools, or whether HBS graduates are as compassionate or moral as those of other business schools. The answers to those questions will not be found in this book. Here the emphasis is on the bottom line: how HBS gets results.

THE CASE METHOD RULES

Many people who claim some prior exposure to, and knowledge of, cases and the case method at Harvard Business School may still not completely understand what cases are, what they are used for, or how they come into being.

Simply stated, a Harvard Business School case study is a written description of any business situation. Students are told to put themselves in the position of decision maker, and they are graded on how intelligently they argue their point of view.

Cases range anywhere from one page to fifty pages in length, and cover a broad spectrum of topics relating to business. Each case is supposed to be a self-contained unit, giving the student exactly what he needs to know, and no more. They're all printed under the Harvard Business School logo, with an author, copyright, and disclaimer statement at the bottom of page one. The disclaimer states that the case is solely for educational purposes and does not describe either effective or ineffective management techniques. There is often a similarity in the way cases are logically constructed, which is known as the "Christensen Method," after Professor C. Roland Christensen, who standardized case research and writing. Professor Christensen is Harvard's leading proponent of the case method throughout the university, and while he used to monitor nearly all cases at the business school, these days no single person or review board exercises editorial control over the final case products.

Ken Auletta, a business author and columnist, wrote *The Art of Corporate Success* in 1984 about Schlumberger Limited and Jean Riboud, the chairman of the French oil service company, which grew out of a series of articles published by the *New Yorker* magazine. An HBS professor, Francis J. Aguilar, who read those articles, liked them so well that he, in turn, excerpted them and portions of the book for a case study. The case, "Schlumberger," was first used in 1985 by Professor Jay Lorsch in the Advanced Management Program (a program that instructs senior corporate executives), where it received good reviews—in fact, too good. One student (who failed to notice Auletta's name below that of the professor who had edited the material) asked Lorsch why other HBS case studies weren't as interesting or as well written as "Schlumberger," to which an irritated Lorsch replied, "Because it wasn't written by a Harvard professor." The following year "Schlumberger" was dropped from the Advanced Management Program curriculum mainly because it made the "real" Harvard cases look bad.

Although the business school spends millions of dollars annually to develop its own case studies, cases come from all kinds of sources, including directly from *Fortune, Forbes, Business Week, The Wall Street Journal, The New York Times*, and a variety of books, including *Iacocca* and *In Search of Excellence*. There is nothing especially magical about a case; with minimal preparation many people can, and do, read, analyze, and write them. Students will state honestly that, with few exceptions, Harvard's case studies are a bit too long, a bit too dull, and a bit too vague.

Other people besides just the professors at Harvard Business School write cases also. Occasionally MBA students write cases about a real business situation of their choice for academic credit. Their instructors in these instances are the sole editors; the school publishes anything deemed worthy by the instructor.

More frequently, however, cases are written either by Harvard DBA (doctor of business administration) students or by staff researchers who have a variety of titles. Researchers are not required to have a Harvard degree, though many do, but all have at least one master's degree. They are hired by individual professors, often directly from the ranks of the MBA program, and they usually spend one or two years on the job before either going into the DBA program, for which they can receive academic credit for the time they spent doing research, or into private industry. Researchers receive salaries that are much lower than what they could get elsewhere (starting at $18,000 per year), with the exception of one special class of researcher known as the "Baker Scholar."

The *Baker Scholar* designation is one that is given only to students enrolled in Harvard's MBA program, and, by definition, indicates a student who has graduated in the top 5 percent of his class. It is equivalent to the *summa cum laude* appellation given by other schools. Baker Scholars command the highest starting salaries of any HBS graduates, and few stay on campus after graduation to work at the school. Those who do stay are accorded very good treatment.

A top student from Stanford or Wharton business schools could, if he was hired by a professor, join HBS as an "associate in research," which is the same title given to Baker Scholars when they join the staff. However, a Baker Scholar would always earn at least twice as much as his Stanford or Wharton colleague, even though they are doing exactly the same type of work. It is the school's way of recruiting MBAs from within, filling the DBA program with its own top students.

After a year of research, most go into the doctoral program, after which they vie for a spot on the faculty, if there are openings. If not, there are always a number of postdoctoral fellowships that remain unfilled each year. The career path is the same for a Baker Scholar's classmate who may have graduated in the middle or bottom of the class, except that the perks for Baker Scholars are a good deal better; they include private offices, faculty mentors, and expense accounts. The school considers itself lucky to get two of the thirty-five to forty Baker Scholars who graduate each year from the MBA program to continue in the DBA program.

One of the most popular misconceptions about HBS cases, which is perpetuated by the school itself, is that there are no "right" or "wrong" answers to cases. As stated in the 1987 MBA admissions catalog, "Harvard cases typically do not have single outcomes or 'approved solutions.' Consequently, the discussion of these cases trains students to make decisions, develop implementation plans, and to explain and defend their actions." When visitors are present in the classroom, professors draw attention to the disclaimer printed on all cases that basically states that HBS is a purely neutral observer.

Regardless of what is said, approved solutions to many cases do exist. Authors of case studies often write a companion document to the case called a "teaching note," which tells instructors how to teach the case, what questions to ask, and what answers to accept. With few exceptions, instructors follow the guidelines set forth in the teaching note when one is available. Students are never permitted to see the teaching notes, and an elaborate system was invented to keep them from falling into students' hands.

Newer professors or instructors, while still following the note, often espouse the purist idea of there being no right or wrong answers, even when one is plainly stated. But seasoned professors often look only for the single right answer. When two different class sections discuss the same case minutes apart, the veteran professors are the ones who complain to each other about how the answer got "leaked" to the second section during the break. Andrall Pearson, who came to Harvard Business School from Pepsico, leaned more toward the center on this issue than his younger colleagues when he told his MBA class, "There may not be any 'right' answers to these cases, but I sure as hell know a 'wrong' answer when I hear one."

Later chapters describe specifically how and why several cases came to be written, but, generally speaking, the more senior a professor is who works on a case, the stronger the agenda is behind it. Student cases are written for academic credit; associates in research and doctoral students write cases to get promoted; assistant professors sometimes write cases given to them by full professors, but usually they write just to be published. Associates and full professors write cases for a variety of reasons, including interfaculty favors, consulting assignments, academic power (i.e., to get research dollars for other projects), academic prestige (i.e., to be on the leading edge of a new trend), theoretical research, or just to reach an arbitrarily set personal quota.

Two kinds of cases exist—field-based and library-based, as noted on the front page of each case. Field cases stem from a case writer's visit to a company, or a telephone call to someone at a company. Library cases, on the other hand, are put together from journals, periodicals, and "general experience," and are often called "armchair" cases.

While there's no particular stigma attached to armchair cases, most professors would prefer students and other faculty to believe they do a tremendous amount of fieldwork. Consequently, they will often make the single phone call that turns an armchair case into a field case. Professors Michael Porter and Ted Levitt rarely do armchair cases, and they set the standard that others want to follow.

Budgets to do research and write cases come from two places: the Division of Research, which is controlled by the dean, or directly from the dean. Until 1986, the division was managed by one industrial-marketing professor, but now that budgetary power is nominally divided among four senior professors who advise the dean on who should get what from the division's accounts. Field research is expensive, and HBS usually picks up the entire tab for case development; while there is never any shortage of funds, certain projects have priority.

Ultimately the dean decides what the school's priorities are, which makes him the single most powerful man at the school. Many professors, especially junior professors, curry favor with him to get money for their research. If it were publicly available, the dean's list of research projects in progress, detailing the amount of money allocated to each by professor, would readily show which junior faculty were slated for promotion. Needless to say, such a list is never circulated.

The bulk of cases are written by researchers and junior faculty, and fewer and fewer cases are written by the more senior professors going up the organization by rank. Some professors claim to write four cases a year, every year. However, it is not always possible to determine direct authorship of a case study simply by looking at the name on the cover page. As in all areas of academia, many senior scholars are along for the ride. Staff researchers often work for three months on a case, hand it to their faculty supervisor, and find that the published case lists the faculty supervisor as the first author. Workers in the Division of Case Services (which distributes, prints, and stores cases) claim that more than half the time the professor whose name is on a case has had little or nothing to do with writing or researching it. No studies have been done to discover the accuracy of this claim, but such practices are commonplace. The system works, and rarely does anyone complain.

Most research takes place in a think tank called "Baker 400," located on the top floor of Baker Library. There, in small cubicles, forty to sixty researchers pore through field notes, documents, journals, and tapes, and produce hundreds of new cases every year. Standard issue is a telephone, a typewriter, an HBS officer directory, and a library card. Each researcher's faculty supervisor tells him or her what to research and when to have the product ready. Once initial drafts are completed, they are handed over to specialized departments at the school for typing, proofing, artwork, and so forth. There is even a specialized department at HBS whose single job is to assign a number to each case.

Unlike news articles, cases make no claims to be entirely unbiased. It often happens that companies agree to have a case written, only to become dismayed at the final result. In those instances, they have been known to do their own editing and rewriting to present a more balanced picture. If that still isn't satisfactory, the company has three options, according to the school's official protocol: HBS will either scrap the case entirely, or agree to teach the case only with a company representative present, or allow the case to be used just once.

Usually companies opt to cancel everything. As one senior executive said, "There's no reason to put Band-Aids on him when the patient is dead." Researchers and professors then attempt to get permission to write a "disguised case," in which the names, dates, industry, and financial numbers are selectively changed. Again, according to protocol, disguised case studies must still be approved by the companies about which they were originally written.

Disguises range from changing every important detail to changing nothing. An ancient HBS trick is for the writer to state on the first page of the case that numbers have been disguised, when in fact they haven't. Competitors sometimes get copies of cases and are amazed by what is openly revealed. It is as if Harvard has tailored a suit that is visible only to students. To everyone else, the company is seen naked.

A marketing professor at the University of Chicago

business school, who was very enthusiastic about the HBS case method, wrote several of his own cases that were modeled on Harvard's. It was his hope, he said, that his would be as tightly crafted and intricate as Harvard's best—which always contained misleading statements, false numbers, and obscure language to throw students intentionally off the scent. The clever students were expected to cut through the morass of disinformation.

One of the directives that case writers are occasionally asked to observe is to use as many examples of successful women and minorities in business as possible. Student groups on campus, especially the Women's Student Association, have often voiced dissatisfaction with the school's administration over the fact that there were too many cases featuring white, upper-middle-class, male executives. Equal representation is never given high priority at the school, probably because those few students who complain are too busy with their classwork and job search to try to mount an effective and sustained campaign. Course heads, who are in most instances white males, can do little to change the imbalance if they want to. Thousands of cases, dating back to the early 1930s, backlog the system and act as both strong impediments and deterrents to change.

Once new cases are taught in the classroom, they either become part of the core curriculum or they're dropped. Most cases get one chance to make it. The Division of Case Services keeps track of sales figures and prints a catalog of several thousand cases, denoting some as "bestsellers" (a designation that brings honor rather than money). The catalog encourages sales from other schools, but does not help to promote new cases within HBS. Word of mouth alone is what makes or breaks a case's chances; instructors often agree to teach a new case based solely on the recommendation of a trusted adviser.

Professors usually prefer to teach cases that they either once used as students or developed directly or indirectly. Professor Michael Porter, for example, uses several key cases in his Competitive Analysis course that he authored or co-authored, combined with a few strategy "classics" sprinkled in. In this way, because he knows the material so well, class preparation time is cut to a minimum, which is an important consideration for Porter and several other highly paid consultant-professors.

The goal in teaching case studies is for students to test each other's ideas, and in so doing, to learn from one another rather than from an instructor. Professor Jack Gabarro said that his concept of the "ultimate" case discussion would be one in which he would appoint a student to lead off, and then let students build on each other's ideas until some logical conclusion was reached. At that point he, the instructor, would dismiss the enlightened class without ever having had to speak a single word. It never happens that way.

Typically, a student will lead off the class by stating his solution to the case's particular problem, and then find himself verbally surrounded by a dozen or more classmates who try to impress the instructor with their knowledge and abilities. The instructor then attempts to prompt the right answers from the class by asking the right questions, hoping that by the time the session ends the class will get the point. If not, it's all laid out in the last five minutes. When the opposite happens and the solution is revealed too early, the rest of the class period is spent on meaningless side issues.

Thousands of brilliant students have learned by the case method, and thousands of them swear by its usefulness. Dozens of chief executives of major corporations return annually to their alma mater to praise the rigorous method that taught them to think and analyze. If testimonials are valid indicators of success, Harvard's teaching methods must be considered successful.

But considering that books, magazine articles, newspaper articles, and consulting reports, all written by non-Harvard-Business-School-trained authors, have successfully been turned into cases, perhaps it is the method that works rather than the cases by themselves. Case discussions force students to think fast on their feet, a skill that stays with them long after they learn it.

Whether eighty-five highly motivated and intelligent Harvard MBA students could get together with instructors for two years and discuss just articles from *The Wall Street Journal, Forbes, Fortune, Business Week,* and other business journals and come out as well as their counterparts using Harvard cases, remains a debatable question.

THE INNER WORKINGS

As at most professional schools, promotion to the tenured ranks of HBS is based primarily on the caliber of research, rather than on excellence in teaching or dedication to the needs of students. Many outstanding and popular associate professors have been denied promotion to the rank of full professor at Harvard Business School because they failed to meet the criteria established by the tenure review committee, namely a "substantive contribution to their field." The criteria are vague enough so that all but the most remarkable candidate (e.g., a Michael Porter) can be excluded from further contention by simply not getting along with someone influential at the school.

Teaching ability is not stressed or even required, and several full professors have not had to set foot in a classroom for years. For them, the school lends its prestigious letterhead to their written products, and they, in turn, add more prestige to the HBS name through their brilliance. Students simply aren't factored into the equation.

Whether or not the professors are good teachers, HBS is still a great institution to attend. The school can afford to, and does, spend more money on facilities and maintenance than some schools spend on faculty salaries. Baker Library is certainly the finest business-school library in the United States. And thanks to a vigorous rehabilitation program, the student dormitories are comfortable and well maintained. What most students notice, especially the executive students, is that things get done. If someone complains that a chair is broken, or that an electrical outlet doesn't work, it gets fixed immediately. The school is remarkably efficient at taking care of the small details, which makes life easier for students and faculty.

Different levels of service are provided to the different student groups, of course, and the double standard has existed for decades. The executive students, particularly the Advanced Management Program students (AMPs), are taken care of first and foremost. The AMPs have first-rate living accommodations and dining facilities separate from the rest of the campus, as well as modern classrooms that have seats designed for comfort. The fact that each AMP student's company pays tuition of $20,000 for the employee to attend the thirteen-week course has a lot to do with the amenities that are provided.

The faculty and staff also enjoy the benefits of working in a place where budgets are apparently unlimited. For example, when Professor Richard Vietor wanted a film crew to come in and tape a presentation by economist Alfred Kahn on airline deregulation, he didn't have to ask how much it would cost to get the job done. In fact, the tally came to something around $10,000, but the professor never saw the bill. The audio-visual department sent the expense report to the comptroller's office for automatic payment.

The pleasant physical surroundings and the tremendously efficient support staff of the school do not make the training at HBS less rigorous. Stories that students tell about ferocious competition and overwhelming demands on time are for the most part accurate. The school makes its programs intentionally tough, and enforces a mandatory curve in grading MBA students in which the bottom 10 percent of each class fails. Thus, students are compelled to work hard in order not to fail, rather than to succeed.

But because the programs are so hard, the prestige so

alluring, and the rewards for getting through so great, only the very best students are successful there. It is for those reasons, not because of the faculty or the facilities, that so many top students apply for admission to the school.

THE THREE BIG DAYS IN THE HBS CALENDAR

MBA Commencement

As spring turns into summer at the Soldiers Field campus of Harvard Business School, fewer and fewer MBA students are seen walking about. The 780 first-year students are there because they have to be, but second-year students, many with firm job offers in hand, take their final exams in early May and spend their last few weeks as Harvard Business School students away from campus—working on independent course projects, preparing to start new jobs, or taking vacations.

Quite suddenly in late May, after the first-year students take their exams and leave, workers begin the annual ritual of assembling the graduation platform in front of Aldrich Hall on the open field between the Dean's House and Baker Library. New sod is laid down, fresh paint is applied to touch up chipped woodwork on buildings, and fresh flowers are planted in flower beds all around the campus, especially around the graduation stage. In a matter of two weeks, the entire campus is resplendent.

In the first week of June, the campus begins to fill up again with second-year students, who load their possessions into cars, sunbathe on the lush green lawns, and stage extravagant beer parties up to the eve of graduation. Graduation day, according to veterans, is usually a little subdued if for no other reason than that the students are mostly "partied-out." The main Harvard commencement takes place in Harvard Yard, where the entire university congregates first, but the MBA diplomas are handed out at the business school campus, and that's what parents and students come for.

The dean is usually one of the first arrivals from Harvard Yard, walking in full academic regalia over the Weeks Bridge to the back side of the HBS campus. As is his custom, he confers with the other business school deans on the podium to make certain that no last-minute hitches occur.

One by one the faculty, staff, and operations people emerge from the buildings to take up strategic viewing positions along the perimeter of the seating area. Professor Ted Levitt, looking dapper in a plaid sport coat, mingles with the arriving parents, giving them both evidence that one of the legends of Harvard Business School exists, and material for stories to tell their grandchildren. Students nervously wander around trying to find their seats, and take one last look at the place that caused them so much anxiety. Looks nice.

The ceremony begins, the deans' speeches are made, 780 names are read off (each one applauded by a private cheering section despite requests to the contrary), and diplomas are handed out. An hour and a half later, it's over. Most of the faculty, including Ted Levitt, leave early, as soon as the names are called, to go back to their offices.

The next day, the stage is dismantled and the (rented) flowers are dug up and taken back to the nursery for later use.

Classes Begin for MBA Students

In early September, the signs that a new academic year has arrived appear first in the parking lot behind Aldrich Hall. It is there that one notices the diversity in economic status among members of the entering class. Prosperous MBA students roll up in new Porsches or BMWs, while their less well-heeled classmates, squeezed in with an odd assortment of personal belongings, climb out of weather-beaten Japanese cars.

The social schedule during the first week usually in-

cludes at least one party per night, where students try to
meet as many of their classmates as possible, mainly to
assure themselves that they are all equally formidable. In
recent years, Boston newspapers have been sending reporters to cover the events and interview the cream of
the crop of American MBA students, and the media attention invariably adds an extra amount of excitement to
orientation.

In preparation for the first day of class, the faculty
undergoes a profound change in appearance. Whereas
during the summer khakis and sport coats are the norm,
few male professors are ever seen after September 1 in
anything except dark, high-authority suits. They are highly
visible, which makes them seem all the more intimidating as they walk the campus.

A little fear goes a long way toward pulling a new group
of raw recruits into line. Organizational Behavior professor Jack Gabarro, one of the shortest male faculty members at HBS, described his method for getting the proper
amount of respect on the first day: "First of all, I'm actually a teddy bear. Not only do I give the appearance of
being a teddy bear, but deep down I really am. That's
why I have to be as lethal and as threatening as possible
during that first session.

"I've found that if I fail to put the right amount of fear
in them—if they see through me and discover that I really
am a teddy bear—then I've lost the game for the entire
semester. But if I get in and really make them sweat that
first day, then I can ease off later on and just be myself
without losing control.

"What I do in the first session is to go in for the jugu-
lar. I'll find the guy who comes to class having read the
case just once, or, better, not at all, and I'll unmercifully
tear him apart as an example to all the others. I become
a real S.O.B.—I mean I can't even stand myself. My students learn not necessarily to hate me, if I can help it,
but to quake at the thought of what I can do if they slack

off. Maybe it's different for finance professors or M.E. [Managerial Economics] professors who teach what are considered here to be 'hard' courses. But O.B. [Organizational Behavior] has this reputation for being 'soft' so I've got to quickly disabuse them of the notion that it is."

Classes Begin For AMPs

The third big day in the academic year takes place in mid-September, when the first session* of the Advanced Management Program begins. Although all 140 AMPs go through only a thirteen-week program that awards each a certificate, rather than a degree, they are accorded the same rights, privileges, and respect as all other Harvard Business School alumni. AMPs are listed in the alumni directory, attend school reunions, and participate in all alumni activities along with MBAs.

The Advanced Management Program is popular with some of the world's largest corporations, many of whom keep their own waiting lists of suitable company candidates who hope, eventually, to attend. More so than the MBA program, it tends to be heavily dominated by men. (Only 19 out of 287 total AMP participants in 1985 were women.)

The AMPs always arrive in a grander style than the MBA students. The parking and entrance areas are well marked out for them with road signs that point them in the direction of Baker Hall, where they live and work. In addition, extra staff are on hand to take care of luggage and answer any questions that may arise.

Like MBA students, the AMPs have their own automobile status symbols to separate the class by economic level. In 1985, for example, one participant drove up in his $100,000 1955 Mercedes-Benz 300SL Gullwing sports car from New York, and parked it prominently in front of the guardhouse of the parking lot, where it received twenty-

---

* The AMP runs two sessions. The first, beginning in mid-September, is always accompanied by more fanfare than the second, which begins in early February.

four-hour protection. Several of his classmates got rides on weekends, which presumably made him one of the more popular members of that class.

Because AMPs are outnumbered by MBA students by ten to one on campus, the latter are all but oblivious to the middle-aged executives who amble about in their space. The same cannot be said of the faculty, who are keenly aware of the arrival of the AMPs. Most go out of their way to be as friendly as possible to the men who wear the distinctive white name tags on their suit coats.

The first day of class for AMPs differs considerably from that of the MBA students. In many respects it takes on the upbeat mood of a party as students are told that they are there not to compete for grades, but rather to learn from the hundreds of years of cumulative work experience they have between themselves. They're instructed to cheer for each other, to help each other out in dealing with problems, and to work together in teams. Rather than use fear as a motivator, professors usually try to make the entire experience very positive.

None of the faculty who teach in the AMP are inexperienced. The school sends its most seasoned men into the classroom. Whereas the MBA students are often taught by assistant professors, or even doctoral students, the AMPs rarely see anyone outside of tenured, full professors with twenty years of teaching experience behind them. The AMPs pay a lot more, and they get a lot more for their money.

AMP class materials are the best also. In one instance, the chief administrator of the Advanced Management Program was told that a new case (which had not yet been distributed) contained a single typographical error in one of the financial statements. Rather than distribute the cases with an errata sheet, as would have been done in the MBA program, the administrator elected to throw away all the cases on hand (which had cost more than $300 to print, collate, and bind) and rush into print a new, corrected version for an additional $600.

CHAPTER 2

The
Strategy
Master

• • •

Michael Porter was panic-stricken. Someone had stolen his briefcase, he was sure, because there was no trace of it anywhere. It was gone. Two months of agonizing effort on a working paper, and irreplaceable interview notes, were in there, and now someone had conspired to remove the briefcase, and the documents, probably for use in a rival's research project.

"Still no sign of it, Professor Porter," reported his secretary. "I called the campus police and they're searching the grounds."

Porter was shaking—beads of sweat began to form over the rims of his glasses. "You tell those bastards to find it," he yelled with a rage that could no longer be controlled. It was an irrational outburst by a man who prided himself on his cool, analytical, systematic, and entirely rational approach to problem solving.

He swept across the second-floor Morgan Hall corridor into his office and violently slammed the door. Inside, and alone, he vented his frustration by grabbing haphazard volumes from his bookcase and hurling them at the wall— a *thud, thud, thud* became audible well down the hall.

Then, suddenly, he noticed in the corner of his office, where he stockpiled six cases of diet cola, a swatch of brown leather hidden behind the cans. A moment later he emerged from his office, clutching the prize to his chest and beaming with victory. Terror had melted away in the moment of discovery, and his professorial demeanor returned.

Michael Porter was driven, and always had been for as long as anyone could remember. Even upon making tenure, an accomplishment that assured continual employment at Harvard Business School and often had the effect of mellowing the recipient, he continued a frantic pace to do more.

Porter was born in Ann Arbor, Michigan, but grew up in Asia and Europe, where has father, an army colonel, was stationed. He distinguished himself early in two areas: golf and mathematics. That combination helped him to gain admission in 1965 to Princeton University, where he studied mechanical and aerospace engineering. He gravitated toward the conservative side of Princeton and, in spite of campus unrest and anti–Vietnam War activities going on about him, joined the army reserve, eventually rising to the rank of captain.

His was a quiet, serious, and determined life, not over-concerned with the currents of political change around him. He joined the golf team and won every major Eastern collegiate golf tournament he entered; in 1968 he was named to the NCAA Golf All-American Team. Porter excelled at everything he did, seemingly without effort, and his extraordinary ability attracted a circle of admirers around him both on and off the athletic field.

In 1969, he graduated with high honors from Princeton with a bachelor of science degree and entertained thoughts of becoming a professional golfer. Burton Malkiel, then chairman of Princeton's economics department, saw in Porter a potentially brilliant academician, and it was he who steered Porter toward Harvard's MBA program.

At Harvard, Porter finally came into his own intellectually. Surrounded by rivals from Harvard, Yale, Dartmouth, and Princeton, he began to see himself as the brightest of them all. It was not conceit that made him believe that; rather, it was the ease with which he cut through the feeble arguments of his classmates. However, he was terrified of speaking in class. More often than not he chose to sit silently watching classmates flounder in ignorance, rather than crack open a case and put an end to their misery. When he did speak, his comments were by far the most insightful of anyone there, and despite his spotty record in class participation, a factor that comprised 60 percent of some course grades, Porter still graduated as a Baker Scholar at the top of his class.

The intellectual stimulation of academic life agreed with him, and he stayed at Harvard to get a Ph.D. in business economics. With single-minded determination he cut the time required to earn the degree to just two years, and afterward was invited to join the faculties of both the Department of Economics and the business school. The dual appointment gave him a unique vantage point that led him to conclude two things: first, that the business school had no systematic method for categorizing and classifying information the way that economists did; and second, that a niche existed in the overlapping area of business and economics where he could apply economic principles to business situations.

The immediate acceptance of his new ideas surprised even Porter. He had methodically staked out his own area of expertise, expecting to receive some notoriety in the process. But suddenly in 1977 he became the epitome of a brash, talented, new generation of academics at Harvard. In droves, senior professors sought him out for advice and information. Lucrative consulting assignments were offered to him with increasing regularity. Invitations of all kinds, from board memberships to country-club memberships, poured in. "Mike, can we get together tomorrow afternoon to discuss that new case?" It was always a ruse to get him alone for an hour to put his enormous brain power to work on their problems.

In 1981, at his elevation to a tenured, full professorship, Porter finally declared an end to his accessibility. He felt he had been used long enough, and he could not tolerate having the "brain drainers," as he referred to professors who ate up his valuable time, taking advantage of, and capitalizing on, his powers of analysis. He stopped eating at the faculty-club dining room, he did not return phone calls, and he adamantly refused to be waylaid. He became, by choice and for self-preservation, a loner on campus.

The inspiration to start his own consulting firm came when he realized that his private consulting work was requiring an increasing amount of time to manage. The methodical side of Porter longed for structure that would organize the disparate projects he was called upon to do. By opening his own firm in an office away from the business school, he could keep the two sides of his life separate. He began by recruiting some of his students, who might otherwise have gone to such prestigious management-consulting firms as Bain & Company or McKinsey & Company, and offered them equity positions in his new company, Monitor.

At first his clients were hesitant to allow him to bring in recent MBAs to work on their problems. They wanted Porter, not a Harvard MBA, and they were willing to pay more than $10,000 per day to get him there, alone. Porter argued that his former students were bright, energetic, trained by him, and hand-picked because of their stra-

tegic thinking abilities. The combination of Porter's tu-
telage and his students' sweat would produce superior results that would more than justify his exorbitant rates.
Besides, Porter had offered them no alternative. Either
they hired Monitor Company, or they hired another consultant.

The company's income more than doubled each year
for the first five years. Yet even the phenomenal success
of the venture, and the publication of a widely acclaimed
strategy book, *Competitive Strategy*, left Porter bored. The
challenge had always been to make a lot of money, but
now that goal began to lose its appeal. He had indulged
his passion for modern art by spending more than $1 mil-
lion to decorate his house with modern sculpture and
paintings. He had even restored a Victorian mansion in
Cambridge, and had installed a Jacuzzi bath in a third-
floor tower overlooking the city.

THE PRESIDENTIAL COMMISSION

Porter confided his growing discontent to his friend John
Young, president of Hewlett-Packard (for which Porter had
done consulting work), who was sympathetic. Young had
just been appointed by President Reagan chairman of a
new presidential commission on industrial competitiveness, whose charter was to identify those areas of the
American economy that might benefit from government
regulation or deregulation. The commission was to cut
through the bureaucracy of government and make recommendations that would have far-reaching effects on the
industrial stability of America.

Without hesitation, Young offered Porter a seat on the
commission and convinced him that it would give him a
vehicle for accomplishing something beyond the narrow
confines of academics and consulting. Government was
an entirely unexplored frontier for him, and one that was
worthy of his talents.

Twenty business leaders and academics were recommended to President Reagan, who accepted the list and officially made the appointments on August 5, 1983. In addition to Porter and Young, other members of the commission included Robert Anderson, CEO of Rockwell International, Dimitri V. D'Arbeloff, CEO of Millipore, Mark Shepherd, Jr., CEO of Texas Instruments, and Ian Ross, president of Bell Labs. Each member was designated chairman of his or her sector. Porter headed up the general category on industrial competitiveness; others headed up sectors that included labor, manufacturing, and technology.

Commission members served at no salary and were expected to appoint one or more employees from their company or organization to work full time on the project. D'Arbeloff, who like most others spent only nominal time heading up his sector, brought two of his senior executives to Washington for a year to conduct interviews and write reports for him. He based his recommendations on their findings. Porter, on the other hand, immediately recognized the potential of the position and petitioned to Dean McArthur to allow him the full access to the student brain trust of Harvard Business School, a request that McArthur eagerly accepted.

Porter established twelve subcategories within the industrial-competitiveness sector and set up a selective admissions process to attract twenty-four of the best students at HBS to work, for free, on his part of the commission report. Of those that were selected, almost half later graduated as Baker Scholars, and the others, all from the top quarter of their class, had specific industry expertise.

Washington quickly lost its appeal for Michael Porter. He had attended meetings of the commission expecting that the force of his personality would turn the machinery of government, but instead he found that bureaucrats shared the same undesirable traits as academics. His chief administrator, a German who was appointed by the commission, often attempted to engage him in mindless debate over economic issues, so Porter learned to avoid him completely. Others on the commission preferred the social and status-related aspects of the appointment to the tough intellectual fourteen-hour days he was putting in.

At Washington parties, Porter invariably found himself talking to the most senior executive in the group, with whom he enjoyed sparring over issues of national importance. His capacity to sit still for prolonged periods, however, was directly related to the sophistication of the person sitting opposite him. He had a very low tolerance for people who could not grasp complicated problems of management and policy. Small talk was out. If someone bored him, Porter said so, rather bluntly, as if the mere assertion of the condition would improve the conversation.

When it became clear that he could not work with the administrator chosen by the commission, Porter called in a former student from Los Angeles, Eric Evans, to take over the administrative duties. Evans, a Harvard JD/MBA who spoke fluent Japanese and dressed in meticulous pinstriped suits, was Porter's protégé and the only other person, besides Porter, who had authority to make decisions. That he could have spent his time working more profitably elsewhere was impressed upon everyone by Porter's solicitous demeanor toward him. But Evans had the level of sacrifice and dedication that was expected. The fact that Porter could find a JD/MBA to do mundane scheduling for him only added to his own reputation.

For four months, Harvard Business School paid the entire cost of Porter's research. Students involved in the project were permitted to travel anywhere within the United States and telephone whomever they liked, so long as they distilled their information into concise twenty-page reports. When it was over, in May 1984, they presented their findings for two days to a group of top executives and government officials who were invited to HBS by Porter for the occasion.

Sitting in a basement lecture hall for nine hours each

day, "mainlining information," as one executive put it, left Porter in an almost euphoric state. His students had, collectively, shifted through thousands of government reports and interviewed hundreds of government officials, past and present. Each report could have exceeded two hundred pages including exhibits, but Porter got only pure, distilled information. He prepared complex questions to plumb the depths of the students' grasp of the information. He challenged basic assumptions, and suggested his invited panel of experts do the same. They, who had spent entire careers in the field, matched wits with Harvard's elite.

Porter believed that an intelligent and highly motivated MBA student could cut through jargon and intricate information to cull key pieces of information from a morass of data, and anyone who could do that successfully deserved to work for him. His students proved him correct. Indeed, those who impressed him the most in presentations were offered high starting salaries with Monitor Company.

TEN SECRETS TO INFORMATION GATHERING

As gifted as Porter was at analyzing information, he was also a master of obtaining information. Data gathering was an art that required keen intelligence and persistence, but it was also a skill that could be taught. In a briefing given to the twenty-four students before the start of the presidential commission work, Porter divulged his ten secrets of corporate information gathering, which he shared so he'd be certain of getting good data. These, with Porter's comments about each, are enumerated below.

1. Always ask questions you already know the answer to. "That way, if you find someone straying from the facts, you can cut the interview short and not waste any more of your time."
2. Know as much about a company as the person you

are interviewing does. Porter suggested reviewing ten years of annual reports and 10-Ks,* as well as talking with industry analysts. "Most chief executives I know spend [very little time] reading the published information from articles, annuals, and journals about their own companies. With twenty hours of research time in the library you can blow them out of the water."

3. Keep your eyes open in their offices. Look for clues to personalities from the furnishings. "If an executive's office is too neat, I know it's not worth my time to get him to air his dirty laundry in front of me. I look for the ones with crumbs on their desks and papers bulging from the drawers."

4. Ask to see information you know a person doesn't have but can get. It is used to establish a precedent for information being passed from a corporation to the researcher/consultant. "I trained one guy to copy every interdepartmental memo and send it to me the day he got it. That's the level of cooperation you strive for."

5. Maneuver the person being interviewed into giving sensitive information by asking a series of non-threatening questions with a loaded question thrown in the series. "Your success at this technique will depend on your ability to lull them into a false sense of security."

6. Write down questions asked during first interviews and ask them again during second interviews. "It's amazing to compare the different answers you get after they've forgotten what they said the first time."

7. When good information is flowing freely, do not interrupt the speaker.

8. When someone is uncooperative, be very direct and tell them so.

9. Never have lunch with midlevel managers. "They

* 10-Ks are reports filed with the Securities and Exchange Commission by all publicly held corporations. These disclose vital financial information to stockholders about a company's financial status.

will try to pick your brain and get you sidetracked when you could be using that hour [more profitably]."

10. Always have lunch with the senior corporate executives. "Not only will they pick up your tab, but often, when they are removed from their office surroundings, they have a tendency to give very confidential information."

COMPUTERIZED DATA BASE

Porter was the consummate pragmatist, and he enjoyed tackling real-world difficulties with cold, hard, rational tools. He believed that systematic approaches to problem solving were always preferable to gut-level decision making. Information was the key to making decisions—the better the information, the better the decision. He had no use for "soft" analysis that was based on perception rather than facts.

Collecting data, of any kind, became an obsession for him. With the aid of Thomas Craig and Mark Thomas, two principals of Monitor Company and both former students of Porter's, he began to look for data that would help to analyze emerging global trends. The task, at first, looked to be beyond the realm of possibility.

The information Craig, Thomas, and Porter determined would be useful included specific data on every major industry, market shares of individual products in every country, and a complete list of all relevant tariffs, laws, and production quotas. Collecting the data, even if it was possible, would have taken decades, by which time it would already have been obsolete.

Porter discovered what he felt was an easier and simpler way to build models that approximated global trends. Based on the assumption that most major changes in the world economy were reported by *The Wall Street Journal*, and that merger and acquisition activity was an approximation of the trends in industries, by collecting and cataloging the published data in the *Journal* one might be able to use it to predict global trends. The task, then, became a matter of mechanically sifting through fifteen or twenty years of *Wall Street Journal* issues to collect the data, and to write a software program that could take the information and manipulate it.

He hired two Baker Scholars, part time, to work on the computer-programming assignment, a full-time researcher to read *Wall Street Journals*, and two other researchers to program the data. In all, the job required ten months of work before the system was operable. Once it was ready, it became one of the most important forecasting tools he had at his disposal.

With the data base he built, he predicted such information as the likelihood of an electronics firm in Japan acquiring a chemical company in the United States, given certain restrictions built into the equation. He also picked out industry trends more easily than ever before, information he profitably used at Monitor Company and in research reports. Thereafter, new data from clients were entered into the system and matched against existing data, and an analysis of the results was included in strategy reports.

When added to the other computerized data bases Porter was building, his ability to spot emerging global trends before any other strategic thinker was becoming unsurpassable. Monitor Company's own long-term strategy for success in the management-consulting field hinges on the expectation that computerized strategic analyses will eventually reduce the number of hours of Porter's thinking time required to complete any project. A machine will never replace his brilliance, but it may, he hopes, expedite his work, leaving him free to take on more projects.

CHAPTER 3

The Success
of a
Strategy

· · ·

When his knock on the door of Dean Lawrence Fouraker's Jerusalem hotel room failed to elicit a response, Professor Joseph Bower turned the handle and let himself in. There before him lay Fouraker, dressed in a smoking jacket and stretched out asleep on his bed.

"Come on, Larry. At least wait until the speeches get going before you take a nap."

Fouraker awoke with a start.

"What time is it?" He glanced at his wrist. "Nuts! I forgot to set my watch ahead."

"It's a few minutes after seven," said Bower. "The others are waiting downstairs."

47

Fouraker rolled out of bed and checked himself in the dim light of the hotel mirror. Fatigued. There was no other word to describe him, a result of jet lag and having to officiate at the class of 1976 graduation some days earlier, where he had had an unpleasant discussion with Harvard University president Derek Bok over his expansion plans for the business school.

"Do you have a comb?" he said. "Mine seems to be missing."

Bower pulled one out of his pocket and handed it to him. Fouraker adjusted his black satin bow tie, put on his dinner jacket, and motioned to Bower to follow him out the door. In the space of five minutes he had rejuvenated himself, becoming once again the lively, sophisticated, and charming dean of the Harvard Business School.

To less dedicated men it would have been a tedious chore to lead a four-hour seminar on the responsibilities of boards of directors with forty-five chairmen and managing directors of Israeli and European companies, and then later that evening play host at a dinner banquet for the same businessmen. But for Fouraker, it was part of the expanded job description that he had made for himself in 1970 when he became dean of the preeminent business school in the world. No one forced him to establish Harvard Business School outposts in remote parts of Asia, the Middle East, and Europe. He did it because it was the right thing for the school to do, and because he had a missionary zeal, even if Harvard president Derek Bok did not.

Several professors who are former colleagues felt Fouraker saw himself among exclusive company, including congressmen and governors. Like the latter, the dean of Harvard Business School had obligations to his constituents, who, in Fouraker's view, were the business leaders of the world. They looked to him for guidance, and he looked to them for money to support institutions such as the Jerusalem Institute of Management. Trevor Chinn, chairman of the Lex Service Group, Ltd. in London, and

Irving Shapiro, chairman of E. I. DuPont de Nemours & Company, had backed the idea from its inception and both had donated substantial sums. Fouraker knew that the success of the new Jerusalem Institute of Management, the first executive-education school in Israel, depended upon how much support it was perceived he was giving it. Shapiro shared board responsibilities with him at Citicorp, and Chinn was a heavy donor to HBS. That was why he came to Jerusalem—to demonstrate to them his support of the idea he had helped to launch using Harvard Business School's intellectual resources and their money.

THE BOK REPORT

The problem Fouraker had with Derek Bok was that he felt Bok lacked a global vision for Harvard's future. Furthermore, he could never quite stop thinking of Bok as the dean of the law school rather than as the president of the university and his boss. Fouraker had been appointed by Bok's predecessor, Nathan "Nate" Pusey, who was a Harvard president in the ancient and honorable tradition of Harvard presidents. Bok reminded Fouraker of someone's kid brother, a precocious upstart whom he could never take seriously. They had never seen eye to eye, from the day Bok was chosen to be president, the year after Fouraker was made dean.

Fouraker's thinly veiled contempt for him antagonized Bok at every meeting they had with each other, and Bok never forgot Fouraker once joking to him, "If you need to learn new management techniques, I'll arrange a private tutorial with some of our faculty." Behind the arrogance of the statement was the implication that Fouraker didn't approve of the way Bok managed the university, which Bok took as a deliberate insult.

The business school, Bok was constantly reminded, operated independently of the university in nearly every respect, so there was seldom any reason for him to venture from the confines of Harvard Yard to visit the HBS campus across the Charles River from Cambridge. With an entrenched tenured faculty and no financial controls over them, there was little he could do to change the way things were run there anyway. His sole power over HBS was his ability to select a new dean, but without justifiable cause he was unwilling to replace Fouraker. Not only did Bok's sense of fair play stand in the way of making a change, but also Fouraker enjoyed the support of a strong contingent of professors who liked the fact that their chief administrator was rarely around to monitor their activities. Fouraker devoted most of his time to traveling and representing the school at social functions, delegating the day-to-day operations to his subordinates. Bok felt that the business-school dean's chief responsibility was to stay on campus and manage the faculty, but it wasn't a serious enough breach of conduct for him to discharge him.

What upset Bok about Fouraker, more than anything, was the fact that Fouraker's main source of personal income came from outside Harvard University, from the eight public companies on whose boards he sat: Citicorp, RCA, Gillette, Jewel Companies, R. H. Macy, Inc., NBC, New England Mutual Life Insurance Company, and Texas Eastern Transmission Company. How could anyone, wondered Bok, effectively run Harvard Business School while sitting on the boards of eight major publicly held corporations, each of which met one or two days each month, not to mention the nonprofit boards he was also on? True, he was the best fund-raiser the school had ever had, but by any definition Fouraker was a professional board member, not a dean, and therefore not someone who was effectively leading the school, either by example or by deed. So Bok began to look for cogent reasons to remove Fouraker, waiting for the moment when he would overstep his bounds, to show that his termination was not due to a personality clash, but because the school needed new management. But when Fouraker made visits to Harvard Yard, as he did for the June 1976 commencement ceremony, Bok made no secret of his displeasure over the policies of the business school's dean, and his free-spending habits.

"What in the world do you need another executive-management program for when you're already losing money on the ones you've got in Europe and Boston?" he said, abrasively questioning Fouraker's plans to start two more programs aboard. The reason was that the development of international programs fit Fouraker's image of himself as the leader of Harvard Business School. The dozens of men he shared board meetings with, like Clifton Garvin, Jr., of Exxon, Thornton Bradshaw of Atlantic Richfield, and Walter Wriston of Citicorp, could boast of international expansion, and so could Fouraker. He ran Harvard Business School like a corporation at which he was the chief executive officer, chairman of the board, and majority stockholder.

He had once brought up the suggestion of buying a small corporate plane to get him from meeting to meeting and country to country, but abandoned it when he realized that it would have been indiscreet for someone in his position. It was his bad luck that he had to fly first class on commercial airliners, a practice viewed by his fellow board members as slumming. Derek Bok, of course, traveled economy class whenever he went by plane, but Bok had taken a vow of poverty; Fouraker certainly had not.

The blister that had grown between Bok and Fouraker in 1976 over Fouraker's expansion plans for international programs began to fester in January 1977, when Bok spent a week with Harvard Business School professor Michael Yoshino on a trip to Tokyo. Their visit had been proposed by Bok as a way to develop new Harvard ties with Japan. Bok, who was from California and a graduate of Stanford, knew that Stanford had done much more than Harvard to attract Japanese students and research dollars, so he selected Michael Yoshino, one of the few Japanese professors at Harvard, and the only tenured Japanese professor in the business school, to accompany him as a translator and goodwill ambassador.

Between meetings with Japanese prime minister Takeo. Fukuda, Secretary General Ohira, and the chairmen of Mitsubishi, Nippon Steel, and Nissan Motors, Bok probed Yoshino for information about the management of the business school, and what he discovered confirmed his worst suspicions. Fouraker was sometimes absent from HBS for weeks at a time, and was said to spend much of his time in Italy, Switzerland, Spain, and Hawaii to meet with executives and to set up Harvard training programs that were under the auspices of the school.

From a leadership point of view Fouraker's influence had become destructive, installing a strong anti-intellectual agenda in the faculty, who knew that to get ahead at the business school they had to be good businessmen, not good educators. Outside teaching seminars for corporations, consulting, and directorships were actively encouraged to bring in corporate money, and those activities occupied more than half the time of senior faculty, a policy that went far toward making the business school less scholarly and more corporate. Also, under the dean's directions HBS began to isolate itself from the academic, achievement-oriented mission of Harvard University, while at the same time cashing in on the prestigious Harvard name. Wealthy businessmen with little rigorous formal education were becoming elite Harvard alumni by passing through one-, two-, three-, or six-week programs, and they went on to become prime candidates for the school's fund-raising drives. All of these discoveries awakened in Bok the desire to oust Lawrence Fouraker from the deanship of the business school as quickly as possible.

Derek Bok was born in 1930, the youngest child of an affluent family, and lived in a house located in an otherwise vacant canyon. His grandfather was a Dutch immigrant, the editor of *Ladies' Home Journal* for thirty years, and author of a well-known social commentary called *The Americanization of Edward Bok*. Derek Bok attended

Stanford University, where he played on the basketball team, and where in his senior year he decided to apply to Harvard Law School.

His decision was based on the recommendation of a graduate resident adviser who lived in the freshman dormitory at which Bok was proctor, William H. Rehnquist. Rehnquist, who in 1986 was named Chief Justice of the Supreme Court, had earned a master's degree from Harvard Law School in 1950, and he persuaded Bok to enroll there saying, ". . . go to Harvard, because you'll never have to waste any time explaining to other people why you chose it." It was, according to Bok, "not a terribly good reason, but it was the only reason I had."

At Harvard, Bok rose to the top of his class and came to the attention of the faculty, in particular his antitrust professor, Kingman Brewster, who had spotted a rising star. After Bok graduated and had joined the U.S. military, Brewster sought him out and convinced him to return to Cambridge. "He came to call when I was in Washington in the army, and invited himself to dinner. He extolled the virtues of the academic life. Since I've always found Kingman irresistible, I decided maybe that was what I wanted to do after all."

In 1958, he finished his service and returned to Harvard Law School as an assistant professor. In his first class were Michael Dukakis, who later became governor of Massachusetts, and Antonin Scalia, who, at Rehnquist's elevation, was appointed to the Supreme Court by President Reagan in 1986. Bok became dean of the law school in 1968, just ten years after joining the faculty, and three years later, during a period of student protests at Harvard, he was appointed president of the university.

Bok immediately saw the need to symbolically break with the outdated traditions of Harvard, and to bring in a new generation of leadership. He was just forty-one, one of the youngest presidents in Harvard history, and came to power during the most turbulent period in postwar history. For safety, as well as for expediency, he chose not to live in the presidential mansion in Harvard Yard, and he carefully nurtured an image of being modest and practical by driving around town in a Volkswagen Beetle. Hearing charges that Harvard was a country club for the sons of the wealthy and an ivory tower for academics made him work to erase those stereotypes. He set an example by playing on a basketball team called "Bok's Jocks," and by walking the campus picking up litter.

The distractions of reorganizing the management of Harvard University during his early years in office led him to overlook the negative reports he received about the business school. Compared with the violence and turmoil in the rest of Harvard, HBS seemed to be going about its business in serene quietude. Until 1976, there didn't seem to be any reason to investigate reports of indiscreet spending, and the decay of the intellectual fiber of the institution, which seemed trivial compared with his other problems. But in that year Bok's close friend, and a former secretary of labor, Professor John T. Dunlop, returned from Washington and, as a "university professor" (which gave him the privilege of working anywhere within Harvard he wanted) set up an office at the business school. It was widely believed that Dunlop was Bok's eyes and ears at HBS, and that Dunlop was briefing Bok on a regular basis about the school's sources and uses of funds. During their visit to Japan in January 1977, therefore, Michael Yoshino only corroborated what Bok had already learned.

When he returned to Harvard, Bok decided that the moment had come to shake up the business school. His sense of fairness and justice prevented him from asking Fouraker to resign; Fouraker was, after all, just the tip of the iceberg. So he decided that the best way to deal with the problem was to circumvent the business-school dean, using Dunlop to establish a new business-government research center at the Kennedy School of Government. The center was to have "parallel professorships," taking faculty from both the Kennedy School and the business school to teach and do research. In that way the growing isolationism of HBS, which had been fostered by the Fouraker administration to keep the university from controlling the school's money, would gradually erode. As Bok saw it, Harvard needed a wholesale reclamation project for HBS to weed out the arrogant, self-righteous attitude of men like Fouraker.

In late 1978, Bok stunned the business school with a blow that was more potent than even he expected by devoting his 1977–78 annual report to HBS. While it was not made public until April 1979, advance copies of the report circulated throughout the school and produced shock waves that reverberated in every office. For the first time, Bok openly criticized the school's case-study system saying, ". . . it does not provide an ideal way of communicating concepts and analytical methods . . ." He also questioned the ethical lessons being taught to America's future business leaders at HBS, and the school's lack of attention to the area of business-government relationships.

The attack was aimed squarely at Fouraker, who felt its impact most heavily, and who tried to assure himself, and those around him, that the report was meaningless and that Bok had no intention of trying to bring about reforms at the school. He was, however, deceiving himself.

The end came on January 19, 1979, when *The Wall Street Journal* published a front-page article called "To Some at Harvard, Telling Lies Becomes a Matter of Course," about a course at the business school that taught students to use "strategic misrepresentation" in business negotiations. To Bok, whose wife taught an ethics course at Harvard Medical School and had just published a book called *Lying,* in which she condemned the practice, the article hit too close to home. Not only did it demonstrate that the school's lack of scruples was tainting the university, but it also publicly stated what Bok knew all along, but was afraid to admit, which was that ethical abuses were rampant among the faculty.

Bok called Fouraker into his office to answer the issues

raised by the article and outline his own plans to remedy the situation, and when he could not convince Bok of his willingness to change the system, which Fouraker thought was functioning effectively, Bok asked for his resignation. He made it clear to Fouraker that he vehemently objected to both Fouraker's attitude and the distorted sense of values that prevented him from understanding the seriousness of the issues that had been raised. Fouraker, stunned to realize that Bok had, effectively, just fired him, arrived back in his office at HBS in a state of semi-shock.

He was, of course, a tenured member of the business-school faculty, which meant that short of gross misconduct on his part, he could not be removed from Harvard. Bok permitted him to stay in his post until a successor was named, which was Bok's way of minimizing the amount of publicity that would come out about the dean's ouster. They both denied that his "retirement" had anything to do with the *Wall Street Journal* article on lying at HBS; Bok felt it would be a dangerous precedent to give the perception that a published article had anything to do with his decision to make personnel changes. It would have implied that he had let things get out of hand to the point where the media had had to investigate. After a decent period of time elapsed, Fouraker announced his early retirement, and Bok used the publication of his report on the school to describe the qualities he was looking for in the school's next dean.

While Fouraker tried to assert an antilying and proethics position by issuing a letter to the alumni and by having the professor whose course stirred the debate send a letter to the editor of *The Wall Street Journal* defending the school's curriculum, it was too little, too late. Bok's report came out on April 29, 1979, and the story, in which he called for a massive restructuring of HBS, was covered the next day on the front page of *The New York Times*. "The report is a first step in a long process of selecting a new dean for the school," he said. But even Bok was surprised by the amount of attention the story began getting in national publications. Ethics in business suddenly became a new topic of debate, in which Harvard Business School, the role model for business schools everywhere, was at the very center of the controversy. That Harvard's president openly criticized the school made many wonder if the decay had gone farther than anyone had expected.

Bok did his best to contain the story. "If you read the report carefully," he said, "you'll find that it is at least 90 percent a description of change already under way in the school." But by June 1979, *Fortune* magazine put the story about the shake-up on its cover, sending Walter Kiechel III, an editor and MBA graduate of HBS, to do an in-depth analysis of Bok's criticisms, adding further fuel to the flames.

What Kiechel found was that the faculty and the dean resented Bok's intrusion into their system of doing things, going so far as to criticize Bok for not basing his conclusions in fact. Fouraker, who had nothing to lose at that point, told Kiechel that he did not think Derek Bok had ever even attended a business school case-study discussion, to which Bok restrainedly replied in *Fortune*, "I have sat in on an occasional class."

THE BOWER REPORT

What was at stake was no longer just the dean's job, which was already stripped away, but the survival of a system that had allowed the tenured faculty to double or triple their academic incomes through the use of contacts generated under the guise of doing research for Harvard. Bok's critique prompted many of the professors to draw up battle lines in what was expected to escalate into an unprecedented academic war. The mere mention of changing or eliminating the case method of instruction sent faculty scurrying to talk with the press to denounce

Bok's suggestion. "Nothing could be less prudent," said Professor James Heskett to *The New York Times*. "The case method has served us perfectly in preparing students to deal with increasingly complex problems."

As the faculty worked to protect its territory from Bok, it found a receptive group of allies among powerful alumni, especially those alumni whose companies heavily recruited MBA students. The group's most ardent supporter was Marvin Bower, who headed the strategic management consulting firm of McKinsey & Company. On May 21, 1979, Bower convened a meeting of the board of directors of The Associates of Harvard Business School, whose membership represented officers of McKinsey & Company and four hundred other companies. Their plan was to form an advisory task force that would formulate a strategy to "help the business school meet President Bok's objectives," and to make a recommendation on whom the next dean of the school would be. The board selected Bower to be the task force's vice-chairman, and appointed fifteen staff members to conduct interviews with the faculty, seven of whom were consultants with McKinsey & Company.

For the next several months, Bower drew his top associates from the New York, Chicago, Washington, and Cleveland offices to return to their alma mater and do field research for the Harvard consulting report. There was to be no margin for error, and no doubt going in what the results would be. It would validate the teaching method that had trained hundreds of McKinsey men, beginning with Marvin Bower in 1928, and put an end to Bok's foolish suggestion that wholesale changes be made at the school.

Of all the companies that recruited at HBS, McKinsey & Company was the one with the most to lose if the case system was cut back or eliminated, so Bower made it his personal mission to keep drastic changes from being made. The school that had been responsible for McKinsey becoming the preeminent management-consulting firm by supplying more than a thousand fresh MBAs from 1937 on, was not about to be restructured based on the flimsy arguments of Harvard's well-intentioned, but ill-advised, president. Bower had spent his entire consulting career working with administration after administration at HBS to secure the best students from each new class of MBAs. He was the living continuity that extended back to the school's earliest days, and the strongest proponent of maintaining the status quo.

His father was a land registration official in Cincinnati, where Marvin Bower was born in 1903. He was the brightest and hardest-working student in his high school class, choosing to attend Brown University from among several other colleges to which he had been admitted. His ambition had been to become a corporate lawyer, and to that end he came to Harvard Law School in 1925, where he did well, though not well enough to make *Law Review*, which was the credential he needed to be hired by Jones, Day, Reavis & Pogue, the most prestigious law firm in Cleveland. Rather than risk rejection by applying directly out of law school, Bower applied to Harvard Business School because he felt the MBA credential would give him an edge, two years hence, over the other *Harvard Law Review* graduates who would be applying then. The strategy was successful, and in 1930 he was hired to be an associate with Jones, Day.

He had never planned to become a management consultant until he met James O. McKinsey in 1933, who was a professor at the University of Chicago business school and the principal of his own firm. McKinsey believed that "management engineers" could bring specialized knowledge to companies in need of advice, and he persuaded Bower to leave the security of his law firm and become McKinsey's one-man New York office. "My colleagues in Cleveland thought I was out of my mind when I left a leading law firm to join an unknown firm in an unknown field," he said.

Almost from his first year with the firm, Bower was the single driving force behind McKinsey & Company's success. James O. McKinsey became chairman and CEO of

Marshall Field & Company in Chicago in 1935, and spent most of his time running that retail-department-store company until his death in 1937.

After McKinsey was gone, and Bower was working for some of the largest corporations in New York, he saw no advantage to changing the name of the company. It would always be McKinsey & Company, and he would always be just a partner. In 1950, he took on the additional title of managing director, and in 1967, he officially retired, although he continued to be the firm's most aggressive business generator and to set all its major policies. Titles meant nothing to him; for as long as he lived he would still be the commander, regardless of what his partners called him.

McKinsey & Company grew rapidly throughout the 1950s and 1960s, spurred on by the large number of Harvard Business School Baker Scholars who were hired to staff new offices throughout the United States. There was a direct correlation between the amount of money Bower gave the school each year and the number of Baker Scholar graduates that the firm was able to hire. As the dollar contributions went up, faculty recommendations and favored interviewing schedules were made available to the firm, and each successive administration allowed Bower the full run of the facilities. In many ways the school became an admissions tool for McKinsey & Company, with students knowing on enrollment that there would be a job waiting for every Baker Scholar there if it was wanted.

Recruiting of top students by McKinsey was done at other prestigious business schools, but never to the extent it was done at Harvard. Bower had a strong preference for HBS Baker Scholars, young men who had been trained to think on their feet. Other graduates from the best schools, Dartmouth, Wharton, and Stanford, were at least as smart as those from Harvard, but they were often not as articulate. Harvard's case system forced students to be glib because their grades depended upon how well they spoke in class. McKinsey consultants' main talent was an ability to use words to persuade, a skill they learned in hundreds of hours of case discussions at HBS. The other advantage that Harvard MBAs had over their rivals was that they had been taught to dive into the middle of confusing and unfamiliar business situations, also the product of learning by cases rather than by textbooks and lectures. Baker Scholars tended to be intelligent generalists who could expound on any issue, and whose natural inclination to remain silent on topics they had no background in had been systematically broken down. In effect, McKinsey paid a premium for students who were good at "winging it."

At the firm, there had always been either the Marvin Bower way of doing things or the wrong way of doing things. Its professionals were the "IBM Men" in the management-consulting field because they dressed alike, talked alike, and produced reports according to rigorously defined formulas. Often the partners were encouraged to move on to work for corporations in order to make room at the top for the younger associates who were always waiting to fill their places.

Despite the suffocating environment described by many former employees, strong alliances between past and present members of the firm developed through "alumni associations" patterned after the Harvard Business School alumni association. At regular intervals, McKinsey "graduates" met to discuss their companies' problems with the current group of associates in the firm, which was one of the primary ways that new business flowed into McKinsey. It was a new old-boy network, once removed from HBS.

Thomas J. Peters, the co-author of *In Search of Excellence*, headed up McKinsey's specialized area in the study of leadership and change in organizations in 1979,* and

* Peters and Robert H. Waterman, Jr., who co-wrote *In Search of Excellence* in 1982, were, in the words of one former associate, "chopped off at the knees." The Bower team approach required partners to sublimate their egos to the greater glory of the firm, something Peters and Waterman were not willing to do, which resulted in both of them leaving the firm.

was a strong influence on Marvin Bower while he was putting together his report for President Derek Bok on Harvard Business School. Peters's main thesis was that leaders of successful organizations often had "lofty themes" that guided the day-to-day activities of their companies and formed the source of their leadership. John F. Kennedy's call to put a man on the moon by the end of decade was one example of how the leadership-through-lofty-themes idea worked. Peters's concept of leadership so impressed Bower that he made it the cornerstone of his report to Bok.

He argued that no other method of teaching would be as effective at making students see the "big ideas," and that forcing them to study theoretical textbooks and listen to lectures would produce a generation of managers with no leadership skills.

On two occasions during his field research, he took time out to meet with Derek Bok and personally impress upon him the need to maintain the system as it had evolved. They talked as one Harvard Law School graduate to another, both determined to see the business school return to the fold.

Bower described to Bok the qualities he should consider in picking the next dean, and explained why the last dean had to be replaced. As Bower saw it, Fouraker was a poor leader because he was an outsider who did not understand the real goals and ideals of the institution, which Bok and he both knew had nothing to do with international expansion. His biggest flaws were that he refused to be a team player, and he consistently set a bad example by delegating his main responsibilities to a staff and by spending most of his time away from campus. Bower's recommendation for Fouraker's replacement was John H. McArthur, a former football player and a successful business consultant. In appearance and style he was the antithesis of Fouraker: overweight, self-effacing, modest. He was the antidote for a decade of absentee management, an argument Bok found persuasive.

The fifty-two-page report, written entirely by Marvin Bower, was presented to Bok on December 3, 1979, and was entitled "The Success of a Strategy." In it he explained that Bok's concerns were "unwarranted," and that there was no justifiable reason for changing the curriculum or the method of instruction. The strategy of using only the case method of instruction, unique among all important business schools, was a resounding success, Bower said, which was borne out by the fact that the school's graduates were in such high demand, and were viewed as the business leaders of America.

Bok was officially unavailable to comment on the report, which contradicted every main argument in his report from a year earlier. There was, of course, nothing that could be said. The Bower report, in a masterful stroke of strategy, was released a month after Bok had already appointed Bower's choice for dean, John H. McArthur. The status quo must be maintained at all cost, it said. Quoting British prime minister Benjamin Disraeli, he wrote, "The secret of success is constancy to purpose," which from Bower's perspective meant keeping McKinsey's supply of trained talent moving through the system.

In 1984, a reporter for *The New York Times* came to Harvard Business School on the occasion of the school's seventy-fifth anniversary and discovered that the Bok report was still a very sensitive topic on campus. "If you raise it with the dean he will be very upset," said the school's director of communications. The reporter explained to him "that the topic could hardly be avoided" because of its significance to the future plans of HBS. McArthur, immediately notified that the *New York Times* article would feature a five-year retrospective look at the Bok report, decided to cancel the long-scheduled interview he had granted with the reporter, forty-five minutes before it was to start.

Leave
It to the
Dean

• • •

Two weeks prior to stepping down from his position as dean of the Harvard Business School, Lawrence E. Fouraker met privately in December 1979 with an alumni group at a black-tie dinner held at the Harvard Club of New York City. For ten years, as dean of HBS, he had officiated at hundreds of similar gatherings, where he made impassioned pleas for funds to complete his latest building project. Standing at the podium, looking almost majestic, he would rally his listeners with the appeal "Give generously, or don't give at all."

Now, on the eve of a forced retirement from the job he had wanted above all others, Fouraker, visible demoral- 65 ized, could not bring himself to deliver the same appeal for funds that usually marked the close of his speeches. His words that evening spoke of accomplishments and ideals, of projects left unfinished and plans never begun.

"If I have erred," he said, "it was always on the side of caution. My contributions to the school will not be remembered as just the buildings I built or the programs I started. Mine was the era of leadership in the true Harvard tradition—an era, I'm afraid, that has come to an end."

Even as Fouraker delivered his final remarks in New York, John H. McArthur was in Boston constructing his plans for an orderly transition to the deanship. According to his design, he would become a new kind of leader who would represent the new generation of academics at the school. The emphasis would be on building an institution that embodied the thinking of the nation's brightest business minds.

In style, as well as substance, he would break with the past. Where predecessors were stern and domineering, McArthur would be unpretentious and friendly. Where they were intimidating, he would be approachable. And where they had been stiff and formal, he would let the prestige of the office imbue its own formal manner around his boyishly unsophisticated bearing. He was President Bok's choice to be the next dean precisely because he would bring new ideas and a new leadership style to the job.

McArthur was from Vancouver, British Columbia, in Canada. He played football on the University of Vancouver team as a tackle and middle linebacker and was good enough to consider a career in Canadian professional football. His family, however, convinced him that he would quickly be pummeled, and that if he did survive for three or more years, there was no future in it outside of coaching. Instead, McArthur used an interest in forestry to gain admission to Harvard Business School's MBA program in 1957. There C. Roland Christensen discovered him and recruited him for a career in academics.

As a case writer, McArthur's unbeguiling manner and large frame made him an easy target for the practical jokers on the faculty. Highly regarded for his intellectual talents, he nevertheless presented a challenge to his colleagues in terms of who could be the most inventive in fooling him. Pearson Hunt, a professor of finance, enjoyed the sport more than most, and plotted ways to have fun at his case writer's expense.

In 1961, Hunt bet Stanley Teele, dean of the faculty, $20 that he could negotiate McArthur into a position where he would make some sort of blunder in front of the chairman of Standard Oil of Ohio. Teele, who thought a great deal of McArthur, raised the ante to $50. To win the bet, Hunt had to prove that he had led McArthur into doing or saying something inappropriate in front of the chairman.

Hunt called McArthur into his office in August to give him his new assignment—to interview the chairman of Standard Oil of Ohio and to write a case on the chairman's capital budgeting system and management policies. He instructed McArthur, who was to leave the following Tuesday for Ohio, to meet back with Hunt on the morning of his departure to get his final instructions. At the appointed hour, on a sweltering August day in Boston, McArthur, dressed in a dark-blue, three-piece pinstriped suit, walked into Hunt's office sweating profusely.

"Where's your hat, McArthur?" asked Hunt incredulously.

"Hat? But I don't wear a hat," he said.

"You can't meet the chairman of Standard Oil without a hat. You'll have to stop off in Boston and buy one."

Dutifully checking in at Brooks Brothers on Newbury Street, McArthur selected a dark-brown fedora. But so unaccustomed to wearing a hat was he that he nearly left it behind twice, first on his way to the airport in the taxicab, and then as he was leaving the plane. When he got to Standard Oil, he finally solved the hat problem by keeping it squarely, and resolutely, on his head, taking it off only when he got to the chairman's office.

After the meeting, and on his way to lunch, McArthur realized that he had left his hat behind, and excused himself to go get it. The chairman, who never wore a hat, laughed uncontrollably. "Are you mad?" he said. "It's ninety-five degrees outside. You can't wear a hat."

Teele paid the $50 to Hunt. Dean McArthur recounted the hat story on numerous occasions. It was, he said, the last time Teele lost a wager on him.

By 1983, McArthur had a strong sense of his own abilities, and a mission to impress his stamp upon Harvard Business School. During his first three years in office he had learned to harness and channel the power that was his. He traded less prestigious directorships with companies like Buckeye Pipe Line Company and National Aviation and Technology Corporation for more prestigious directorships with Chase Manhattan, Teradyne, Rohm & Haas, and People Express Airlines. The office had transformed the duckling into a swan and had made McArthur a man to be taken seriously.

As the school's chief fund-raiser, he found that his ability to raise money was directly related to the quality and amount of information he had. He started a comprehensive computerized filing system, which kept track of personal information on every donor, and potential donor, that he came into contact with. At fund-raising events he broke away at odd times to jot down information he had learned. Children, hobbies, business contacts, and anything that might be useful to know later on, went down on little note cards. The information was fed into the system and stored. Arriving at parties thoroughly briefed, the dean dazzled the guests with his total recall of the large and small details of their lives. That, and a warm handshake, was his secret to raising money.

With fifty-two thousand living alumni in the school's directory of former students, getting a large number of

small donations was relatively easy. The challenge was
to identify the potential million-dollar donors from both
corporations and alumni. Several previous deans had
cultivated successful businessmen over a number of years
and upon their deaths went to their widows with suggestions for new buildings to be constructed to honor their
husbands. It was a system that struck McArthur as a fund-
raiser's form of ambulance chasing, and he refused to do
it. He wanted gifts from living people, and active corporations, who would give generously over a long period
of time.

McArthur began to call on alumni with increasing regularity to suggest that classes work together to establish
class chairs. Through the school's alumni associations he
recruited men who headed up prestigious investment
banks and consulting companies, whose businesses were
built on contacts, to become reunion gift chairmen. In
1985, Richard Menschel '59, partner, Goldman, Sachs &
Company; Harold Tanner '56, managing director, Salomon Brothers; Marvin Bower '30, managing director,
McKinsey & Company; and George Weiss '20, retired director of Bache Group Inc., formed the main contingent
leading the drive. Albert Gordon '25, chairman, Kidder,
Peabody, who was one of the school's most generous donors, and whose company heavily recruited MBAs, declined the honor of being the class of '25 gift chairman.
When all the donations were tallied up from the 1984–85
fund drive, $9.89 million had been raised, including
$100,000 each from Weiss, Tanner, Menschel, Bower, and
Gordon.

McArthur's real talents for fund-raising were at an intellectual rather than operational level. He understood that
people usually gave large sums under two circumstances:
either to honor a family member through naming a
building or chair, or because the school honored them for
their dedication or service. Gratitude for receiving an
award, he had seen, was often paid back by a large donation.

Handing out awards for service had several advantages over the traditional fund-raising methods of attending meetings and making speeches. Not only would business-men work diligently to get awards by donating money themselves and getting others to donate, but once awards were handed out, the school could count on continued support from the winners over a long period of time. And even when they did not give large sums out of their own pockets, they often controlled corporations that could do-nate in increments much larger than the individual could.

Looking at his options in 1980, McArthur decided to make better use of two awards the school conferred, the Alumni Achievement Award and the Distinguished Ser-vice Award. The Alumni Achievement Award, created in 1968, was given at commencement each year by the Har-vard Business School alumni association. The first recip-ients were graduates who had achieved outstanding success in business or government as a result of their HBS educations. They were men who had come up the hard way, like Robert McNamara, MBA '39, former U.S. sec-retary of defense, and Charles F. Myers, Jr., MBA '35, chief executive officer of Burlington Industries. The award was the business school's honorary degree, but under a differ-ent name because only the university could grant honor-ary degrees.

From 1980 on, McArthur handed his selections for the Alumni Achievement Award to the alumni committee, which approved the selections and sent the list back to McArthur. However, instead of picking just one or two recipients, as had been the custom before, the dean chose four annually. Where there had been fifteen winners in the award's first twelve years, during McArthur's first seven years twenty-five alumni walked off with the prize.

So Roy Huffington, chairman and president of Roy M. Huffington, Inc., and Jaquelin Hume, chairman of AMPCO Foods, joined Richard Malott, chairman and CEO of FMC Corporation, and John C. Whitehead, senior partner of Goldman, Sachs & Company on the dais, and the money came in just as expected. William McGowan, chairman of MCI Telecommunications Corporation, winner of the award in 1985, gave $100,000 to the 1984–85 fund drive, as did John Whitehead, a 1980 winner, and C. Peter McColough, a 1986 winner, both of whose gifts were matched by their companies.*

McARTHUR'S INNER FUND-RAISING CIRCLE

As McArthur considered other ways to raise money, he called in two of the school's distinguished, and most generous, alumni to discuss fund-raising strategies: Albert H. Gordon and Marvin Bower.

Gordon was a national co-chairman of the Harvard University campaign to raise $350 million,† had spent six years on the business school's visiting committee, and was chairman of the Harvard Business School's Associates Program, which raised more than $2 million annually exclusively from corporations that recruited at the school. Marvin Bower, who had been the managing director of McKinsey & Company, was chairman of the HBS fund for two years, a member of Harvard's board of overseers and the HBS visiting committee, and was a board member of the Associates Program.

At a meeting in late 1981 with Dean McArthur, Bower and Gordon both asserted that, in their opinion, the school had done all it could at a national level to raise money, and that attention should be focused on building a grass-

---

* The 1985 co-winner, John R. Shad, MBA '49, chairman of the Securities and Exchange Commission (SEC), donated $20 million of his personal fortune in 1987 toward the establishment of a new $30 million ethics program at Harvard Business School.
† Harvard University's $350 million campaign began in 1979 as a $250 million fund drive to rejuvenate undergraduate teaching programs. The money raised by 1985 when the campaign ended (in excess of $350 million) was earmarked to pay increased salaries for undergraduate professors and to bolster the university's scholarship funds.

roots network of regional support through clubs in each state. The New York City club, in which both Bower and Gordon were active, was the model for the new network they proposed, and would provide a clear signal to other clubs of how money could be raised by those who were adept at the art.

They decided that the New York City club would set the example by establishing its own service award, based on the precedent of the main awards given each year at commencement that were given to alumni who raised large sums for the school. To show their commitment to the idea, Bower and Gordon each agreed to donate money through the Harvard Business School Club of New York to establish the Bower-Gordon Award. Other clubs would use it as a prototype to get their own alumni members to work at raising money.

On April 6, 1982, at the New York club's annual awards dinner, Secretary of the Treasury Donald Regan delivered the keynote address as the recipient of the club's Business Statesman Award. Previous winners of that honor had been David Rockefeller, C. D. Dillon, Henry Ford II, Robert McNamara, Felix Rohatyn, and Walter Wriston. All men of finance, they were chosen in order to attract large crowds of alumni who would be targets for donations to the HBS fund, and to guarantee that a number of prominent New York businessmen would be there to keep the HBS business-contracts network alive.

When the winners of the new Bower-Gordon Award were announced, it became clear that the pair's plans had backfired. The board voted unanimously. The winners were Albert Gordon and Marvin Bower.

Neither man had been present at the meeting at which the award recipients were chosen. Gordon, for his part, was amused at getting the prize, and although he would have preferred another choice, he decided that the award had gone to the right ones after all. He commented wryly to the crowd gathered at New York City's Sheraton Center: "Now to those members of the club that are here tonight, I want to let you in on a secret. I want to tell you how you can get the award at some future time. If you work hard enough for the club, and if you live long enough, you'll get it."

Marvin Bower, too embarrassed to pick up his award, used the convenient excuse of a snowstorm that evening to telephone his regrets at not being able to come.

CHAPTER 5

An Introduction
to Power
and Influence

. . .

Away from distractions of mundane commerce, business scholarship is generally thought to exist at Harvard Business School in a pure, unfettered form. But along the corridors of Morgan Hall, where Dean McArthur, his staff, and a few senior professors roam, chance conversations turn not to routine matters of pedagogy, but to power. Who's got it, who's getting it, and how to get more of it. Those are the issues that occupy the waking hours, and stir the imaginations. Power, in all its varieties, drives productivity forward, and McArthur packages, brokers, and distributes it, alone.

Upon meeting Dean McArthur for the first time, most

people profess to be disappointed. His voice is too high, his face too pudgy, and he walks with a distinct waddle. In sharp contrast to his predecessors, all men of poise and social standing, McArthur is most in his element at sporting events talking to alumni. His 230-pound physique does not cut a dashing figure at formal social gatherings, where, he readily concedes, he would rather not go.

To offset his social shortcomings, McArthur uses cash and craftiness, rather than standing and good breeding, to harness and channel power. On becoming dean, he established a budgetary system in which he controlled all the school's research funds. While many privately disdained the mild, short-sleeved dean, those who hoped to do research submitted themselves obediently to that budget power.

The dean's informal method for dividing the school's considerable discretionary dollars is known by some in the organization as "hallway summits," a term used behind his back to mock the gravity with which he conducts the distribution process. Each morning that he is in residence at Harvard, at precisely nine-thirty, Mc-Arthur emerges from his paneled, book-lined office at 124 Morgan Hall to engage in stand-up conversation with one or more waiting professors. Endowed chairs, corporate sponsorship, and major consulting contracts, in that order, are on the agenda. By being instrumental in bringing one or more of those items to the dean, professors gain power—power that has a multitude of internal and external uses, including large expense accounts, prime office space, better committee appointments, larger staffs, and public-relations boosts, among others.

Success at the door leading to the dean's office frequently results in the quick transfer of large sums of money. The game, as it is played, consists of establishing one's power in the organization by marshaling as many of the school's resources as possible for one's own purposes. Those with aspirations for research dollars are obliged to queue up at McArthur's office or face the dreaded, bureaucratic Division of Research, which is indirectly controlled by McArthur. The dean makes himself available to hear out the protagonists and, in a semipublic way, announces to the small community who is winning.

The dean's private accounts contain, at times, more than $25 million, which is the accumulated donations from corporations, foundations, and individuals. Money from Atlantic Richfield Company, Bendix Corporation, the Gillette Company, Albert Gordon, The Grace Foundation, Merrill Lynch & Company Foundation, State Farm Companies Foundation, Texas Eastern Transmission, Unilever, and Zurn, as well as scores of lesser-known entities, pours into the accounts.

Funds are directed into and out of research accounts, depending upon which professors and projects are in favor. The accounting is complicated, though there has never been a hint of misappropriation of funds. Indeed, such is the nature of research that almost any item can be justified.

Convincing McArthur to transfer money from the accounts requires negotiating skill and precise knowledge of what motivates him. He does not easily part with it; he has to be cajoled into opening the coffers. Seasoned veterans do not even consider approaching him until they have a solid lead on a chair, corporate sponsorship, or major consulting contract.

Research legitimizes the whole process. New chairs lead to new research, and new research creates opportunities for industry contacts, which lead to sponsorship, consulting contracts, and eventually, more new chairs. Education aside, the school is set up to perpetuate academic research as a means for obtaining money and power for the institution through individual professors.

The grease that turns the wheel of research is the case method. Its genius lies not in pedagogical effectiveness, but rather in its business-generating power. At one time or another, nearly every *Fortune* 500 company has been asked to open itself up to scrutiny by Harvard Business School. Most welcome the call eagerly and even consider it a source of pride to be selected. That attitude was summed up in a statement by Richard Eamer, chairman and chief executive officer of National Medical Enterprises, a company chosen for a study, when he said, "Harvard realized that we are the driving force in our industry."

If Michael Porter or Theodore Levitt is on the other end of the phone, the contact is viewed as almost miraculous. It is the esteem in which HBS is held by corporate executives that puts real power into the hands of Harvard's professors, power that carries with it advantages such as access: "In my entire case writing experience," boasted Professor Jay Lorsch, "I have never had my call to the chief executive of any company screened. I can pick up my telephone, at any time, and get through immediately to any CEO of any major corporation."

The case method is the business school's Trojan horse, welcomed into the enemy camps, exalted by the ranks, and allowed to stand unobtrusively as it analyzes the secrets of the army and infiltrates the command post. Harvard Business School's files contain more than twenty cases on IBM, twenty-five on General Electric, nineteen on General Foods, and five on Pepsico. Not coincidentally, these same companies are among the school's most generous corporate sponsors.

Here's how it works: Once HBS professors get inside major companies, they stay inside. The corporations themselves, predictably, enjoy the use of the professors' thinking power, friendships develop, and eventually the professors indicate that donations to HBS would be welcomed. Many times they don't even have to ask; corporate executives know that the more they give, the more they get. It isn't extortion on the school's part; rather, it is letting the companies have what they want, which is a working relationship with the school.

Having a case written at no expense is the hook that gets companies interested initially. After that, they discover that closer ties bring other tangible benefits. Benson Shapiro, professor of marketing, wrote a booklet that is distributed to companies and explains those benefits. His list includes the ability to watch hundreds of intelligent students simultaneously work on the company's problems; to "develop relationships" within the school; to recruit MBAs; and to make a "substantial contribution to management education."

Not only does the school benefit, but the individual professors benefit also. Marketing professor Robert Buzzell bluntly explained to an interviewer the sequence followed in going from case writer to consultant to board member. "It's kind of like having a date before you get married," he said. Buzzell sits on the boards of Chelsea Industries, U.S. Shoe Corporation, General Nutrition, and VC Corporation.

Several hundred new cases are written every year, the majority of which are written for purely academic reasons. However, many dozens are written for purely business reasons, which include a professor's consulting contract, enlistment of corporate sponsorship, or a recruiting tool for one of Harvard's management programs. A handful of new cases (perhaps three to five each year) are written for no other reason than that the school hopes to attract a $1.5 to $2 million endowed chair.* These are the so-called major cases in which the school's investment is $150,000 or more; they are always approved by the dean before the work begins. Cases on the Korean companies Daewoo, Samsung, and Goldstar were three examples of this.

---

* An endowed chair results when a lump sum of money (minimum of $1.5 million) is donated. The money is invested in long-term negotiable securities, and the annual income from those investments ($120,000 to $150,000) is used to pay for a professor's salary, expenses, and small research budget. The chair is named in honor of the donor.

THE CASE OF THE CHAIRMAN'S NEW SUIT

In mid-1983, Dean McArthur, acting on the advice of his top strategic advisers, issued a policy statement directing the general management department to research Korea with the eventual goal of endowing two new chairs from that country by 1986. The directive had two effects. First, $500,000 was allocated for the project, and second, the school recruited a Korean national visiting professor, Dong Sung Cho. Cho was the "insider" who knew Korean corporate leaders and who was able to narrow the field of contenders to three diversified giants: Goldstar, Samsung, and Daewoo.

A team was assembled at Harvard, contacts were established in Korea, multiple field visits were made, crates of data were shipped to Morgan Hall, and by early 1985 final drafts of the cases were complete. All this preparation was the groundwork for visits by the three corporate chairmen, the first being Woo-Choong Kim of Daewoo Corporation, for whom a full schedule of events was provided:

MONDAY   10:00 P.M.   Arrival at Logan Airport via New York and Seoul, Korea.

                10:30 P.M.   Limousine ride to Harvard Business School.

                11:00 P.M.   Dinner and overnight accommodations for Chairman Kim and traveling party at the Dean's House.

TUESDAY   8:30 A.M.   Breakfast with Dean McArthur and Dean of Admissions for MBA program at Dean's House.

9:30 A.M.	MBA class discussion with Professor Richard Hamermesh on Daewoo Corporation case. [All ten sections, 780 students, were assigned the case for this day.]
10:30 A.M.	Private screening of AMP videotape on Daewoo Corporation, filmed a day earlier.
10:50 A.M.	AMP class discussion with Professor Jay Lorsch on Schlumberger case.
12:00 P.M.	Luncheon with twelve faculty at the faculty club private dining room.
1:30 P.M.	Question and answer session with seven hundred MBA, AMP, and PMD students with film crew present.
3:00 P.M.	Tour of campus.
6:00 P.M.	Dinner at the Ritz-Carlton Hotel in Boston with ten senior faculty and Dean McArthur.
9:00 P.M.	Limousine to Logan Airport for departure.

All the best-laid plans, however, went awry. The jeans-clad, diminutive Chairman Kim, chain-smoking American cigarettes, arrived two hours late on Monday evening. Worse still, the airline lost his only suitcase between New York and Boston. No toothbrush, no shoes, no suit, and for Harvard, no chair.

On Tuesday morning the problem was solved when a tailor from the university's department store, the Harvard Cooperative Society, was called in to do an emergency fitting in Harvard Square before the store opened to the public. By 8:00 A.M., a $400 suit had been altered to fit Chairman Kim, courtesy of the dean.

Both Kim and McArthur had prepared for that morning's meeting, but McArthur was at a clear disadvantage because he spoke no Korean. Kim, on the other hand, understood English well but used an interpreter anyway. With the interpreter slowing the conversation to a snail's pace, McArthur, as expected, began to show signs of frustration. Tiring of the slow progress of the meeting, at 9:10 A.M. he decided to go boldly in for the prize.

"Would the chairman be interested in furthering Harvard's research into the Far East through the establishment of an endowed chair?"

An equally polite reply was made by Kim through the interpreter: "Chairman Kim says he believes in support of academic excellence throughout the world. He says his personal goal is for one thousand Ph.D. working for Daewoo Corporation by year of 2000."

The dean, foiled in his first attempt, persisted.

"Does the chairman see the benefits to a Woo-Choong Kim chair of business administration at Harvard?"

An agonizing pause followed the interpreter's translation of the question into Korean. McArthur squirmed. Chairman Kim sat quietly for what seemed like several minutes, as if in a trance, before he answered.

"Chairman says he is modest man."

At this response the dean's face became flushed, partly from embarrassment and partly because he could not seem to make himself understood.

"Would the chairman like to establish a permanent relationship with the school?" asked the exasperated McArthur.

"Chairman thanks dean for generous offer. Would be willing to send three workers yearly from Daewoo to study MBA program at Harvard."

McArthur slumped back in his chair and glanced at his MBA admissions director. More frustrating attempts to cajole a chair from Kim were foiled, and McArthur finally agreed to make available 2 (out of 780) MBA places to Daewoo Corporation to fill each year, for five years, with company-selected applicants. In return, the company held open the possibility of eventually endowing a chair.

Conspicuously absent from that evening's dinner at the Ritz-Carlton Hotel was the dean. Something had come up, was the excuse, and he just couldn't make it. Professor Samuel Hayes III accepted the Korean chairman's token gift on behalf of the dean. Kim knew there was no reason for McArthur to be there. The deal was already struck, the discussions were over, and the dean had lost. There was no press conference scheduled to announce the establishment of a new Korean chair. The MBA admissions director had quietly noted the results, and the dean made a note to himself to try again later.

Unlike all other academic institutions, Harvard Business School has the luxury of a tool that guarantees steady communication between itself and industry. While most schools wait for alumni to grow up and become wealthy enough to donate money, HBS takes the proactive approach of setting two- to five-year plans to attract chairs in new areas of interest.

Scholarly research is the heading for the school's research and development, and no business school spends more on it than HBS. Other schools scrimp on amenities for guests, choosing to portray an impoverished image, but Harvard goes just the opposite way. Nothing is too fine for its distinguished guests, and no expense is spared to get a sale.

Hospitality is not wasted on lesser lights, however. When the school attempted to get the chairman of Goldstar Company in Korea to make the same trek as Chairman Kim of Daewoo, the bait was left on the hook. Instead, Goldstar sent the president of its American division, Mr. P. W. "Peter" Suh, from Huntsville, Alabama. Harvard's itinerary for the division president contrasted sharply with Chairman Kim's. Needless to say, mere corporate presidents do not breakfast with Dean McArthur or dine at the Ritz.

FRIDAY	1:30 P.M.	Arrival at Logan Airport via Huntsville, Alabama.
	2:00 P.M.	Taxi to Hyatt Hotel, Cambridge.
SATURDAY	9:30 A.M.	Taxi to Harvard Business School.
	9:45 A.M.	AMP class discussion on Goldstar case.
	12:30 P.M.	Lunch with AMP class in student dining hall.
	1:30 P.M.	Taxi to Hyatt and airport.

SPENDING INTO POSTERITY

"You can't save yourself into posterity, although I'm not entirely sure that you can't spend yourself there," said marketing professor emeritus Malcolm McNair once, and it ought to be the motto of the business school. The power that HBS commands in corporate America exists precisely because the institution is willing to spend large amounts of money on facilities, research, and salaries to attract the nation's best faculty and students.*

From an organizational point of view, the system works because everyone is vested. Professors hire researchers whom they believe will do work to enhance their chances of making tenure, getting endowed professorships, or achieving financial success. From the ranks of the MBA program the most promising students and Baker Scholars (top 5 percent of each HBS class) are recruited to spend

* As of January 1986, the school employed 86 full professors, 22 associate professors, 57 assistant professors, 16 visiting professors, 58 research fellows and associates, and 126 research assistants. Annual expenses exceeded $100 million.

a year writing cases, doing research, finding leads, and selling the system. Some professors promise to hand out the odd consulting job to Baker Scholars to help augment their low ($45,000) starting salary. In return, they affix their names to the product of that labor, reformat it into a book or article, and sell it into the business press as original research.

Far from frowning on the use of school facilities and research budgets for personal and professional gain, the school encourages such practices. Professors who are clever save large sums of money to lavish on the appropriate client, or their favorite pastime. Research accounts are used for a multitude of purposes, which may, or may not, directly relate to research. Season tickets to the ballet and travel expenses in New York were both justified by one enterprising academic as necessary expenses for case development on managing artistic performers. Three weeks in West Germany to study the competitiveness of German industry happily coincided with the arrival time of another professor's preordered Audi. Abuses such as these, unfortunately, cast doubt upon the validity and usefulness of HBS's other research activities, many of which are important and justifiable.

There are built-in incentives for using school research budgets to gain access to corporations. Many professors earn far more than their business-school salary through part-time consulting work. Indeed, an organized consulting firm, called Marketing Science Institute (MSI), which operates under a nonprofit charter, acts as a clearinghouse for surplus consulting contracts in the marketing department.

A majority of tenured faculty members have private clients and do not rely on one of the several in-house companies for leads. Rates are set individually with Michael Porter, at $10,000-plus per diem, billing at the top rate. Full professors in accounting or general management charge between $4,000 and $6,000 per diem, travel and expenses not included.

Part of selling a consulting contract is done on specu-

lation. Professors offer to do cases using funds from research budgets, but once they are inside they look for reasons to follow up. Senior corporate officers, usually the
president or chairman and staff, are invited to Harvard
to watch their corporation being dissected by a class of
MBAs, or by managers in an executive-education class.
Luncheon or dinner with the senior faculty member of
the project at the club or a Boston restaurant provides a
second chance to sell the features and benefits of a Harvard Business School consulting assignment.

The lengths to which professors go to secure such work
vary. Some are content to let Harvard's prestige, and their
own reputation in a given field, draw random clients to
them. Others spend large sums to remain conspicuous in
front of likely prospects. Chief among this group is Professor Michael Porter, who once shipped 375 copies of his
book *Competitive Strategy*, via express mail, to top executives in corporations around the world. While it was un-
doubtedly flattering to receive an advance copy of his new
book, the recipients probably had no idea that they themselves were the objects of Porter's competitive strategy to
foster consulting work for his Cambridge-based firm,
Monitor Company.

CHAPTER 6

Personages
of the
Faculty

• • •

An open secret known to every female member of the faculty of Harvard Business School is that the school is set up and operates organizationally as a gentlemen's club. The preponderance of men is seen in the faculty-club dining room, where aging male professors huddle together to debate fluctuations in the equities markets, and at meetings of the tenured faculty, where two women sit among their eighty-four male peers.

The school is a fraternity built on relationships that began decades ago. The example of Stephen H. Fuller, an expert in labor relations, demonstrates how strong those ties can be. Fuller left the faculty after twenty-four years in 1971 for a higher-paying job as the vice-president of personnel at General Motors. Although he was technically no longer affiliated with Harvard Business School from the moment he quit, he knew that a job was waiting for him at the school if he ever wanted it. In 1982, he let it be known to Dean McArthur that indeed he did want to finish out his career at the school, and the dean unfalteringly brought him back for four years, until his retirement, as the first incumbent of the new Tiampo Chair of Business Administration.

Because tenure is so permanent, the faculty makes every effort to see that the wrong sort of people don't intrude. That sentiment meant, for a long time, that no females were allowed. Active discrimination against women dated back to the earliest years of the school. No women were admitted to the MBA program until 1959, and no women rose above the rank of associate professor until 1961.

Henrietta Larson, who taught business history, joined the school in 1928 and was finally granted tenure in 1961, not coincidentally a year before her retirement. Her colleague Elizabeth Abbott Burnham, who came to the faculty in 1927 and taught business administration, never rose above the associate level, even after working for more than thirty years.

While women were excluded from the tenured ranks, they were encouraged to manage the school's administrative affairs. The school promoted women up to the level of associate dean, and gave them the major responsibility for running the school's machinery, from case records to student registration. There was no lack of women at HBS; there was, however, a lack of real institutional power in their hands.

The first woman to break the tenure barrier was Regina Herzlinger, who did so in 1980. Unlike many of her female predecessors, Herzlinger was fortunate enough to find a male professor willing to be her mentor, and was clever enough not to be perceived as a threat to her male colleagues.

Within HBS, mentors (senior faculty with academic power) act as shepherds to a chosen few. Mentors make certain that the junior associates under their supervision do the kind of work that will be viewed favorably by their colleagues on the tenure committee. Working with the right mentor, such as C. Roland Christensen, virtually guarantees eventual promotion. Few on the senior faculty are mentors. Some, like marketing statesman Ted Levitt, never establish mentor relationships because they prefer to work by themselves.

Herzlinger's mentor was Robert Anthony, a senior professor of accounting. Between 1971 and 1978, Anthony and Herzlinger co-authored numerous *Harvard Business Review* articles, as well as a definitive book on accounting for nonprofit organizations, which won the James Hamilton management book of the year award. Low-key and always professional, Anthony had enormous influence with the faculty as a result of his long and distinguished academic career. He was, perhaps, the most popular member of the faculty among his colleagues. Nevertheless, according to recollections of the tenure review proceedings, Anthony was obliged to call in a number of favors to sway the vote and get Herzlinger appointed to a full professorship.

Most professors vehemently denied that they were the least bit chauvinistic. They maintained that Herzlinger's appointment proved that when a qualified female was reviewed for tenure, she was scrutinized just the same as her male colleagues. The reason that there weren't more tenured women like Herzlinger, they claimed, was that there weren't enough qualified candidates.

Herzlinger's accomplishments, besides her work with Anthony, included prior employment with several business and government agencies, such as the Federal Power Commission and the Massachusetts Office of Human Services, raising a family, and running a successful manufacturing business with her husband. When another Herzlinger appeared on the scene, they said, the faculty would honor her with the same distinction.

The next woman to come before the tenure committee in 1981, Barbara Bund Jackson, fell short of the mark. She was turned down twice before finally leaving the school and filing suit against Harvard Business School for sexual discrimination in 1984. Jackson's suit charged that women faculty members were disparaged, sexually harassed, received unequal pay, and were continually denied other benefits granted to men, namely mentors. The case was still in litigation in 1987.

While the allegations in Jackson's suit were denied by Dean McArthur and Harvard Business School, the co-defendants, the Jackson case had the effect of sensitizing everyone in the administration of the need to remedy the imbalance in the senior faculty, and to give more visibility to the women who had ties to the institution. The result was that in early 1984 McArthur suggested that the Committee of 200 (a national organization that supports women in business) hold one of its semiannual meetings on the HBS campus.

Carol Goldberg, an AMP graduate whose family owned the Boston-based Stop & Shop Companies, chaired the planning committee. On the dean's recommendation, the committee selected entrepreneurship as the theme of their HBS conference. McArthur volunteered the lecturing services of professors Howard Stevenson and Walter Salmon, and for three days in May two hundred businesswomen were accorded the cordiality of the school.

While the conference was a boon to public relations, it did nothing to change the growing discontent of the female junior professors. To them the real issue was inequality, and the conference was perceived as a token gesture. While no one confronted McArthur directly, rumblings were heard to the effect that many of these professors supported Barbara Jackson over HBS in her lawsuit. It became increasingly clear to the dean that the time had come to make some forceful statement in support of fair representation. Another woman had to be granted tenure immediately.

None of the potential women candidates on staff was felt to be strong enough, either because a male colleague in the department had seniority, or because the female aspirant lacked notoriety in her field. The risk in promoting to a tenured position a woman whose candidacy could in any way be challenged was that her disappointed male challengers would have been given grounds for a reverse-discrimination suit. The logical answer, then, was to go outside HBS to hire an indisputable expert in a business field not already filled by a male HBS faculty member.

The advantages to having the Harvard Business School name to use in recruiting a new faculty member became readily apparent to the subcommittee empowered by McArthur to fill the slot. The subcommittee limited its search solely to tenured female professors on the faculties of other prestigious graduate business schools. The theory was that anyone would grab the chance to join the most influential business school in the world, as assumption that proved to be correct.

The woman selected by the subcommittee was Rosabeth Moss Kanter, a tenured professor at Yale's School of Organization and Management. In addition to being one of the preeminent managerial theorists in the country, Kanter had several other qualities that made her the obvious choice. She had written two influential books on management—*The Change Masters* (1983) and *Men and Women of the Corporation* (1977)—and she was one of the few women consultants who was accepted by chief executives of *Fortune* 500 companies. That was the primary reason she got the job.

Kanter's rise to prominence was as much a result of her hard work as it was of her willingness to take risks. Born in Cleveland in 1943, she studied sociology at Bryn Mawr and enrolled in the Ph.D. program at the University of Michigan in 1964. In 1967, she taught sociology at Brandeis University while living in a collective near Boston. At the same time she also worked on the Cambridge Institute New Cities Project, the purpose of which was to create a new kind of commune in Vermont. The project failed, but it sparked in her an interest in organizations. "A lot of the sixties phenomena—the collectives, the alternative institutes, the small enterprises—were entrepreneurial activities," she told *Business Week* in 1986.

Her interest in business picked up considerably in 1972 when she married Barry Stein, a Ph.D. consultant who worked for the firm of Arthur D. Little. Together they founded a Cambridge-based management-consulting firm called Goodmeasure that rapidly attracted such blue-chip clients as Honeywell, IBM, General Electric, and Xerox. At the same time that Goodmeasure was getting off the ground in 1977, she joined the faculty of Yale's School of Management and began commuting between New Haven and Cambridge.

The increasing demands on her time only encouraged her to accomplish more, and she added public speaking to her already overburdened schedule. Kanter became one of the rare women who was able to balance teaching, writing, consulting, and lecturing while still finding time to raise a child.

As her consulting business grew, so did her popularity. For 1986, Goodmeasure, Inc., projected revenue of $5 million, and Kanter's personal-appearance fee on the speaking circuit rose to $15,000 per speech. According to *U.S. News & World Report*, in 1984 she received 440 requests to speak, and made 107 appearances.

At first glance, Kanter did not look like a particularly dynamic speaker, but, in fact, she was. One woman who came to see her address an HBS student organization put it this way: "When she steps up to the podium you ask yourself, 'Who is this short, frumpy professor?' But when she starts to talk, you forget completely what she looks like. She's totally spellbinding."

That was the sort of woman who belonged on the faculty of Harvard Business School, said John McArthur. He offered her tenure and the Class of 1960 Chair of Business Administration, and Kanter jumped at the offer. The message to junior women on the faculty was clear: If their credentials stacked up favorably next to Kanter's—two best-selling books, successful consulting and lecturing businesses, board memberships, advisor to Massachusetts governor Michael Dukakis and Colorado senator Gary Hart, and mother of a seven-year-old child—then they could expect a call from the dean also. The tenure requirements for women at HBS were thus firmly established.

THE MARKETING LEVIATHAN

For several years during the mid-1950s the marketing department of Harvard Business School had great difficulty hiring its quota of qualified staff members to teach the first-year marketing course. The problem stemmed both from a shortage of marketing instructors nationwide and also from the irascible chairman of the marketing department, Malcolm McNair. McNair, who once seriously suggested doing away entirely with the teaching of organizational behavior at HBS because it lacked sufficient importance, was so demanding as a boss that few of the new recruits who joined his department lasted past their first academic year.

By 1958 the situation reached a critical stage. The school tried to fill the vacancies by calling on its alumni to return to HBS as instructors. Noting that "tenure guarantees lifetime employment," and that "the annual salary for the tenured faculty is between $12,000 and $18,000," the alumni magazine tried vigorously to drum up interest. Few alumni, if any, responded.

Among the unpromising new enlistees in 1959 was a thirty-four-year-old business consultant from Chicago named Theodore Levitt, who, by his own admission, was generally unqualified to be there. "You should understand that I had never taught marketing before, never read a book on marketing before, and never taught by the case method before," disclosed Levitt jokingly twenty-four years after the fact.

As inauspicious as his preparation to be a marketing instructor was, Levitt nevertheless had the intelligence and perseverance that was required to survive the difficult first year under McNair. Once his talents in marketing became apparent, Harvard Business School kept him for the remainder of his professional career.

Theodore Levitt fled Nazi Germany with his family at the age of ten and grew up in Dayton, Ohio, where, in 1940, he became a naturalized citizen. After two years in the U.S. Army, Levitt returned to Dayton in 1945 and enrolled at nearby Antioch College, in Yellow Springs, where he received his bachelor's degree in 1949. He continued his postgraduate studies at Ohio State University, earning his Ph.D. in economics in just two years.

Levitt embarked on what quickly became an unspectacular academic career. He joined the faculty of the University of North Dakota in Grand Forks, where he taught business economics for four years and achieved little notoriety in the field. He abandoned academics altogether in 1955 and started a new career as a business consultant in Chicago.

The Lonely Crowd, a book by the noted social scientist David Riesman, changed the course of Levitt's career. Responding to what he felt was Riesman's misinterpretation of the future of American capitalism, Levitt fired off an article to the *Harvard Business Review* called "The Changing Character of Capitalism," in which he said, "I believe a thoroughly convincing case can be made for the continued and growing vitality of American capitalism—and not just in spite of what Riesman says, but because of it!"

Levitt's commentary was eagerly received by the *Review*'s editor, Edward Bursk, who featured it as the lead article in the July/August 1956 issue. The commentary led to a long-distance friendship between Levitt and Bursk and to the publication of a second *HBR* article in 1958

entitled "The Dangers of Social Responsibility." The following year Bursk and others at HBS encouraged Levitt
to come to the school as an instructor.

Despite the fact that he had little formal education in
the area, Levitt ably applied his economics training and
practical business experience to mastering the principles
of marketing, even as he was teaching them to his students. So successful was he in his first year that he immediately produced what has been called the single most
influential article in marketing thought, an article for the
Harvard Business Review called "Marketing Myopia."

According to Levitt, the idea for the article came to him
almost spontaneously. "I never made any notes or wrote
anything down, nor did I ever really think about it, as far
as I can remember. But one night at home, sitting at the
kitchen table, I started writing. Four or five hours later,
the first draft was done. The original title was 'Marketing
Myopia and Growth Companies.' With his enormous in-
sight and wisdom, Ed Bursk, the editor of the *Review*, did
the right thing. He just kept the first two words of the
title and dropped the rest. Beyond that, he hardly changed
a word of what I had written."

"Marketing Myopia" launched Levitt's career and made
him a business celebrity virtually overnight. Upon publication, thirty-five thousand reprints were sold to one
thousand different companies. By 1983, with requests
continuing to pour in, more than a half million had sold
in all. It is easily the most successful article in the *Review*'s history.

While Levitt was never able to duplicate his early writing success, it made no difference to his career. Within
three years he was promoted from lecturer—the bottom
rung on the teaching ladder at HBS—to full professor of
marketing, an unprecedented rise. Sixteen years later he
became the first incumbent of the Edward W. Carter Chair
of Business Administration.

The marketing department, which had labored for decades in obscurity, came into its own with the rising

prominence of its junior member. Levitt wrote numerous marketing books and articles, including eighteen that were published by the *Harvard Business Review* between 1964 and 1983, more than any other single contributor did. By virtue of his highly acclaimed writing ability he rose to become the most famous and most respected member of the Harvard Business School faculty.

Fittingly, the career that was started by the *Review* came full cycle in 1985, when Levitt was named its editor. The transition from scholar, researcher, and consultant to magazine editor was, as he saw it, "a commitment I'm going to have the fun of mastering . . . Now, for those who might say of people like me, 'They can instruct, but can they do?' I am very fortunate that, at my advanced age, I have a chance to make a meaningful response."

THE MISSIONARY ON WALL STREET

Like Rosabeth Kanter, Samuel Hayes III came to the notice of Harvard Business School once he had achieved success at another top business school. Widely viewed as the most influential member of HBS's finance department, Hayes used a knack for persuasion and a boundless energy level to catapult into a successful career at the leading edge of America's money centers. "If he had not been a professor," said one of his colleagues, "he would have been a missionary. He's got the same zeal for spreading new ideas in capital markets as Christian ministers do for spreading the Gospel to heathen savages."

Hayes grew up in Philadelphia and attended Swarthmore College, where he majored in political science and studied cello and pipe organ. At twenty-two, he enlisted in the U.S. Navy, where he continued his amateur musical career as an assistant director of the navy's Blue Jacket Choir. His family encouraged him to pursue banking, and he attended the MBA, and then the DBA program, at Harvard.

He joined the faculty of Columbia's Graduate School of Business rather than Harvard because of its proximity to Wall Street, the source of his research interests. At Columbia, he immediately became that school's top finance professor, earning outstanding teaching honors and full tenure as an associate professor in less than five years. It was an achievement that caught the chairman of Harvard Business School's finance department by surprise. He invited Hayes to return to Harvard for two years as a visiting professor, and before he left Hayes was offered a substantial raise, tenured standing as a full professor, and the promise of a chair within five years if he would forgo Columbia. It was an offer that acknowledged his superstar status in the world of finance, and that assured him complete control over his academic destiny.

As his reputation grew, so did his influence on Wall Street, where his recommendations of Harvard MBA students carried significant clout with the major firms. Recruiting was big business on the campus of Harvard Business School, and was a ritual that, until it was controlled, went on throughout the academic year.* Starting salaries for Harvard MBAs on Wall Street approached $70,000 per year by 1986, luring 25 percent of each class into firms such as Goldman, Sachs, First Boston, Morgan Stanley, Drexel Burnham Lambert, and Salomon Brothers.

Faculty recommendations were especially important in the initial screening process, and in marginal cases, where two or more candidates were closely evaluated. At informal private meetings, faculty met with recruiters, who were often their former students, to discuss insights into personalities of new recruits. Grades were never dis-

*In the early 1980s, the school established rigid guidelines for the hundreds of companies that recruited MBAs. Those guidelines told them the exact moment when recruiting season began (after first-year exams in January), and the first day they were permitted to make permanent job offers. Breaking the rules resulted in suspension of a company's on-campus recruiting privileges.

cussed, since most people applying for the jobs were at
the top of their class anyway. Recruiters wanted to know
how students reacted under pressure, how well they got
along with members of their section, and, especially, how
persuasive they were in arguing their positions. Hayes and
other faculty had spent hundreds of hours with each class,
and were in a better position to answer those questions
than a recruiter who could spend no more than an hour
with each candidate in an interview. Hayes sometimes
suggested names of students who, for a number of reasons, might not have been considered candidates. He had
passed judgment on thousands of MBA students during
his academic career, and was a far better judge of the
characteristics necessary for success in investment banking than any junior partner or associate.

Hayes's recommendations were, by no means, the final
word on candidates. Those who were serious about investment banking had to impress recruiters at formal
dinner parties in downtown hotels, to which students were
shuttled back and forth from campus in a caravan of lim-
ousines, and later in an interviewing process that sometimes required twelve separate trips to New York or Los
Angeles to meet with partners of a single firm. First-year
summer-job interviews were as important as second-year
interviews, since a student with no background in the field
stood little chance of convincing a firm to take a chance
on him. Those who thrived in the frenzied first-year recruiting season, and an equally stressful twelve weeks on
Wall Street, often returned to Harvard for their second
year with permanent job offers in hand, even though such
early offers were expressly forbidden by Harvard.

The sensitive job of being the investment banks' unofficial screening mechanism was a position protected by
Hayes, who eschewed consulting work with major Wall
Street firms to guard against any charges of favoritism.
Every major investment bank donated heavily to the school
both as a member of the Associates Program and as a
provider of matching gifts by alumni. Goldman, Sachs &

Company, especially, was a heavy donor, giving more than $200,000 to establish the John C. Whitehead/Goldman, Sachs & Company Faculty—Business Executives Exchange Program which paid HBS faculty to spend up to a year gaining on-line experience in business. Even members of the firm who were not HBS alumni gave generously. Geoffrey T. Boisi, head of mergers and acquisitions, Robert E. Rubin, arbitrager, H. Corbin Day, Pieter A. Fisher, Stephen Friedman, James P. Gorten, George M. Ross, and several other partners gave a combined total of more than $210,000 to the business school's capital fund in 1984. Such generosity could not be alienated under any circumstances. If it was rumored that First Boston had Samuel Hayes III on its payroll, Goldman, Sachs, Drexel Burnham Lambert, Morgan Stanley, and every other Wall Street investment bank would be up in arms about the "payoff." It was a situation Hayes chose to avoid entirely by refusing all offers that came along.

For the same reason, Hayes also refused to do case studies on any of the major investment-banking firms. His contacts at Goldman, Sachs and Morgan Stanley ran into the dozens, and the doors to the super-secretive, deal-making world of investment banking were always open to him, but he was above temptation. He was one of the notables of the school who had the integrity to buck the system.

MR. CASE METHOD

C. Roland Christensen was an uncompromising ascetic. Raised in the 1920s in Tyler, Minnesota, the son of two schoolteachers, he decided early on to enter his parents' profession, though not to sustain himself. To earn a living he intended to buy a farm and raise livestock. The business of husbandry would provide a safe source of income, he decided, so he entered the University of Iowa to study agricultural enterprise. While there, he worked hard and demonstrated a superior organizational ability, which helped him to get into Harvard Business School.

Compared to the sons of industrialists with whom he sat at Harvard, he stuck out as a callow country boy. As time went on during his two years in the MBA program, he gradually began to fit in as he pushed himself to dress, speak, and act the role of an Ivy League intellectual.

Graduating in March 1943, he was inducted into the army and spent four years as a quartermaster officer. It was his first position of responsibility and he relished it. His assignment kept him away from the dangerous battle zones and ensconced in an administrative bureaucracy where he organized a new, more efficient, and faster system of routing supplies. The experience was a minor victory that taught him he could solve complex logistical problems using some of the skills he'd learned at Harvard. On completing his military service in 1946, he decided to return to HBS.

In order to thrive in the socially prominent circles of the business school, Christensen developed two distinct personas. In the company of peers and superiors he was an exemplary scholar who had the ability to write arcane academic papers at will, and who was willing to discuss minor teaching problems at length. Friends and business associates saw him in a less formal light. To them, Chris was a regular guy who swore, chewed tobacco, and mocked the pomposity of his colleagues at Harvard.

The Christensen Method

In 1953, Christensen made the academic breakthrough that shaped the entire course of his career. Realizing that Harvard's case method of instruction, which used case studies to approximate real business situations, lacked a systematic structure, he concluded that he could become the school's resident expert on case writing and teaching by introducing a new format for cases that others would follow. He immersed himself in the hundreds of examples in the school's library and began to devise a unique approach to writing cases based on the most effective elements he identified in previous works. In 1954, when the then professor of retailing and chairman of the marketing department, Malcolm McNair, compiled a book on the case method, Christensen impressed him by volunteering to write a chapter on the administrative aspects of case production.

Having identified the importance of cases to the school, Christensen used it as the basis for furthering his career at HBS for the next three decades. He established himself as the unofficial editor of all cases that went through the system, a position that gave him a catbird's seat to review his colleagues' research before anyone else. Controlling the content of new cases in the system allowed him to suggest new projects, and to pass judgment on junior faculty whose works he edited. Almost imperceptibly, he maneuvered into a position where he managed the flow of information through the school, and had veto power over who got promoted and who did not.

When Dean Donald David complained in 1953 of the inadequate screening process for selecting Baker Scholars to work as researchers, it was Christensen who volunteered to personally do the job. Henceforth, new recruits were sorted out by him.

Christensen's technique, which he successfully used from then on, was described by a former inductee this way: "Five of us drove up to his house in New Hampshire to stay for two days. He told us that he wanted to get to know each of us personally, and introduce us to his style of life away from Harvard. We went fishing, we rented canoes and paddled around a lake by his house, and at night we sat around a campfire and told stories, just like boy scouts. He invited us to drink, smoke, and relax, if we liked, and to swap dirty jokes. By the end of the weekend, the guys who had the best time didn't get asked to work at Harvard."

If his screening methods were unorthodox they were, at least, effective. Those who made the cut proved to be hardworking, conscientious, and straitlaced. Several, like John H. McArthur, went on to successful administrative careers at HBS, and all shared Christensen's zeal for writing cases.

He was credited with making the case method uniquely adapted to Harvard Business School by inventing a procedure for gathering information that all others, including reporters, analysts, consultants, and even corporate insiders, could not follow. Researchers who handed out Harvard Business School cards were welcomed by chief executives, who gladly spent hours, and sometimes days, with them, pouring out their innermost business secrets. Case writers became academic confessors, who redeemed chief executives from a world of ambiguity. The presumption that researchers and professors were, like Switzerland, neutral and gnomish, and able to guard precious secrets, allowed the school to go in clean and fresh at any level and come out with the product.

The school's Division of Research sent all problem cases, and problem case writers, to Christensen. He made sure that the work got done and that it was up to standard. Gradually his influence was seen throughout the system in products that followed a regimented formula. The Christensen-style cases were bland enough to pass the scrutiny of the executives whose companies were being studied, but the leftover data gleaned in the research process was used by professors to build information bases for their own purposes.

Each new group of assistant professors brought to Harvard Business School were required to attend Christensen's seminar on case writing and case teaching. He was introduced to them as "Mr. Case Method," a term that paid homage to him as the dean of the school's teaching methodology. As he did with the thousands of MBA students who had gone through his classes, Christensen sized up the new assistant professors and made recommendations for their promotion. It was from that early encounter in their careers that he based his decision, years later, on who would get his approval for tenure.

CHAPTER 7

Communications
and
Public Relations

. . .

During the summer of 1985, media interest in Harvard
Business School had reached an all-time high; international newspapers, magazines, and television reporters
converged on the campus, bringing with them techni-
cians and their assistants to film, photograph, and interview at length. On one memorable occasion, two different
camera crews had set up in front of Baker Library at the
same time and, thinking they were MBA students roam-
ing the scenic landscaped grounds, inadvertently photo-
graphed each other's crew members. It began to look as
though the school's public relations firm, Hill and
Knowlton, had done its job a bit too well—the school was

on the verge of becoming a three-ring circus.

That, at least, was how the administration wanted the faculty to see the situation. The issue was control, not publicity. It was fine to have reporters and film crews running from one building to the next doing interviews, which was the intent of hiring a public relations firm in the first place. But the flow needed to be carefully orchestrated and monitored lest the school become overexposed, or find itself in a position where faculty would accidentally deviate from the company line. It would never do to have two professors from the same department contradict each other in the same article, or even in different articles, so a mechanism was invented to handle those situations. Now when a reporter wanted a quote on a marketing issue, he would be given one name; if a different reporter, calling months later, wanted a quote on the same issue, he would be given the same name. In addition, media companies were handed a precise protocol that reporters were warned not to deviate from; the punishment for doing so was to become part of a list of reporters who were not to be given press passes or to be aided in any way.

Faculty, too, were warned to play by the rules. Responding to what he perceived to be a growing loss of regulatory power over faculty members, Dean John McArthur instructed his associate dean, Thomas Piper, to send off a memorandum to all faculty on September 6, 1985, about "media inquiries." It began, "Media interest in the Harvard Business School continues to be high. Handled well, it can be a strong plus for the school. However, we also recognize the risks and vulnerabilities." Attached were seven pages of official faculty ground rules, which spelled out procedures for dealing with the press. The following excerpts are taken from that memorandum:

- If called unexpectedly, you need not feel obligated to respond [to a reporter] at all or at once. Some faculty members find it useful to call the reporter back at a later, more convenient time. Besides providing opportunities to think about the questions, this can also allow time for a check by the News Bureau on the reporter's connection with a publication.

- Unfortunately, some reporters may not take the time to do the homework necessary to make the interview productive. If the reporters are not as well prepared as they should be, you can sometimes tactfully use this as an opportunity to lead them to discuss topics you feel would be more productive.

- On rare occasions, you may receive a request from a reporter to visit class. All of these requests should be referred to the News and Information Service. Unless there is some useful purpose to be served by such visits, the News and Information Service will not make such requests, in recognition of the general desire to avoid inhibiting classroom discussion.

- Videotaping, photography, and filming in HBS classrooms, dormitories, Library and Kresge Hall [dining hall] by outside agencies is prohibited.

- Also, please contact Bill [director of communications] whenever any outside individual or agency wishes to interview you. He is very knowledgeable on the various reporters, news services, and periodicals, and he can provide important insights and advice that may increase the effectiveness of our relationship with the press.

Public relations and communications was a double-edged sword. True, the publicity enhanced the institution's image as the top business school in the country, but it also occasionally backfired, as happened when a *Boston Globe* reporter interviewed Michael Porter and dwelled excessively in the published article about Monitor Company, Porter's private consulting company. Too much of that sort of press could rapidly tarnish the image of HBS as a purely academic-driven organization.

There were safe topics, and in response to queries related to these, the school willingly released information and handed out lists of professor-contacts who could be called. Anything to do with "global trends" of any kind was encouraged. However, inquiries about the school's $200 million–plus endowment, or the use of any research monies, raised automatic red flags. Not only would a reporter who asked those types of questions have his credentials scrutinized, but he would also discover that a screening mechanism had been put in place alerting everyone on staff not to talk with him. Memos would be fired off that explained why it was vital not to give out internal information; Dean McArthur was the only person qualified to respond, and he, unfortunately, was unavailable for comment.

In April 1986, a British magazine called *Business* attempted to write an article on "The HBS as a Business," but the author was not permitted to see any of the school's balance sheets, nor was she allowed to interview any administrative officials. Because she was unable to gain access, her three-page article focused on the school's ties with George F. Baker, president of the First National Bank of New York (Citicorp), who gave money in 1924 to build the original campus.

For anyone who cared, the news-and-public-information office was always ready to give out news and statistics about Harvard MBA students. They were a sanctioned topic, guaranteed to keep the school in the public's eye in a positive way. Even when one first-year MBA student placed a World War II hand grenade in another first-year MBA student's mailbox as a practical joke, forcing the Cambridge fire department's bomb squad to investigate the emergency call, the incident was shrugged off by the administration. MBA students were high-spirited, after all, weren't they? You had to expect that sort of thing from precocious future captains of industry. Members of the press were invited into Aldrich hall to film the scene of the incident, but few bothered. HBS was being a little too candid about it; obviously there was no story there.

Annual placement statistics for each graduating class were routinely released to the major news agencies, who used them to write stories about the record-high starting salaries offered to America's top business students: AVERAGE INVESTMENT BANKING JOB OFFERS AT HBS EXCEED $45,000— MANAGEMENT CONSULTING FIRM OFFERS ONE HARVARD MBA $90,000, TO START. To which the official school reaction was, "Isn't it terrible that the press focuses so heavily on the salaries our graduates are getting? Why don't they look beyond to see the other good things we're doing?" The answer, of course, was that the press was working from carefully prepared press kits that failed to provide anything of substance on any topics except placement statistics. Few reporters had the time or opportunity to investigate more sensitive issues, and those that did saw their sources of information quickly evaporate.

When John McArthur became the school's new dean in 1980, he soon realized that the press had established a quota of articles that would be written about the Harvard Business School simply because it was the Harvard Business School. Editors wanted news about the goings-on there, and reporters were instructed to come back with whatever was current. Eventually, McArthur believed, they would tire of doing stories about MBA placement, and begin to ask questions about what MBA faculty did outside of the five hours they spent each week in class.

POSITIONING ENTREPRENEURSHIP

What was needed was an entirely new topic, one that would allow HBS to control the flow of information about itself, to guide the media into new and more "productive" areas. Toward the end of his first full year as dean, McArthur decided that the new thrust would be on entrepreneurship.

He had consulted primarily with Michael Porter, C. Roland Christensen, and Marvin Bower, among others both inside and outside the school, about possible new themes to promote. Originally it had been Christensen's idea; he championed it, sold it, and agreed to raise money for it, if McArthur would go along. None of the other ideas, which ranged from global strategy to marketing planning, had as much cachet or support as Christensen's entrepreneurship theme, but still, McArthur was cautious about giving it his full endorsement. A final decision on whether to extend the promotion of the entrepreneurship theme in the press would have to wait until the strategy began to prove itself effective. If the press did not take to the idea after a year or so, then a new idea would replace it.

As Christensen saw it, entrepreneurship was an excellent agenda to promote precisely because it was not something Harvard Business School was associated with. Typically, MBAs left Soldiers Field for New York or Chicago to work for *Fortune* 500 companies, the biggest they could get into, where they would climb the corporate ladder of success for twenty or thirty years. Barring that, graduates gravitated toward the financial capitals of the world to become employees of large financial service companies such as Goldman, Sachs & Company; Kidder, Peabody & Company; and Chase Manhattan. Already it had become knowledge that there were more presidents and chief executives of the *Fortune* 500, and leading financial firms, with Harvard MBAs than with any other graduate business diploma.

Christensen felt that there was no point to drawing further attention to those facts. It had already begun to look like a conspiracy to control certain industries, and the school had only fueled the fires by allowing reporters in the Cole Room of Baker Library, where twenty enormous volumes, carefully laid out on a table, were filled with computer sheets that listed the names and titles of HBS alumni, divided and listed by company for the benefit of MBAs looking for corporate contacts. Within those pages one could quickly see that an anonymous firm such as Air Products & Chemicals Corporation in Allentown, Pennsylvania, had more than thirty graduates in top levels of management, and that some major industrial giants, like Ford Motor Company in Dearborn, Michigan, boasted literally scores of MBAs, AMPs, and PMDs* on staff, including Edsel B. Ford II, who had a PMD diploma. The object, said Christensen, should be to downplay the idea that a growing elitist club of graduates was commanding preeminent positions in important industries. If one chose a theme such as global strategy, eventually it would rebound and encourage questions about who would use the strategies, which would, of course, be the major industries populated with Harvard MBAs. What better way to silence such mischievous inquiries than to give the press an exciting and timely issue to sink its teeth into—entrepreneurship.

Few graduates ever left Harvard Business School with the express idea of starting their own company. MBAs were, by nature, a risk-averse group who shunned the wild idea of setting up a speculative enterprise. The classic profile of an entrepreneur had been someone like Stephen Wozniak, co-founder of Apple Computer, who had an engineering talent but had not finished college, let alone gotten an MBA. Nevertheless, a fair number of Harvard MBAs had started their own companies, either because they had lost their jobs or because they had become dissatisfied with working in a large corporation, and a disproportionate number of them had become wealthy and successful.

With McArthur's permission, Christensen set about in early 1981 to line up funds for a new chair, the incumbent of which would specialize in the study of entrepreneurship. The man who would fill that chair had already long since been decided upon by Christensen; it would be Howard Stevenson, for whom Christensen had served as mentor for nearly twenty years, and whom he had decided would be the inheritor of his position of power at the institution.

Stevenson was born in Holiday, Utah, and attended

* See glossary for definition.

Stanford University, where he excelled at mathematics. His objective had been to study the new field of data processing from a business perspective, and in 1963 he came to Harvard as an MBA student. He and Christensen became friends and partners, the latter using Stevenson's strong analytical skills to develop new research materials involving financial analysis, and Stevenson looking to Christensen for guidance and support.

In 1969 he received his doctorate and an appointment to the faculty, but he found that he could not support his growing family on Harvard's modest assistant-professor salary, so a year later he joined a Houston investment-banking and consulting firm run by an HBS alumnus. Christensen convinced Stevenson to return in 1970 by assuring him he could earn as much money consulting and teaching part time as he could working in Houston, and he was right. Stevenson began an eight-year consulting relationship with Preco Corporation, a paper manufacturer in Springfield, Massachusetts, and this supplemented his Harvard salary dramatically.

Dean Lawrence Fouraker announced in 1977 that because of a serious financial constraint, the first in Harvard Business School's history, the school would be unable to add more tenured professors to the faculty, which meant that Stevenson was out. It was a crushing disappointment, and it had everything to do with Christensen's lack of authority at that moment. The decade of the 1970s was Fouraker's, a period that saw the erosion of the base Christensen had worked for twenty years to build. Christensen still had power to lobby with his many friends on the faculty, but at that moment it was Fouraker who decided which faculty were given lifetime tenure, and he decided that Stevenson was not to be one of them.

Christensen resented Fouraker, a man who had never received a single Harvard degree, and who had come to HBS from Penn State under a Ford Foundation fellowship in 1959. Fouraker joined the faculty in 1961 as a lecturer, and within seven years was promoted to full professor and director of the Division of Research. From the very beginning of Fouraker's term in 1970, Christensen let it be known that he was unhappy with Harvard president Nathan Pusey's selection. He challenged Fouraker's absolute position of authority, and the two kept clear of each other as much as possible.

Fouraker was not inclined to do favors for someone who worked at cross purposes with him, and he certainly was not going to grant tenure to someone so squarely in Christensen's camp, all of which left Stevenson with no choice. In 1978 he left Harvard Business School to become chief financial officer of Preco, but he kept in close contact with his ally at HBS, hoping for an opportunity to return.

The task of getting a tenured professorship for Stevenson was greatly simplified in 1980, when Lawrence Fouraker was replaced by John McArthur. McArthur was malleable, he owed Christensen favors, and he was willing to listen to Christensen's advice. They were friends and, even more, they saw eye to eye on the need to have Stevenson return. The school needed more Stevensons, men who were good at selling the image HBS wanted to project: tough, hardworking, resourceful, intelligent. But even McArthur didn't have the budget in 1980 to bring Stevenson back as a tenured professor. John Kotter and Michael Porter, among others, were up before the committee, and they took precedence. There was a very real chance that by delaying their tenure the school would lose both of them. Stevenson was already gone; the worst that could happen had happened. The goal now was to prevent further damage to the talent pool.

By selling McArthur on the theme of entrepreneurship, Christensen maneuvered into a position where he could, at last, get Stevenson back. With single-minded determination, he attacked the problem, seeing it as a critical test of his power in the organization. McArthur may have been the titular head of Harvard Business School, but if deals were to be made behind the scenes, if strategy was to be determined, Christensen wanted to be in the middle of it. He knew that if he was unable to get sufficient support to finance a single chair for entrepreneurial studies, he certainly would not be in a position to guide the school's major decisions during the McArthur administration. At that moment, he needed demonstrable proof that he still had power at Harvard Business School.

The first alumni-entrepreneurs Christensen approached in 1981 about the possibility of donating $1.5 million, or more, to endow a new chair for entrepreneurship were noncommittal. The school had done little to aid in their success as entrepreneurs, and they were hard pressed to think of a viable reason why they should make such a magnanimous gesture toward the institution. They were entrepreneurs in spite of their Harvard training, not because of it, and although they felt it was a good idea to promote entrepreneurship, Harvard Business School, of all business schools, was the least likely institution to lead the charge.

The strongest interest in making any sizable contribution came from Fayez Sarofim, MBA '51, who was president of Fayez Sarofim & Company, a Houston investment-management firm with accounts of $5.5 billion. Sarofim was born in Egypt and came to America in 1946 to study at the University of California at Berkeley. After getting his MBA at Harvard in 1951, he joined the finance department of Anderson Clayton, a Houston conglomerate, and nine years later he left to start his own investment-management firm, picking up such major accounts as the pension funds for Ford Motor Company, CBS, Alcoa, and Standard Oil of Indiana, and others where his Harvard ties were useful in getting business.

Sarofim's network extended beyond just companies that used his investment services, to the companies in which he placed his own and his firm's money. One major repository for those funds was Cooper Industries, Inc., headquartered in Houston, a producer of engines, turbines, oil and gas industry equipment, and pumps; a company whose board C. Roland Christensen had been on since 1971, and which was run by Robert Cizik, MBA '58. Christensen's 200 shares in Cooper Industries paled next to Sarofim's 2.729 million shares of common stock and 606,000 shares of preferred, but Christensen was nevertheless a valuable ally to have on the board. There was no need to antagonize him unnecessarily, but there was also no reason to give Harvard Business School $1.5 million either. Sarofim told Christensen that he would consider the donation of a large gift only after he had talked with his friend, classmate, and frequent business partner, Arthur Rock.

Their careers had paralleled each other and, like Sarofim, Rock had become a self-made millionaire and entrepreneur. He was born in Rochester, New York, and graduated from Syracuse University before coming to Harvard Business School in 1949. His first job out of school was as an analyst, and six years later he was hired by Hayden Stone to work in its investment-banking department, where he helped to set up Fairchild Semiconductor Corporation in 1957. Four years later, he left to start his own firm in San Francisco, Arthur Rock & Associates.

He was one of the first venture capitalists to finance start-up computer companies in Silicon Valley, California, using money from such trusted business contacts as Fayez Sarofim. Their friendship, which had begun at Harvard, grew stronger as each made money for the other. While the bulk of Sarofim's portfolio went into blue-chip companies, there was always a small percentage, enough to diversify the securities mix, to channel into high-risk, high-return ventures such as Rock's. Rock was shrewd and completely trustworthy, and the odd $100,000 invested in computer companies hand-picked by him paid unbeatable returns that helped bolster Fayez Sarofim & Company's earnings during down years in the market.

Rock and Sarofim both viewed Harvard Business School the same way: It had been a valuable place to make contacts, and had helped to open doors to profitable careers in finance, but their success as entrepreneurs had been due entirely to their own talents, rather than from anything they had gained during two years of graduate studies. Notwithstanding their ambivalence toward making $1.5 million cash donations to Harvard Business School individually, they were inclined to consider donations of $750,000 each. Three quarters of a million dollars was not so onerous a burden when one thought about it, and besides, it was going to a worthy charity. So in recognition of their thirtieth class reunion coming up in October 1981, they notified Christensen that the money he requested would be forthcoming at that time. The donation, however, would not be in cash, something they were loath to part with; it would be in shares of stock from companies that they had invested in as start-up ventures. There was no reason to be foolhardy while being generous. Harvard Business School could sell the shares if it liked, or use the dividend income to pay the salary of the new professor of entrepreneurship.

That left only one happy problem for them to solve, which was whether the chair should be named Sarofim-Rock or Rock-Sarofim. Professor Hugo Uyterhoeven, the dean of external relations, went to San Francisco in mid-1981 to work out the particulars of the donation, and Rock asked him how the chair should be named. Since they were equal donors of the gift, Uyterhoeven suggested flipping a coin. Rock got Sarofim on the phone in Houston and Uyterhoeven flipped; Sarofim won: Sarofim-Rock.

Howard Stevenson returned to Harvard Business School in December 1981 just in time to help develop a new course offering called Entrepreneurial Management, for which part of his chair's endowment had been earmarked to provide case-development money. He had, of course, no firsthand experience as an entrepreneur, but there were lots of them out there to study. He would get his training in the subject as he went along, and by the time he had enough material to teach the course, he would be qualified to talk intelligently on the subject.

Just as Christensen had predicted, entrepreneurial

studies became a hot topic at HBS. The press, eager for a new story to tell, and amply supplied with information from the school, played into the hands of a full-scale public relations strategy in which Stevenson became the focal point. McArthur, convinced that the topic had expandability, gave Stevenson carte blanche to study Harvard Business School's entrepreneurial alumni on the condition that Stevenson take what information he gleaned and promote it in road shows for alumni and the press.

Stevenson's findings were not encouraging. Based on surveys that had been taken of reunion classes during 1982 and 1983, less than 11 percent of the alumni called themselves "self-employed" (the widest possible definition of an entrepreneur), and the numbers rose only gradually after that. Stevenson's computerized analysis proved conclusively that Harvard Business School trained managers, not entrepreneurs, and while more than 80 percent of the surveyed participants said they would have liked to have been self-employed, they were not.

Undeterred, Stevenson began to campaign vigorously for the school on the issue of entrepreneurship, stopping at clubs across the country, and making presentations at carefully organized, HBS-sponsored seminars on entrepreneurial ventures. He was the spokesman for a group of people who admired entrepreneurship when they saw it, though they themselves were not so foolish as to become entrepreneurs. The presentations were well attended by both alumni and the media, but there were few converts. Back at Harvard Business School, Stevenson's message was well publicized in student publications also, and in this case, when the new course he developed was offered for the first time, in 1984, more than three fourths of the second-year MBA class signed up to take it.

Once the idea had been planted, it was as if it had always been there. Was Harvard Business School a breeding ground for entrepreneurs? Of course. One need only look at the publicity given to entrepreneurial alumni in the school's alumni magazine.

Stevenson himself had come to think of the genesis of

entrepreneurial studies at Harvard Business School as dating back many more years than it actually had. In June 1986, he was quoted in a *New York Times* article about Wharton, a school that began offering courses in entrepreneurship in 1973, where he noted an alarming trend: "I get a little nervous about how many schools have suddenly discovered that most of their rich alumni were entrepreneurs, so they come up with that as a flattering catchword for getting their support."

CHAPTER 8

Welcome to HBS, Professor Pearson

• • •

An anonymous note written in lipstick was taped during the night to Andrall Pearson's office door in May 1985, and it succinctly expressed the sentiments of the female MBA students in his Section C class. It read: EVEN ONE OF THE 10 TOUGHEST BOSSES IN AMERICA HAS TO GO TO THE SUPERMARKET SOMETIMES!! YOU OWE US ALL AN APOLOGY. But before Pearson arrived that morning, the offending missive was taken down and thrown out by his secretary, thus sparing him from further rebuke.

The incident began with what Pearson thought was a harmless question. The class was discussing a consumer-products company's proposal to put a new household 117 cleanser into mass distribution, and Pearson casually asked a female student whether she would consider buying the product in a supermarket. That was the final straw, as far as the class was concerned. The question, directed as it was to a female student, clearly demonstrated the former Pepsico executive's overt chauvinism. Bad enough that he had often, matter-of-factly, referred to women as "gals." But the implicit assumption in this latest comment was that a female student was more likely than a male student to be in a supermarket at all.

The women of Section C met after class to consider lodging a formal complaint of discrimination against Pearson, but instead decided to wait until they had confronted him with their evidence, which they did at the next class session. One student, however, was unable to wait that long, venting her frustration as she did in the note on her professor's office door.

Pearson was stunned by their accusation that he had consciously or unconsciously maligned the female class members with his question. He had called on the woman not because she was a woman, but because he knew her from discussions outside of class, where he had learned that she was a single parent who did all her family's food shopping. She had, in fact, once mentioned that she purchased Pepsi in supermarkets and rarely anywhere else. He would have asked a male, he said, but it seemed more expedient to call on someone whom he was sure visited supermarkets. Case closed.

But the class refused to close the case that easily. They had smelled a rat, and their eyes and ears were alert from then on for him to step across the line again. At the final class session of the semester, the women of Section C presented Pearson with an apron and a shopping basket, reminders of his indiscretion. It was also a direct and humorous way to show him that at Harvard Business School, students were not going to take any of his corporate-style, old-boy fanny slapping. This was a place where all MBA students were created equal, at least until the job offers came in. Pearson, blushing, put the apron on to show them that he was a good sport about the whole thing. But it was humiliating, like a fraternity hazing, and he endured it in order to quiet the stomping of eighty-five out-of-control MBA students. He even endured a Pepsi-challenge test during the same class session, where he proved that he could distinguish Coke from Pepsi. They had him there, their captive, and could play with him as they liked. Pearson excused the class early that after-noon, and was the first one to leave the room.

Teaching cases to MBA students had never been Pearson's lifelong ambition, but the job had opened up and been offered to him at an opportune time in his career. He had led Pepsico through an enviable period of growth for fourteen years, but then, nearing retirement age, he felt the subtle pressure from three young executives, John Sculley, D. Wayne Calloway, and Michael H. Jordan, as well as from Donald Kendall, the chairman and chief executive officer, to step down. Opting for an early retirement so he could work at a less prestigious company for seven years until he reached age sixty-five was a possibility, as was the option to start his own company. But Pearson was a loyal, dedicated, hardworking company man, not an entrepreneur, and he liked the challenges of working in competitive, complex organizations. Kendall would never have come right out and asked him to retire, because he was, in fact, doing everything expected of a president and COO. But he knew that the company had major expansion plans that did not include him, and that Calloway and Jordan were Kendall's hand-picked successors for Kendall and Pearson. When McArthur called in 1984 to ask whether he would be interested in going back to Harvard as the Class of 1958 Professor,* it took Pearson exactly one afternoon to make up his mind.

Andrall and Richard Pearson, identical-twin brothers, were born in Chicago in 1925, and attended the Univer-

---

* For complete details on why Dean McArthur chose a nonacademic to fill the Class of 1958 Chair, see Chapter 15.

sity of Southern California. During the war, the Pearson twins joined the V-12 officers' training program at USC, where both earned the grade of lieutenant in the U.S. Naval Reserve. In 1945, they enrolled together in Harvard Business School, and two years later Andrall joined the consumer-products marketing division of Standard Brands in New York, where he remained for five years.

McKinsey & Company brought him in as an associate in 1953, and he rapidly rose to the rank of principal and director there. In 1967, Pepsico, Inc., contacted McKinsey to review some proposals made by its chairman, Donald Kendall, which advocated Pepsico's entering the bottled-spirits industry, and Pearson was sent in to head up the consulting team.

Kendall was a gruff and impulsive leader, who had started at Pepsi after the war as an $80 per month delivery man, and had climbed his way to the top by becoming the company's most aggressive marketeer. He was imposing and intimidating when he wanted to be, and had earned the reputation of being unwilling to compromise, which resulted in his being selected for the toughest assignments. In 1959, Kendall was sent to Moscow to represent the company at an international trade show, and in a publicity coup he convinced then-vice-president Richard Nixon, who was on a diplomatic mission for Eisenhower, to bring Nikita Khrushchev to the Pepsi booth at the show. With photographers from the world press gathered around, Kendall deftly held up a bottle of Pepsi to the cameras while Khrushchev and Nixon sampled the product. Khrushchev liked the product—and Kendall—so well that he permitted Pepsi-Cola to become the first manufacturer to build a bottling facility in the Soviet Union. It was a media bonanza, especially for Donald Kendall, who became a celebrity and the undisputed leader of the company.

In hiring McKinsey & Company to review his plans, Kendall made it clear to Pearson that he didn't want, or need, a Harvard-trained consultant from New York City to tell him how to run his own company. The board of directors had refused to approve his plans until he had hired an outside consulting firm to study their feasibility, which, as far as Kendall was concerned, was a waste of the company's money and of his time. But there it was, they were stuck with each other, and he ought to at least know the score going in.

Pearson was only five feet, eight inches tall in shoes with two-inch heels, and could seldom complete an entire sentence without stuttering on a word, two qualities that helped defuse Kendall's natural hostility toward him. He was undeniably intelligent and clever in a business sense, but he didn't fit the Kendall image of the tall, arrogant, Harvard MBA–trained McKinsey consultant. Kendall, six feet, two inches tall, didn't feel the least bit intimidated by Pearson, and with time their friendship and mutual admiration grew. In many ways they were opposites that attracted. Kendall was large, brash, and self-educated; Pearson was rational and Harvard-educated, the only person who could have persuaded Kendall to forgo his plans to buy a distillery.

The limited management-consulting project, which was expected to take a matter of weeks, stretched into a major study that lasted for three years. Kendall valued Pearson's opinions so highly that he sent him out to study every operating facility in the company, and to report back directly to him with his findings. It was a familiar pattern among senior consultants: Companies became addicted to receiving their special brand of filtered information and offered top positions to the senior consultants working on their business. McKinsey men, burned out in their midforties from excessive travel and unreasonable deadlines, often took the offer, even though it usually meant a cut in salary, which is exactly what Pearson did when Kendall offered him a job. Kendall had backhandedly made the proposal to Pearson by telling him that it was cheaper to have him on staff full time than to hire him as a consultant, but that was only a ruse; Kendall had begun to think of him as a surrogate son, a member of his family, and he could not imagine working at Pepsico without him. Within a year, Pearson was promoted to president and chief operating officer, was appointed to the board of directors, and was earning more than $400,000 in salary, bonuses, and stock options.

Pearson had his own reasons for wanting to join Pepsico, and these had nothing to do with his friendship with Donald Kendall. The company was dominated by operations people who, like Kendall, made decisions based on gut-level reactions to changing circumstances. Unlike McKinsey, where everyone had an MBA, Pepsico was a place that had scarcely heard of the degree; the job of heading up operations there was a major challenge. Here was a place where he could impress his own personal stamp on an organization, a fertile, virgin territory whose potential was incalculable. As hard as Kendall had worked to keep those slick, slide-rule-carrying highbrows out, Pearson would work to bring them in, the results of which would speak for themselves.

With Kendall's permission to run Pepsico as he liked, Pearson began hiring at least two Harvard MBAs each year to work in key managerial positions, a move that gradually transformed the entire culture of the organization. He had changed the rules for promotion; to get ahead at Pepsico you needed street smarts and an MBA. Line workers, like Kendall, were now much less likely to rise up the corporate ladder. The smart, aggressive staff managers who cleaned their fingernails and spoke with conviction about corporate strategy and planning systems were the ones who got the raise and the bonus.

As the complexion of Pepsico's management changed, Pearson made more attempts to impress upon his boss the value of those changes. He began to invite Kendall to functions of the Harvard Business School Club of New York, where he was on the board of directors, and he encouraged Kendall to socialize with his circle of acquaintances, Harvard MBAs like T. J. Dermot Dunphy of Sealed

Air Corporation, and John F. McGoldrick from American Can Company. In 1978, the club's dinner committee, of which Pearson was a member, gave Kendall the honor of introducing the keynote speaker for the annual Business Statesman Award, Robert O. Anderson, chairman and CEO of the Atlantic Richfield Company. The following year, when Pearson succeeded Dunphy as chairman of the club, Kendall received the 1979 award and the traditional Steuben glass bowl engraved with his name and professional accomplishments. It was a subtle form of bribery, and Kendall knew it, but still he keenly appreciated the honor. He had never received a bachelor's degree, yet there he was on the dais with Harvard Business School's leading alumni, a member of the club. From then on, people would assume that he had attended HBS. Kendall liked that, and he liked Pearson for giving it to him, which made him look the other way as Pearson systematically undid the management structure that Kendall had worked years to cultivate. It was still his company, no matter whom Pearson hired, and the bottom line was still good.

Pearson had always known that his own potential tenure as chairman and chief executive officer at Pepsico would be either short or nonexistent. When Pepsi-Cola Company merged with Frito-Lay to form Pepsico, Inc., in 1965, Kendall had been the first and only chief executive officer of the new company. Pearson, who was less than five years younger than Kendall, would have only the difference of their ages in the top job when Kendall retired in 1986, which, in some ways, would have made him a lame duck CEO.

Pearson might have been willing to live with that situation, but Kendall was not. If Pearson took over Kendall's job, Pepsico's high-flying young senior executives would grow stale and bored while waiting for him to reach age sixty-five. Worse still, there was a good chance that they would grow restless and start looking for their own companies to run.

John Sculley, D. Wayne Calloway, and a fast-track executive Pearson had brought with him from McKinsey & Company, Michael Jordan, were the three who had emerged from the pack in the 1970s to take over Pepsico after Kendall. Sculley was the most obvious choice to become the new CEO, since Kendall was the one who had convinced him to give up a career in architecture and enter the MBA program at Wharton, and then to join Pepsico in 1967, even after Sculley had married and divorced Kendall's stepdaughter. Sculley was a marketing superstar, who invented the Pepsi-challenge campaign, caffeine-free colas, and two-liter plastic bottles. But he was also a renegade in a company that had a conservative bent, and his competition was equally formidable: D. Wayne Calloway, who was a standout in the Frito-Lay division, and Pearson's choice from McKinsey, Michael Jordan.

They were equally formidable competitors, but the edge was Calloway's because he was more of a statesman in Kendall's image. As Sculley knew, there could be only one chief and if he wasn't it, he wasn't going to wait around for somebody to tell him. So in early 1983, when headhunter Gerry Roche, chairman of Heidrick & Struggles, approached him about becoming president and CEO of Apple Computer, he jumped ship, leaving the succession problem behind him.

Sculley's decision to go solved only part of Kendall's dilemma and heightened his anxiety about who would succeed him. The more time that elapsed before a decision was made about whether Calloway or Jordan would get the job, the greater was the likelihood that someone else like Gerry Roche would make the choice for him. Sculley's departure made it imperative that Pearson step aside before further damage could be done. He was the odd man out—too old to be chairman and CEO, and too young to retire, so Harvard made the decision for him and he opted to resign and start a new career.

Industry leaders were pleasant enough to have around so long as they recruited, donated money, and didn't overstay their welcome. Putting one on the tenured faculty was another matter entirely, and Dean McArthur considered the possible negative repercussions. The executive chosen might be a terrible instructor and an embarrassment to the institution, or he might take advantage of the situation by looking upon the job as a sinecure.

The pros and cons of appointing a distinguished executive like Reginald H. Jones of General Electric or David Rockefeller of Chase Manhattan Bank were hotly debated. Jones was felt to be too senior to be on the faculty, and he chain-smoked, even when he was talking with a class of MBAs, as he had been invited to do on occasion. Rockefeller, on the other hand, was thought to be too celebrated, a person who would create public relations problems for the school if he arrived for class each day in a chauffeur-driven limousine. Chief executives who held Harvard MBAs, like James E. Burke, '49, chairman & CEO of Johnson & Johnson, were ruled out also because it was felt that they would turn the job down. The executive chosen would have to be a sure bet to take the job, because if it was public knowledge that a Harvard Business School professorship was being offered "on the street," the reputation of the school would suffer. This was not an easy task; it was a matter of damage control.

McArthur finally decided on Andrall Pearson as his first choice. Marvin Bower liked Pearson a lot and that was enough. But Pearson was also friendly with many faculty members, having been on the visiting committee, having recruited, and having been a solid, loyal alumnus who had raised a lot of money through the HBS Club of New York. When he called to offer Pearson the job, the meager salary of $100,000 per year was mentioned only as a footnote. Pearson didn't need the money, and McArthur knew it. He also knew that Pearson wasn't likely to be at Pepsico much longer, information that had been passed to him by a member of the HBS Club of New York who kept up with that sort of thing. It was a safe bet to ask him if he wanted the job, because even if he didn't he would be discreet enough to keep quiet about it.

The dean appointed him to the school's heavyweight department of general management, which boasted people like Michael Porter and Joseph Bower. Pearson would become one of the anointed few who would formulate strategy with Porter and write articles for the *Harvard Business Review* on global strategy. However, by appointing him there, the dean was also obliged to find him suitable office space in Morgan Hall, which housed the department.

Space on the even-numbered side of the building, the dean's side, which had the building's only elevator, was filled completely, and no one was scheduled to move out for at least two years. Putting him on the odd-numbered side, away from the power center where Porter, Levitt, Bower, and Christensen worked, would have been like sending him into exile, a place from which he could never hope to return. The solution was to move a secretary out of Morgan 330, which was at the end of a dark corridor next to the ladies' room and a water cooler.

In January 1985, accompanied by Dean McArthur, Pearson toured his new office, which, at fifteen feet by fifteen feet, was smaller than the antechamber leading to his former office at Pepsico's Purchase, New York, headquarters. It was, at least, a corner office, with a pleasant view of the tennis courts. Pearson wasted little time moving in a desk, a plant, and three chairs, as well as two books (one each by Porter and Kotter) to fill an empty floor-to-ceiling bookcase that occupied an entire wall of the office.

The first thing Pearson noticed when he began work was that there was more traffic down his corridor than any of the others. The ladies' room adjacent to his office was the only one on either the second or third floors, and was used continually by the forty secretaries in the building. Had the wall between Pearson's office and the lavatory been soundproof, it would not have been so noticeable, but it wasn't, so Pearson found himself in the embarrassing situation of having to explain the incessant plumbing noises to people who visited or called him.

"Joining the church as a cardinal," as Pearson referred to his appointment to HBS while he was still at Pepsico, was not as satisfying as he had hoped it would be. He was envied by many on the faculty who could not understand why he gave up a job that paid him close to $1 million each year to teach at Harvard Business School. They were willing to be civil, but after a two-week honeymoon period during which every department head lunched with him at the faculty club, he was on his own. If he had still been president of Pepsico, the pretense of accepting him as an equal would have lasted longer; but he wasn't, and they knew it, and there seemed to be no reason to waste time on him. The ones who did seek him out because of his contacts at Pepsico, General Cinema, TWA, and McKinsey, companies at which he was or had been a director, he soon learned to avoid. They were the faculty who had been tenured in the 1960s and whose academic careers had never taken off; they wanted to use him to their financial advantage. So Pearson began to spend more of his time at HBS alone, and in time only came to the campus when it was essential that he be there. Board meetings, where he met peers who still considered him to be a top-flight corporate man, occupied an increasing amount of his time.

PART II

RAISING
MONEY

• • •

CHAPTER 9

The Industrial Bank of Japan Chair of Food Service

• • •

Kaneo Nakamura, the president of the Industrial Bank of Japan (IBJ), was a man accustomed to getting his own way. A ferocious competitor, Nakamura had directed the growth of IBJ's international-banking operations in London, New York, and Washington, helping, in the process, to propel his bank's ranking in the world to number sixteen, with $80 billion in assets. Nakamura had been fortunate enough to make friends with some of Japan's postwar industrial geniuses at a time when they were just starting their careers. Among others, Dr. Takeshi Mitarai, president of Canon, and Akio Morita, chairman of Sony, knew Nakamura personally, and as those relationships developed, so too did the companies and IBJ.

During forty years of international-banking work, Nakamura had held to one fundamental rule of business: Banks don't lend money, bankers do. That conviction ultimately led him to Harvard Business School, a place where contacts were made, the primordial swamp that was the genesis of an international-banking elite. If banking was built on contacts, then there was no better place in the world to make them than there.

In 1966, he joined 160 corporate executives in Harvard's Advanced Management Program, the fiftieth class, as only the second Japanese businessman ever to attend the program. It turned out to be a profoundly humbling experience for him; not only were his classmates ignorant of the Japanese culture and business environment two decades after the war, but he was seen as an outsider, a situation he never thought possible. Thrown into the forum with managers from mostly American industrial corporations, he saw that even though he was brighter than they, their bias against Oriental companies and industry would not be overcome in thirteen weeks of exposure, through him, to Japanese methods. Even his roommate, A. W. Clausen, then an alert young executive with Bank of America who went on to become president of the World Bank, showed only a modest inclination to learn the dynamics of Japanese business relationships. Nakamura's presence in the class did result in converts, but he had not enrolled to do missionary work at Harvard, a place renowned for its liberal thinkers. He came away from the experience on the whole more impressed by the school's faculty than by his fellow classmates, an impression he conveyed to his company on his return.

Yoh Kurosawa, a managing director of the Industrial Bank of Japan who attended the eighty-third class of the AMP in January 1980, consulted with Nakamura before coming to Harvard. His decision to enroll in the program was based on many of the same considerations that Nakamura's had fourteen years earlier. But fourteen years had seen the explosive growth of Japanese industry, giving Kurosawa the advantage of a growing Japanese lobbying effort at the school that expanded with Japan's increasing importance. A cultural bias still existed, but Harvard had begun to use at least a few course materials that gave recognition to Japan's prosperity. Other Asian countries, Singapore, Taiwan, and Hong Kong, were represented in the program too, and together they formed the nucleus of a small, but formidable, contingent.

It was Kurosawa who first had the idea of donating a chair to Harvard Business School. He approached one of his professors, Hugo Uyterhoeven, who was the director of Harvard's corporate fund-raising effort, to discuss the feasibility of such a donation. In Uyterhoeven's experience, a current student, even an AMP, had never seriously inquired about donating a chair. His first response was to say that, of course, Harvard Business School would be glad to establish a chair to honor the Industrial Bank of Japan, the price tag of which would be in excess of $1 million.

Discussions never went beyond a preliminary description of what the chair represented, but Kurosawa was already convinced of its merit. Returning to IBJ in Tokyo, he laid out to Nakamura and other senior executives the advantages of donating a chair to Harvard Business School: It would be, he said, the first donation of any appreciable size to the school from any Japanese company. That alone would set IBJ apart in Western capital market centers. Publicity surrounding the donation would reach many of the world's influential businessmen who may never have heard of the Industrial Bank of Japan. Looked at as a purchase of media, it would be an inexpensive and efficient way to reach the target audience of influential businessmen and entrepreneurs who did business internationally.

Nakamura was unsure. His own Harvard Business School experience had done little to dispel the impression that the school's alumni were, as a group, unimpressed by gifts of great magnitude to their alma mater. But he did believe that an old-boy network existed, and that one Harvard alumnus would be more likely to do business with other Harvard alumnus, even a Japanese whom he had never met. If a large donation would guarantee the admission of more IBJ executives to the graduate programs, with the effect that more bank employees would be wired into the network of large international-banking deals, then it might, in fact, be a good idea.

Under the condition that a "fruitful relationship" developed between Harvard Business School and IBJ, Nakamura was willing to consider the gift. Up to that point, in 1980, only he, Kurosawa, and two others from the bank held HBS degrees of any kind, a number that hardly represented an impressive showing for a fourteen-year relationship. Kurosawa relayed this information to Uyterhoeven and explained that if the business school was to lend IBJ access to its executive-education programs, a chair would most certainly be forthcoming. Uyterhoeven responded that no company, including IBM or Xerox, could send more than one student per year to the AMP, which was a policy to keep the classes from becoming dominated by a few large companies, resulting in a loss of heterogeneity. However, IBJ could, at its discretion, send one person to the AMP and one person to the PMD (Program for Management Development), which was geared toward younger executives. Officially there would be no guarantees of admission, but Uyterhoeven would explain the situation to the admissions directors of the AMP and PMD, and with a wink and a handshake the deal would be struck.

Over a five-year period a "fruitful relationship" did develop, during which time eight senior managers went through the AMP and PMD. But by that time the price of a chair had increased to nearly $1.5 million, and Matsushita Electric Company beat the Japanese competition to the punch by donating a chair in early 1983. Even so, the benefits were becoming increasingly apparent as each new group of managers returned to Japan with new American, European, and Asian contacts, and an Asian-HBS old-boy network was beginning to form.

Nakamura, who had been promoted to the presidency of the bank, determined that the time was right in June 1984 to send HBS the check. Dean McArthur, elated over the fortuitous turn of events, used the occasion of this newfound wealth to bestow the chair upon his associate dean for educational programs, Professor Thomas Piper, a selection that, if unpopular with the HBS faculty, caused no stir elsewhere in the university.

THE SECOND ROUTE

The appointment of a professor to a chair symbolically represented the recognition of outstanding achievement in that person's field, and often was made after twenty or thirty years of work. Walter Salmon, for example, who became the Stanley Roth, Sr., Professor of Retailing, had been on the boards of several major retail chains, including Sears, Zayre, and Carter Hawley Hale, and had spent twenty-five years in the field of retail merchandising before being named to the chair. Likewise, the great majority of endowed chairs were given to cap off long and distinguished careers. John Kotter, best-selling author, did not hold an endowed professorship, nor did Michael Porter, internationally known strategist, nor Thomas K. McCraw, 1985 Pulitzer Prize winner. Their chairs would be waiting for them, after a decade or two.

Thomas Piper discovered a second route to a chair, a nonacedemic one, which was based on using his business contacts to financially benefit the school. It was a new approach by someone who had avoided the conventional academic track. Piper attended Williams College and received his MBA from Harvard in 1962. He joined the doctoral program and spent eight years working toward his DBA degree in the analytical side of finance.

His interests led him away from academics and toward

administration and consulting, where there was less pressure to perform heroic feats of analysis. He took on committee assignments, which he found easier than writing finance books. He was popular in the finance department because he agreed to write or revise the short, single-issue case studies on companies like Cyclops Cement Company, Dana Pharmaceutical, and Crown Corporation, which, though necessary, were tiresome to write and equally tiresome to read. It was that willingness to do drudgery that led the tenure committee to award him a full professorship in 1977.

Having achieved his objective of winning permanent work at HBS, Piper turned his attention to consulting. At a 1975 alumni-association gathering he met Richard Marriott, MBA '65, a vice-president of the Marriott Corporation, the hotel-and-restaurant chain founded by Marriott's parents. The two of them hit it off immediately, and Marriott offered to put him on retainer to Marriott to work on ad-hoc assignments. It was a standing offer that Piper was unable to take advantage of until 1978, when he was freed from case writing and other academic burdens.

What started as a business relationship blossomed into a friendship between Professor Piper and the Marriott family. With increasing frequency the Marriotts invited him to attend formal and informal family meetings, and within two years he found himself making multiple visits each month to Washington, D.C., and Bethesda, Maryland. Piper decided that, for the sake of expediency, a case should be developed on Marriott Corporation that would enable him to write off his frequent visits. After two years, a fifteen-page case study was completed at a cost, for field-based research, in excess of $35,000.

As work with Marriott progressed, Piper considered other ways to forge new ties between Harvard and the company. Marriott had been making a concerted effort to compete in the food-service business, which supplied food to hospitals, schools, airlines, and hotels, and Piper suggested that the company take a look at Harvard Business School's food-service operation with an eye toward running the entire operation. When Marriott's operation team toured the school's facilities in mid-1981, it was apparent that the Kresge Hall's dining facilities, built in 1950, were inadequate. Piper recommended that Harvard and Marriott strike a joint-venture deal whereby the cost of renovating Kresge Hall would be split between the two, and in return Marriott would agree to provide full food service for the dining hall, the faculty club, two snack bars, and all HBS functions, a contract valued at $4.5 million per year. An agreement was quickly reached in September 1981. The Marriotts, for their part, were so pleased with the outcome that they offered Piper a position on their seven-member board of directors, beginning January 1982, at $12,000 per year and $900 per meeting.

Renovations to Kresge Hall began in May 1983 and were completed in September 1983 at a cost of $3.4 million. Marriott's food-service division reorganized the entire food-provision operation at the business school, bringing in six of their most experienced managers to run it. Hourly workers in the school's dining hall were invited to join Marriott's food-service operation under the condition that they renounced membership in their local union. Given the alternative between working with Marriott at Harvard or not working at all, most went along with the demand. Harvard Business School, which had had a long history of trouble with its food workers' union, stayed entirely out of the negotiations.

The efficiency of the food-service operation at Harvard Business School exceeded all expectations. Marriott understood that the school played host to some of the country's most influential business leaders on a consistent basis, as well as providing service to 1,600 executives each year in executive-training programs of all kinds. With this in mind, Richard Marriott had directed the management team of the HBS operation to spare no expense in making the school a showcase for the company.

If they had to lose money to do it, they could still expect the full support of the company. The result of that directive drastically improved the diets of 1,400 MBA students and an equal number of faculty, staff, and visitors.

Everyone on campus noticed an immediate change. Now when a professor ordered coffee, tea, and doughnuts for a seminar of twenty students at 7:30 A.M., the order arrived at 7:15 A.M., the coffee and tea piping hot, the doughnuts fresh, and the entire bill coming to less than $10. And if the lunches were not free, they were at least affordably priced. A three-course luncheon in the posh faculty-club dining room averaged $2.75, with no tips allowed to the waiters. And lobster and steak dinners became the standard fare for the Advanced Management Program students during their thirteen-week stay at the school; they, on average, went home smarter and ten pounds heavier. Seldom, in business history, had a customer received so much value for so little cost.

While Marriott was demonstrating its production and operations expertise to the business school faculty, the company was also recommending a series of new ideas, all of which were summarily vetoed. McArthur protested most vehemently when Piper came to him with a request from Marriott to install a Roy Rogers minirestaurant in place of the student snack bar in the east wing of Kresge Hall, an idea that McArthur felt, would "commercialize" the school and set a bad precedent. In all other respects, however, the dean was quite pleased with the outcome of the joint venture and contract. Service and quality of food had never been better, and what had been a sore spot for the school became a source of pride. In appreciation of his work in bringing in Marriott Corporation, McArthur selected Piper to be his senior associate dean in December 1983, and the first Industrial Bank of Japan Professor in June 1984.

Piper's connection to international finance, particularly banking in Asia, was tenuous. He had taught as a finance professor for several years, and had spent two years teaching in Harvard's International Senior Managers Program (ISMP) in Switzerland. Unquestionably he was an able finance professor, but he knew little about Asian banking or finance. Many on the faculty were appalled at the dean's cronyism in selecting his associate dean, an administrator, for such an important academic assignment.

The Industrial Bank of Japan, in its enthusiasm to donate the chair, had neglected to ask whether any stipulations could have been put on the chair. Had the bank been better informed, it could have demanded that the chair be given to a member of the faculty with strong ties to the Orient. Or that an Asian finance professor from another school be chosen (since Harvard had only one Oriental full professor, who was in general management). Both suggestions, while voiced by the faculty, failed to be mentioned to Yoh Kurosawa at the moment he made the donation, which left McArthur free to appoint virtually anyone he wanted.

There had been a brief moment when the dean considered bringing in someone from outside HBS to fill the position. The net effect of such a move would have been to keep the school's operating budget virtually in the same position. The faculty size would have increased by one, but the budget would have increased by an amount to just cover that increase. McArthur estimated that if he appointed Piper to the chair, the IBJ would provide him with an additional $100,000 per year, a sum representing Piper's former salary and expense account, to use as he wished. Since the business school operated as a separate business entity from Harvard University, the dean would have full discretion over the use of that newfound cash, which would not have been true if an outsider was hired to fill the chair.

McArthur chose Kaneo Nakamura for the school's 1985 Alumni Achievement Award, reasoning that if the Industrial Bank of Japan was generous to the school for doing so little, it could be even more generous given the right incentive. New large donors were always more difficult to cultivate than old ones who had proved their loyalty and generosity. A second chair was a remote possibility, but there was always the Associates Program to consider, where an unrestricted gift of $20,000 or more each year gave the donating company membership in a club with IBM; Goldman, Sachs & Company; Sony; and twenty-seven international-consulting firms, investment banks, and corporations. Then again, the school would be needing some large corporate sponsors in the near future for a major new building program, for which a feasibility study by the architectural firm of Moshe Safdie & Associates had just been completed at a cost of $100,000.

CHAPTER 10

The Master Plan

• • •

The most ambitious building project at Harvard Business School since 1927 (when the campus was built) was unveiled in June 1986 before several thousand graduates at the school's annual alumni-day celebration. It was called "the master plan," a project of imaginative scope and vision that would add almost twenty new buildings by the year 2000 at a final cost estimated to be in excess of $150 million. When it was finished, it would result in a doubling of the size of the campus, and a doubling of the school's capacity to do new research, initiate new executive-education programs, and play host to an international corps of business leaders. In short, it was the road map for a generation of growth at the school.

Cost had never been factored into the equation in 1925, when Dean Wallace Donham retained the exclusive architectural firm of McKim, Mead & White of Park Avenue, New York City, to design the original campus. Nor did Donham have difficulty raising money to complete the project; George F. Baker, president of the First National Bank of New York, agreed to give the entire $5 million needed to build the campus if Harvard would name the school after him, which it did. Henceforth it was called "George F. Baker Foundation—Harvard University—Graduate School of Business Administration," a name that appeared on all stationery but has long since lost its significance.

The fund-raising campaign turned out quite well, ending successfully as it did in 1924, two months before it was to start. That was the way it was hoped things would go in 1986 when the new plans were unveiled, although it was more than anyone could hope for that one man would pick up the entire building cost. One couldn't expect that kind of enthusiasm toward a school that was already in a mature phase of growth, but it wasn't implausible to believe that the full amount could be raised before a single spade of dirt was turned over.

Moshe Safdie, the Woodner Professor of Architecture and Urban Design at Harvard University's Graduate School of Design, was selected by Dean McArthur to prepare the plans for the new campus. He was a professor who had taught at Harvard for nearly a decade, but who was chosen not for his academic credentials but because, like McArthur, he thought big. Safdie's design for the Coliseum Project, which was done for Mortimer Zuckerman's Boston Properties development company in 1985, won a competition against two of the world's most prestigious design firms, Skidmore, Owings & Merrill; and Helmut Jahn. The design, which was part of a $455.1 million proposal by Zuckerman to the City of New York, called for a pair of towers, one fifty-two stories high, and the other seventy-two stories high, to be built on the southwest side of Central Park in Manhattan. It was a colossal venture that would take years to complete and would earn millions of dollars in fees for Safdie's firm. On the basis of his work on the Coliseum Project, Safdie earned membership into a small group of architects who designed the world's largest development projects.

He was born in Haifa, Israel, in 1938, and moved to Canada at age seventeen to study architecture at McGill University. In 1964, he acquired dual Canadian–Israeli citizenship, founded his own architectural firm, and shortly thereafter was selected by the Canadian government to design housing for Montreal's Expo '67. "Habitat '67" was bold and innovative, a prefabricated concrete housing complex unlike any piece of architecture ever built. Cost overruns and design flaws marred the two-year construction of it, but "Habitat" was an aesthetic and cultural success, and led to Safdie's appointment on Yale's faculty and then on Harvard's.

Safdie was the only architect McArthur had met who could imagine the strategic importance of developing a new far-reaching expansion plan. They had discussed what the consequence of the project would be, and agreed that no cost ceilings would initially be established. Harvard constructed buildings to last for centuries, and the school couldn't enter a major development program with cost restrictions in mind. The new had to harmonize with the old; that was the only restriction. Safdie agreed that the construction would provide a focal point for the school's new activities. Furthermore, the vibrant sounds of bulldozers and construction crews would be healthy to have around; it rallied morale and spurred production, so there was no reason to hurry through to completion. "The master plan," said McArthur, "might take a generation or more to complete, but when it's done Harvard Business School will be a world-class business education organization for the future."

Changing the physical orientation of the campus was

the thrust of the new proposal. McKim, Mead & White architects had faced the school in a northerly direction, toward the Charles River, Harvard Square, and Harvard Yard. That had been fine for the first sixty years or so, but new buildings behind the original campus had been springing up since then, and the original plan had begun to lose its intent. Now guests arrived by car at the rear of the school, next to the loading docks, the parking lot, and the service areas of Baker Library, which was the least attractive part of the campus. No amount of trees and flowers could hide the fact that the school's entryway looked, at times, like an industrial trailer park. What was needed, said Safdie, was a new entrance for the rear of the school, in addition to the greatly expanded square-footage requirements that were part of his basic instructions.

New buildings floated off his drafting board that, in terms of cost, had no grounding in reality. There was a new athletic and fitness center with a price tag of $25 million if it was built in 1987 and $40 million if construction was delayed for seven or eight years. A series of symmetrical buildings along the southern border of the campus to house a bank, post office, bookstore, and student dormitories were each priced between $15 and $25 million. The first project Safdie wanted to work on, the new southern facade for the rear of Baker Library with a courtyard, fountain, and underground parking, was a multimillion dollar enterprise. He underscored his special interest in this by posing for the alumni-magazine photographer in front of the grease-stained Baker parking lot. This, he said, was the first impression visitors had of the great Harvard Business School, an impression that could not help but be negative, and required immediate attention.

Future buildings would eventually swallow up all of the school's athletic fields and parking lots. The plan called for all parking to be built underground and all buildings to be connected by tunnels the way many of the original buildings were. It would be a convenience for visiting dignitaries, who could drive into the subterranean parking spaces in the dead of winter, walk without an overcoat to their meetings with faculty, to lunch, to a class, and finally back to their car, without ever having to go outside.

Several other buildings for which no use had yet been identified but that, seen on the scale models, created a pleasing harmony, were incorporated into the plan as surplus space. Ample opportunity to find uses for them would be discovered when the time came to build them. Perhaps they would be for needs that had not yet even been identified. The job of an architect was only to suggest an aesthetic design that fit the customer's specifications, it was not to prescribe how to use the space.

One of those as-yet-unidentified buildings was a massive granite-and-brick building, which, when it was completed in 1995 or so, would cost approximately $60 million. It would be the new administration building, perhaps, or a new center for entrepreneurial studies, depending on how it was funded and what the space requirements of the faculty were. Until it was built, McArthur chose to call it McArthur Hall, a name that would honor the man who had the vision to make it and all the others a reality. There was very little chance that it would be dedicated as McArthur Hall. That honor was reserved for the person who gave the most money to have it built, not for an administrator who had conceived of building it. That was a minor point anyway, for the glory of dragging Harvard Business School into the second millennium would be his. None of the other deans since Donham had thought of updating the master building plan. They had put up a hodgepodge of buildings when the whimsy struck them, without ever realizing that there were limits to the space behind the library. Safdie's architectural renderings would change all that, even if he wasn't around to see the finished product. They would remember that far-sighted dean whose legacy was in every building constructed after 1986.

The only problem with the building program was that it presupposed a dramatic increase in the amount of income the school would generate during the years 1986 to 2000. Annual fund drives were expected to yield $10 million to $15 million, but much of that was already earmarked for special projects and upgrading selected facilities. As it was, the current discretionary income was more than adequate to meet the current operating expenses for new expansion activities, with a little left over at the end of the year to add to the capital-improvement fund. But the master building plan required an equally grand financing plan that would open up previously untapped sources of funds.

THE GOLDEN TOUCH OF GOLDMAN, SACHS

Heading the dean's list of ways to raise new money for building was a plan to designate Goldman, Sachs & Company to be the lead organizational sponsor and fund administrator, an idea that, from the dean's point of view, made eminently good sense. In 1986, Goldman, Sachs was one of the two largest private investment houses in the country, with capital of more than $1.3 billion and annual profits for its seventy-nine general partners of a reported $400 million. A plurality of those general partners were Harvard MBAs, and the fact that they were each worth between $6 million and $25 million, and that they owed their professional careers to HBS for providing the credentials needed to work for Goldman, meant that they were wealthy enough, and had good reason, to support such a large-scale project. Moreover, the primary function of the Goldman partners was to raise money for other people, a job they excelled at above all others, so it was natural to think in terms of putting the firm onto such a major fund-raising effort.

The school's ties with Goldman, Sachs ran long and deep, stretching back to the early 1900s, when HBS was still housed in Harvard Yard. Walter and Paul Sachs, sons of the co-founder, Samuel Sachs, were both Harvard-educated and partners in the firm until Paul Sachs left to join the faculty of Harvard University, and both supported the fledgling business school with gifts of cash that included a $100,000 donation in 1927 to commemorate the building of the new campus. It was, however, under the leadership of Sidney J. Weinberg, who headed Goldman for forty years until his death in 1969, that the firm forged its strongest ties with the school. Realizing that Goldman was, to a large extent, dependent upon the business school for each new crop of young associates, he cultivated the relationship at every opportunity. With time, Goldman and Weinberg became the first recourse for the school's dean in the event of any major cash requirements. Whenever a couple of hundred thousand dollars was needed on short notice to put a new chair or a new project over the top, the call went out to Weinberg, who was glad to oblige. He was capable of preserving prudent silence when it came to matters of money, never asking that the chairs bear either his or the firm's name. Those who really counted would know who the benefactor was anyway, so there was no reason to take public credit for the gestures of goodwill.

Weinberg liked the idea that he was not only a Harvard Business School benefactor, but also a significant employer of the school's graduates. It gave him a sense of satisfaction that he, who had never graduated from high school and who had spent a childhood in poverty, could buy and sell such prestigious commodities as Harvard MBAs. He was born in 1891, the third of eleven children of Polish immigrants, in Brooklyn, New York. Forced by financial pressures to leave school after the eighth grade, Weinberg took a job at the age of sixteen as an assistant to the janitor at Goldman, Sachs & Company, where, in 1909, Walter Sachs discovered the boy's flair for finance.

Weinberg's was a Horatio Alger story, literally going from rags to riches. By 1920, he had been promoted to the professional staff at Goldman as a bond trader. By 1925, during a period of unusual prosperity, he became financially independent and bought himself a seat on the New York Stock Exchange for $104,000, and within five years became a senior partner and lead investment banker in the firm with a one-third equity position by plowing his profits back into the partnership.

As the head of Goldman, Sachs, Weinberg delighted in playing the role of an ordinary, unsophisticated man on the street. In 1936, when Franklin D. Roosevelt wanted to reward him for helping to finance Roosevelt's successful presidential campaign, and offered him an ambassadorship in the Soviet Union, Weinberg turned it down, explaining to his friends, " . . . I don't speak Russian, so who the hell could I talk to over there?" The fact was that Weinberg's power was in New York, where he was a member of the board of directors of thirty-five major corporations. Power was what motivated him, not prestige, and he found that he could enhance that power by soliciting money from friends, partners, and fellow board members for such charities as Eisenhower's, Kennedy's, and Johnson's campaigns, and for Harvard Business School. The financier John Hay Whitney said of Weinberg's methods, "Sidney is the best money-getter I've ever seen. He'll go to one of his innumerable board meetings— General Foods, General Electric or General Whatnot—and make no bones about telling everybody there what he wants. Then he'd say, 'Come on boys, where is it?'—and up it comes."

Throughout Weinberg's tenure, Goldman hired at least one Harvard MBA each year, gradually increasing that number to twenty. Only one in ten of the new recruits ever became a partner, odds that were mentioned to them when they were hired, but investment banking was built on personal contacts and networks so it was profitable to hire well-connected Harvard MBAs who, even when they didn't become partners, fanned out into the financial markets and often became valuable allies. That, at least, was the official justification for having so many of them around. In fact, they were excellent feeder stock, which, through a process of natural selection, created a top level of superior management at Goldman. The harder they worked, the easier it was for Weinberg to exaggerate his own myth of being a patriarchal adviser who made decisions based purely on instinct.

In 1966, Harvard University awarded Weinberg an honorary doctorate in appreciation of the millions of dollars that he and his firm had raised for Harvard Business School. He framed the document and hung it in his office next to his eighth-grade diploma from P.S. 13 in Brooklyn. He would point to these, saying that he couldn't decide which one he was prouder of.

John C. Whitehead, a Harvard MBA, and John Weinberg, also a Harvard MBA and Sidney Weinberg's son, were the next generation to carry on Goldman's tradition of supporting the business school. Whitehead was the son of a telephone lineman, and had worked as an accounting instructor at HBS for U.S. Navy training classes held at the business school during World War II. In 1946 he entered the MBA program, becoming, as he liked to joke, the first person ever to go from being a faculty member there to being a student. He completed the program in just eleven months, and went to New York to work for Sidney Weinberg at Goldman, Sachs.

Whitehead's first intern was John Weinberg, the boss's son, whom he met for the first time in 1948, the summer before Weinberg started at Harvard Business School. Despite the fact that he had a three-year jump on Weinberg at Goldman, their careers paralleled each other as the two made partner, joined the management committee, and became senior partners on the same days. In 1977, Weinberg and Whitehead, known in the firm as "the two johns," were made co-chairmen, a situation that remained until 1985, when Whitehead stepped down to become deputy secretary of state in the Reagan administration.

Beyond their shared interest in making Goldman, Sachs

prosper, each held the strong conviction that the long-standing relationship with Harvard Business School should be nourished at every opportunity. Goldman's competitors, which were comprised of the investment-banking firms of Morgan Stanley and Salomon Brothers, were equally avaricious in skimming off the cream of each MBA class.

They were more polished, had better contacts, and were smarter, on average, than any other repository of raw talent anywhere in the world, and Goldman had the inside track at recruiting them, a privileged position that had been protected for fifty years.

Weinberg and Whitehead made recruiting the number-one priority at the firm, particularly the recruiting of Harvard MBAs. They established a new scholarship fund at HBS to honor Sidney J. Weinberg, and recommended in 1983 that every partner, whether he had attended Harvard Business School or not, donate money to the annual fund drive. And as a commitment to their determination to hire them, John Whitehead and John Weinberg each agreed to interview five of the top student prospects from each class, a demonstration of solidarity with the other partners, who individually spent an average of twenty-five hours with each of the thirty MBAs hired yearly.

In February 1985, Whitehead donated more than $200,000, with the firm contributing an equal sum, to establish the John C. Whitehead/Goldman, Sachs & Co. Faculty—Business Executives Exchange Program, which was to pay the salaries and expenses for junior HBS faculty to switch places with executives in industry for up to a year. The idea was to improve the real-world experiences of faculty members while HBS students benefited from the experience of businessmen, who participated by teaching or doing research.

The exchange program cemented the Goldman, Sachs–Harvard Business School relationship since this setup required the dean to consult Goldman each year about the best candidates to participate in the exchange. From then on, the firm had only to sit back and wait for the phone to ring, rather than always being the initiator.

But the exchange was only one of several schemes that brought HBS and Goldman closer together. In 1984, John Whitehead thought up the idea of collecting and writing a series of case studies that demonstrated how private-sector companies tackled such problems as unemployment, poverty, and urban decay. Whitehead's plan was to gather the cases into a book form and distribute them to company managers and boards of directors as provocative ideas for consideration. Rather than doing the project himself, however, he interviewed and hired HBS students to gather case materials and write the book. It was done just the way Harvard Business School professors did it, except that he could afford to pay the MBA students a lot more.

After Whitehead, a succession of younger partners in the firm, all of whom were actively engaged in recruiting activities, became the next to carry on as HBS fund-raisers. Richard Menschel '59, who was a member of the firm's eleven-member management committee, was appointed in 1983 to be the chairman of his class's twenty-fifth reunion. The class of 1959 was Dean McArthur's class, one of the last two all-male MBA classes at the school, and a group whose five hundred members had become some of the country's most successful investment bankers and venture capitalists. Charles P. Waite, president of Greylock Management Corporation, James Wolfensohn, president of the investment firm of Wolfensohn, Inc., and J. Morton David, chairman and CEO of D. H. Blair & Company, an investment-banking and venture-capital firm, were just three of the class notables. Menschel carried the mantle of power and prestige that was Goldman's, which made him the most qualified to lead the fund-raising drive. Classmates could hardly insult him by refusing to pledge less than a paltry $5,000; what was $5,000 to a man who handled billions of dollars in transactions each year? It was more difficult to make small donations to someone like Menschel than someone like Wolfensohn, who, though equally prosperous, didn't have the same organization behind him as Menschel did.

In 1984, Menschel raised $1.5 million and set a class-participation record by convincing 80 percent of his classmates to donate. It became the Dean John H. McArthur Discretionary Fund of the Class of 1959, the first in a series of donations that would be raised at the thirtieth, thirty-fifth, and fortieth reunions. Other classes gave chairs to hire and promote professors; the class of 1959 demonstrated to everyone that it could give the equivalent of a chair if it wanted to.

The dean's new discretionary fund would be husbanded with the help of Menschel. There would be semiannual accountings, of course, and meetings with McArthur to be sure that the fund wasn't being depleted, all of which would, in a new way, bring Goldman closer to the school. McArthur could do with the money what he liked, said Menschel on making the donation; from then on they were partners, which was fine as far as McArthur was concerned, since he had his own reason for wanting a direct conduit to Goldman, Sachs—namely an expensive new building plan.

THE HBS ALUMNI-CLUB CIRCUIT

The amount of money required to complete the master building plan was, of course, much higher than could be realized from annual fund drives, even with Menschel and Goldman leading the campaign. The other way to raise money through the firm, besides direct solicitations, was to enlist Goldman's support in issuing tax-exempt bonds for the purpose of building the new campus additions. The precedent for such a move was that in 1983 Goldman, Sachs had been the lead underwriter in a $350 million bond issue to build an electricity-generating plant for Harvard Medical School, an offering that was fully subscribed. The problem with raising money that way was HBS would have to pay interest on $100 million to $200 million, whatever the final price tag for the construction would be, permission for which the university's corporate officers would not give lightly.

Another alternative that McArthur considered, either in addition to or instead of his plans to involve Goldman, Sachs, was to turn to the school's growing alumni clubs for increased support. There were clubs in every major U.S. city, as well as in Singapore, Nigeria, Thailand, and all the European countries, and most of these were composed of well-heeled members. Those in New York City and Los Angeles boasted membership lists that included people like James D. Robinson III, chairman and CEO of American Express, Clifton C. Garvin, Jr., chairman of Exxon, and Albert V. Casey, retired chairman and president of American Airlines, who were major sources of money both as individuals and as determiners of how their corporate funds would be given.

Bert W. Twaalfhoven, MBA '54, was the sort of club member that McArthur sought most actively to befriend. Twaalfhoven had spent several years on the executive council of the Harvard Business School Association, the organizational body that oversaw the member clubs, and had served as president from 1984 to 1985. He was president of his own company, N. V. Indivers, an Amsterdam-based holding company that owned manufacturing facilities in Asia, the United States, and Europe, but he devoted, when necessary, more than half of his professional schedule to HBS club business.

Twaalfhoven's special talent was fund-raising. He was appointed in 1983 to be co-chairman of his class's thirtieth-reunion gift committee, where he was put in charge of canvassing donations from the foreign students in his class. Using his own money, he paid for special trips throughout Europe and Asia to solicit funds from those he identified as the most promising. In Japan, he paid a visit to Shintaro Ota, president and CEO of the Toho Mutual Life Insurance Company in Tokyo, whom Twaalf-hoven had discovered was a multimillionaire. He had come to Tokyo with the expectation of asking Ota for at least $25,000, but when he arrived at the company headquarters he found out that Ota was wealthier than he had suspected; the forty-story office building that housed the Toho company belonged to Ota personally. By the time he reached Ota's office, he'd made up his mind to ask him to become a Leadership Fellow by donating in the top category, $100,000-plus. Ota, who didn't feel the same way toward HBS that Twaalfhoven did, decided to make a donation in the second top category: $50,000–$100,000.

In McArthur's plan, alumni like Twaalfhoven, who were eager to fund-raise on their own time and money, and of whom there were many hundreds, would be mobilized to go after the potentially large donors, like Ota. The reason they would be willing to take on such a thankless job was that it had fringe benefits, as Twaalfhoven found out. Many of the alumni were in a position to become business partners or customers. Other alumni volunteers were motivated out of the assumption that their work in raising money for Harvard Business School would help their offsprings' chances of gaining admission to the MBA program. Since it was school policy that alumni offspring, whether their parents worked for or gave money to the alumni association or not, were to be given preference in admissions over all other candidates, it made no difference to the dean if these dedicated alumni wanted to spend their free time raising money. If by working on the school's business they thought they were doing something extra to foster good family relationships with HBS, he certainly was not going to be the one to dissuade them.

It was not difficult to construct a plan for raising many millions of dollars from alumni clubs. As a practical matter, hundreds of members were both willing and able to give between $5,000 and $10,000 annually without much hesitation. Taking the higher figure and multiplying it by ten years resulted in $100,000, which was an amount that showed a dedication to, and active participation in, the ongoing improvement of the educational objectives of the institution. Thus, according to this one, of many, planned giving schemes, as few as a hundred people could team up to fund a single $10 million project, and, with matching donations from corporations, that figure could rise to $15 million. So in addition to the annual alumni fund drives where class chairs were becoming the norm, there could be class buildings, or even club buildings, in which a group of alumni, tied together by a common geographic location, could give in tandem. All that was required was a fostering of a financial commitment from a large number of alumni over a period of time, something the alumni clubs and association were in a unique position to do.

McArthur decided, therefore, to make annual tours of the major alumni-club meetings, and put together either a slide presentation or movie to use in conjunction with his appeal for funds for the building project. Those who wanted to be immortalized in the hallowed halls of Harvard Business School could, if they so desired, have a hall named after them for a lump sum of $100,000 or so. A single dormitory room might be as little as $30,000, and the bronze plaque affixed to the door would be a constant reminder of that donor's generosity. The presentation would show the alumni exactly what their dollars would buy, which would be a tangible, tax-deductible, reminder of their ongoing commitment to the institution.

Between consulting work for numerous companies and government agencies, Dean John H. McArthur of Harvard Business School still found time to serve on the board of directors of half a dozen multinational corporations, as well as to raise millions of dollars for HBS. His master building plan, prepared by the world-famous architect Moshe Safdie, was to be a lasting memorial to himself.

Brilliant, high-strung, and a spellbinding lecturer, Michael E. Porter turned a best-selling strategy book into a tenured professorship and a multimillion-dollar consulting business. His impressive collection of modern art, and his ability to effortlessly best his competitors in all fields, awed his colleagues.

Dean of Harvard Business School from 1970–1979, Lawrence E. Fouraker was said by some to run HBS like a corporation. It was such corporate-style management that ultimately led to strong disagreements with Harvard president Derek Bok, and to Fouraker's early retirement.

Clasping the medal presented to him by President Derek Bok at Harvard's 350th celebration in 1986, Marvin Bower listens attentively as his contributions to the school are enumerated. As managing partner of McKinsey & Company, Bower cultivated close ties with HBS deans for four decades to skim the cream of each MBA class.

Although the business school was one of the most successful, prominent, and wealthy graduate schools at Harvard, university president Derek Bok was disturbed to find in 1978 that it showed lackluster support for business ethics. Discovering that he had limited direct power over the school, he looked for subtle ways to institute control.

Holding his portrait at the dedication of Harvard University's multimillion-dollar Gordon indoor-track facility, Albert Gordon, chairman of Kidder, Peabody, is one of Harvard Business School's largest individual donors. His long-standing generosity has made him an important adviser to successive deans at HBS, and his advice and donations continue to be eagerly sought.

The first woman to break the tenure barrier at HBS, Regina Herzlinger prevailed over a seventy-year tradition of discrimination at the male-dominated institution to earn her permanent seat on the faculty. Despite her top credentials, her influential mentor, Robert Anthony, was forced to use every bit of persuasion he had to get his reluctant colleagues to admit her to the club in 1980.

Six years after first granting tenure to a woman faculty member in 1980, Dean McArthur bowed to growing pressure to do more. His solution was to raid Yale's School of Management to bring Rosabeth Moss Kanter to Harvard Business School. A successful business consultant, corporate lecturer, and best-selling business author, Kanter is more than a match for her peers on the faculty.

Language proved no barrier to Woo-Choong Kim, chairman of the conglomerate Daewoo Corporation and wealthy Korean philanthropist, as he went in to deal with the unsuspecting dean of Harvard Business School. Kim, playing his cards close to his chest, won a new suit and two coveted MBA places for Daewoo.

Founder of Matsushita Electric Company and the wealthiest man in Japan, Konosuke Matsushita was persuaded by his closest friend to donate a chair to Harvard Business School in 1981. When the school planned a media bonanza to publicize the gift, Matsushita's strong sense of honor led him to quietly quash the plans.

Theodore Levitt was immortalized by the Harvard Business Review *for his discovery of the concept known as "marketing myopia." Once he was elevated to the top of the profession, few remembered this economist's shocking lack of marketing credentials.*

After failing to make tenure in the late 1970s, in 1981 Howard H. Stevenson was hired back from exile at a Massachusetts corporation to fill a new chair of entrepreneurship made possible by his strong HBS mentor C. Roland Christensen. Not an entrepreneur himself, Stevenson quickly became the school's leading spokesman on the subject while brushing off suggestions that he and the school used the entrepreneurship theme to raise money from wealthy alumni.

After losing out to D. Wayne Calloway (seated, left) as the successor to Donald Kendall, chairman of Pepsico (seated, right), Andrall E. Pearson (standing, left, next to Sharon Rockefeller and Arnold Weber) was offered an academic golden parachute: full tenure and an endowed chair. His meteoric rise to power made him a target for the school's old guard, who took pot shots at him to see if Fortune's *assessment, "one of the 10 toughest bosses in America," was correct.*

Industrial Bank of Japan president Kaneo Nakamura paid Harvard Business School nearly $1.5 million in 1984 to endow a new chair, the first step in his plan to solidify his bank in the school's old-boy network.

(Left to right)
Thomas Piper, senior associate dean; Yoh Kurosawa, Industrial Bank of Japan managing director; Hugo Uyterhoeven, senior associate dean; John H. McArthur, dean; and Tatsuo Yoshida, Industrial Bank of Japan general manager, celebrating the new Industrial Bank of Japan Chair of Finance and the beginning of a "fruitful relationship" between the bank and HBS. Piper was recipient of the chair, an honor earned through an unusual and unconventional method.

As co-chairman of Goldman, Sachs & Company, John C. Whitehead forged closer ties with Harvard Business School by personally donating large sums of money and by encouraging his partners at Goldman, Sachs— including those who never attended HBS—to follow his lead.

Bruce Scott (left) and George Cabot Lodge II in happier times, posing for a publicity picture on the steps of Baker Library for their book on U.S. competitiveness. This unlikely duo launched a calculated media campaign to warn of an impending financial crisis. When a sudden upturn in the economy punctured their balloon, they parted company.

Chairman and chief executive officer of General Cinema Corporation, Richard A. Smith brought HBS senior associate dean and professor Hugo Uyterhoeven to his company's board of directors in 1980. While watching Uyterhoeven teach the General Cinema case study for more than ten years, Smith was able to put the top financial minds of Harvard Business School to work on his company's business. The results produced explosive growth for the company.

Chairman of Carter Hawley Hale Stores, Inc., Philip Hawley got a great deal more than he bargained for when he asked one of his board members, Harvard Business School professor Walter J. Salmon, to assist in finding a "white knight" to ward off a threatened takeover by The Limited, Inc.

A. Alfred Taubman, real estate developer, owner of Sotheby's, and winner of the Harvard Business School Club of Detroit's 1983 Business Statesman of the Year Award, refused for the first time ever to back his long-time business partner, Leslie Wexner, in Wexner's bid for Carter Hawley Hale in early 1984. The Detroit award made Taubman keenly aware of the HBS community, of which Hawley was a member, and Wexner was not.

CHAPTER 11

Doing Business with Harvard Business School

• • •

MARVIN BOWER AND THE MATSUSHITA CHAIR OF LEADERSHIP

Following Derek Bok's example, McArthur became the first business-school dean not to move into his official residence, a palatial brick mansion in the center of the campus, and for a time he even refused to move into the dean's office in Morgan Hall. He also let it be known that he intended to be more visible than his predecessor: "I'll be spending a lot of time right here," he told a reporter a few months into the new job. But as for Bok's criticism of the case method, "The solution is to manage it, not to abandon it," McArthur said.

He was Marvin Bower's dean, not Derek Bok's, a fact that became more obvious with time. Superficially, he appeared to be his predecessor Lawrence Fouraker's opposite; philosophically, however, they were twins. As Bower explained to him, Fouraker's problem was that he was injudicious in dealing with Bok, so he cautioned the affable McArthur to stay on the president's good side and to avoid appearing to disagree with him. Bok, of course, had no power to make changes at the business school, except through the hiring and firing of the dean. If McArthur avoided controversy, Bower said, he could keep his job indefinitely.

Halfway through McArthur's first year, 1980, Bower visited with him and his newly appointed associate deans and staff to discuss new fund-raising strategies for the school. He asked McArthur where the new money in business research would be going in the 1980s, and thinking briefly on it, McArthur replied that he expected it would be in the study of the growth of Japanese industry. Bower picked up on the idea, and began working with it, eventually building a new proposal around it:

"What would you say, John, if I were able to arrange for a Japanese company to finance a new chair for the school to study Japanese industry?" He stopped and looked at McArthur.

"I'd say that was great, Marvin," said McArthur, half laughing as he said it.

"As I've mentioned to you on more than one occasion, my company has a Tokyo office, and we've been working with a major Japanese bank to restructure their organization . . ." He broke off and turned to the new associate dean of external relations, Hugo Uyterhoeven. "By the way, a chair is how much, now?"

"A million, two."

Bower took out a pen from his coat pocket and jotted the figure on the note pad in front of him. He resumed, "You know, the Japanese have a wonderful sense of honor and duty, much different from how Western businessmen behave. Once you win their trust, they remain loyal to you forever. This bank I mentioned was losing money all over until we came in and saved it, and the chairman, a wonderful man by the way, more or less said he owed me one if I ever needed it." He looked at McArthur. "If they were to donate a new chair to you, John, I think it would, in a subtle way, get your new job off to a good start. What do you think?"

McArthur shrugged his shoulders. "You make it sound so easy. Where do I come in?"

Bower stood up to leave. "You don't," he said. "I'll take care of everything."

The bank that Marvin Bower's firm had saved was the Sumitomo Bank based in Osaka, the third-largest bank in Japan, which grew out of the sixteenth-century Sumitomo family copper-refining business in Kyoto. The bank's honorary chairman was Shozo Hotta, an octogenarian just three years older than Bower, who had asked Bower to consult with Sumitomo in 1977 after a catastrophic series of losses a year earlier nearly forced the bank under. A team of McKinsey men rushed in and proposed a radical reorganization plan, the results of which began to have an immediate beneficial effect. The bank turned a healthy profit the following year and largely credited McKinsey with the turnaround.

When Bower met with Hotta in December 1980 and broached the subject of the bank's donating a chair to Harvard Business School, Hotta's first reaction was that he was flattered by the offer, but that he did not feel he was worthy of such distinction. Not everyone had the privilege of being asked to give a chair, which, as Bower had explained, signified a high degree of professional attainment. Such an honor, said Hotta, should be reserved for someone who was truly deserving, a man whose life was exemplary and represented the best of Japanese management. He said he would talk to his longtime personal friend, the wealthiest man in Japan, Konosuke Matsushita.

He was born in 1893 to a wealthy family in the Wakayama Prefecture, southeast of Osaka. His father, a farmer by trade, speculated unsuccessfully in wholesale rice futures in 1897 and was financially ruined, forcing his family to seek work in the city of Osaka. Matsushita left school at the age of ten and drifted through a series of unproductive jobs, eventually making his way to the Osaka Electric Company, a manufacturer of electric light fixtures. In 1918, when his idea to manufacture a double-ended socket was turned down by Osaka Electric, he quit and went into business to manufacture them himself, using 100 yen (then equivalent to $50) to set up a shop.

Matsushita's success was immediate, and within four years the company employed fifty people, diversifying into the manufacture of an array of electric products. The rising fortunes of Matsushita Electric Company prompted the president of Sumitomo Bank in 1927 to offer the founder a loan of 20,000 yen (equivalent to $500,000), which Matsushita declined, saying that he was loyal to his own bank. But a severe depression that year forced several Japanese banks out of business, including Matsushita's, which led him to reconsider Sumitomo's offer to start a new banking relationship.

Shozo Hotta, deputy president of Sumitomo, first met and became friends with Matsushita during the Allied Occupation of Japan after World War II. Matsushita's factories, reduced to rubble by Allied bombing, were rebuilt with Hotta's help, bringing renewed prosperity to the company and a strengthening of the bonds between Hotta and Matsushita. For all his personal wealth, Matsushita always considered Hotta his equal, and credited him with helping to launch the company's most popular brands, which included Quasar, Technics, and Panasonic. It was, therefore, not an unusual request that Hotta made of him in January 1981 when he asked him to give money to Harvard Business School. If Hotta felt it was a worthy charity, then that was enough. It was Matsushita's distinct honor to be permitted to support his friend, and he accepted the offer with great humility.

Marvin Bower christened it the "Matsushita Chair of Leadership," although he had originally expected that he would call it the "Sumitomo Chair of Leadership." The word *Leadership* would have been tagged on no matter who had given the chair. He planned a media extravaganza on the campus of the business school to which Mr. Matsushita would come and present the chair to the dean and then receive an honorary Business Statesman Award. Unfortunately, Matsushita wouldn't go along. The chair was meant to honor his friendship with Hotta, not become a public relations tool for either his company or Harvard Business School. If HBS wanted its chair, it would have to come to Japan to pick it up.

In April 1981, professors Abraham Zaleznik and C. Roland Christensen visited with Konosuke Matsushita to try to persuade him to make the donation within the ivy-covered walls of Harvard. No, he said, he would not go to Harvard Business School under any circumstances. In November, Dean McArthur went to Japan to pick up the check.

The tangible benefits that Marvin Bower expected would accrue to him and his firm for having delivered the new money to Harvard Business School did not arrive on the schedule he had planned, and by 1983 it began to look as though they never would. In the highly competitive field of big-time management consulting, a firm's most prized property was its supply of expensive young associates. The value those associates had to a firm could not be overstated. It was often said, by companies like McKinsey, that the firm's assets put on their hats and walked out of the office at 9 P.M. every evening.

There was little to differentiate one management-consulting firm from another besides the reputations of its best management-consultant associates, who, at McKinsey, were nearly always Baker Scholars (top 5 percent of each class) from Harvard Business School. The decades of the 1940s, 1950s, and 1960s belonged to McKinsey & Company at HBS, but during the 1970s Bower had watched an alarming trend as more of the school's thirty-five Baker Scholars each year opted for Boston Consulting Group (BCG) and Bain & Company, smaller and higher-paying firms. The Matsushita chair was supposed to stem the tide of competition by impressing upon the school McKinsey's outstanding leadership role, but it didn't.

THE EXPLODING FELLOWSHIP

As Bower knew, there was no way for the faculty and staff to force HBS's top students to take McKinsey's $55,000 job offers over Bain and BCG's $65,000 job offers. Until those two firms entered the market, McKinsey had always paid the top price for Harvard's Baker Scholars, but resolutely refused to get into a competitive bidding situation with them to prove that McKinsey would pay the most. The only winner in that type of high-priced auction would be MBAs, and Bower was not about to reward them for his competitors' avarice. He believed that the best students would go with McKinsey because of the firm's outstanding reputation, not because they paid the highest starting salary in the field. Students saw it another way; McKinsey became the old-fashioned firm, Bain and BCG the places to be.

There were, however, ways to give the best students the right incentive besides bidding up the starting salary for associates. When they talked with their professors about the pros and cons of working for McKinsey & Company or another firm, as Bower believed many of them did, those faculty members could point them in the McKinsey direction. All that was required was that the dean make a short announcement at a faculty meeting (which he did shortly after he returned from Japan, in early December 1981), stating that McKinsey & Company had been very nice to the school, and that the school ought to be nice to McKinsey. They weren't stupid; they knew exactly what

McArthur's intent was. Nevertheless, the subtle approach produced no discernible benefits. McKinsey's yield of Baker Scholars declined in the 1982 and 1983 recruiting seasons, forcing the firm to hire a large number of second-tier students. McKinsey's reputation was founded on its being able to buy the top students at wholesale prices, repackage them, and sell them at retail prices to clients that were willing to pay $250,000 per month to have a four-man team go in and do an analysis. Its customers were fussy; for them, there was no substitute for the best of the best, and if some other firm besides McKinsey had them, then that was whom they would hire.

The problem stemmed from the aggressive recruiting tactics of McKinsey's competitors. Bain & Company, a Boston-based firm that hired Baker Scholars almost exclusively, had begun offering "exploding bonuses" in 1980, which gave students a large lump sum of cash for signing with the firm on the day the job offer was made, but the size of the bonus declined each day that it was not taken. The high-pressure strategy was the most effective tool ever used by a firm recruiting at HBS, and in its first year eighteen out of eighteen Baker Scholars who were offered the bonuses accepted them immediately.

Marvin Bower was livid over McArthur's refusal to force Bain to end the practice, and even more upset when McArthur suggested that McKinsey begin emulating Bain's technique, or apply one of its own. Bower said that it was the dean's responsibility to end the problem.

Despite Bower's anger at McArthur, there was, in fact, very little McArthur could do to control the actions of Bain & Company. Ultimately his response to the situation was to "disinvite" Bain from making a recruiting presentation to the MBA class that year, and to call on the firm to work out a compromise solution, which they were unwilling to agree to. It amounted to a slap on the wrist, and in the following season the bonuses continued to be offered and accepted.

The other disturbing information Bower received about

where all the school's Baker Scholars were going was that a growing number were hired by Monitor Company, Professor Michael Porter's consulting firm in Cambridge. The athletic and brilliant Porter was siphoning off the top Baker Scholars for himself, using as a recruiting tool his own charismatic personality. The ones Porter was not able to convince to join Monitor Company ended up at either Bain or Boston Consulting Group, where Porter had a number of very strong ties; among other things, he had co-authored with partners from both firms several strategy articles that were published in the *Harvard Business Review*. Young, impressionable Baker Scholars were smart enough to see that as far as Porter was concerned, Bain and BCG were "in" and McKinsey was "out," even if he would never be so foolish as to state that in so many words.

Bower wanted McArthur to reprimand Porter for taking the school's most valuable product for himself, but McArthur, who saw nothing wrong with what Porter did, followed through in a halfhearted fashion. Bower was his friend, and one of the largest individual donors at the school. Porter also was his friend, and the school's brightest luminary. He was caught between two power figures, and there appeared to be no way to extricate himself from the situation without risking the goodwill of one or the other. So Marvin Bower decided to tip the scales in his own favor by using the one weapon that Monitor Company, Bain, Boston Consulting Group, and all his other competitors could not match.

In 1984, Bower announced to McArthur his own answer to Bain's "exploding bonus" system. He called it an "exploding fellowship program." While MBA students benefited by signing with Bain, in this new scenario HBS would benefit when students signed with McKinsey. Unlike Bain's scheme, the Marvin Bower Fellowship Program was to be incentive-oriented, rather than penalty-oriented. It was to start with the endowment of $2 million, and would grow by $500,000 each year that McKinsey reached its quota of hiring HBS Baker Scholars. There was to be no penalty if McKinsey failed to meet its self-determined quota; however, additions to the endowment would grind to a standstill. On the other hand, there was no ceiling on the up side. If, for example, McKinsey's arbitrary quota was met for ten consecutive years, the endowment would grow to $7 million [$2,000,000 + (10 × $500,000)].

The particulars of the fellowship were never made public. Ostensibly the program was designed to pay the salaries of four junior faculty members from business schools other than Harvard, for one year, to come to HBS to do research and study. Professor Theodore Levitt was named director of the program, and was given the job of selecting candidates with "demonstrated outstanding achievements in scholarship, productivity, influence, and leadership." If the program fizzled, as the first $200,000 Bower Fellowship had in 1968, it was to have no effect on the "exploding" contributions. The fund would revert to the dean's general fund, to be used as the dean saw fit.

In the recruiting process, finding students for summer jobs between their first and second years at HBS is more important than recruiting second-year students just before they graduate. Students who perform well during the summer are frequently offered permanent jobs before they return to HBS for their second, and final, year. The top prospects, therefore, are often out of the hiring pool by the end of the first summer.

If a consulting company knew how well the first-year students had done at the same time that the students themselves knew, the firm would be able to make its choices for summer associates earlier. Thus, instead of weeding through hundreds of unproductive interviews to find the top prospects, the company could concentrate its efforts on recruiting from among the top 10 percent.

In theory, students who received job offers before returning for their final year at HBS would have no incentive to excel during their second year. However, Baker Scholars, for reasons of pride and status, are competitive under all circumstances and work up to capacity anyway. Over many years, it was found that there was nearly a 100 percent overlap between those students who were at the top of their class after the first semester, and those who were named Baker Scholars at commencement. In any case, those who did not do well during their first semester had very little chance of reaching the top-5-percent category by the time graduation arrived. Therefore, it was a very safe bet to recruit the top 10 percent first-year students in each class, since the Baker Scholars would almost always be drawn from their ranks.

One of the most talked-about recruiting efforts in early 1985 among first-year MBA students from the class of 1986 was the special attention from McKinsey & Company. On the first day of recruiting season, approximately one hundred students received invitations from the company to meet with the firm's partners to discuss summer employment opportunities. Résumés and photographs of MBA students were sent to all interested recruiting companies, but McKinsey acted on the information soonest. By comparing notes, some MBA students noticed that McKinsey had singled out the top ones from each section. Not much was made of this, however. In the following days, invitations from other companies began to pour in and no one felt left out. Whether the school showed favoritism to McKinsey was never brought up as an issue by students or competing recruiters.

The result of McKinsey's recruiting in 1985 was that during that summer the firm had more of the top students from the first year's class working for them than they had had the year before, and most of these students accepted job offers from the firm and began full-time employment in June 1986. Nearly all graduated as Baker Scholars. On July 9, 1986, the enlarged $2.5 million Bower Fellowship Program announced its selections for the four 1986–87 fellows.

THE IBM WAY

Next to companies like McKinsey that gave large lump sums, the greatest advantages went to companies that were members of the Associates of HBS, whose criterion for admission was an active interest in HBS activities and a willingness to invest unrestricted amounts of money in the school's ventures. Newly invited members received glossy promotional catalogs explaining how the system worked: "Traditionally, Associate companies have taken advantage of opportunities for close relationships with the School on a number of fronts. For instance, many recruit actively in cooperation with the Office of Career Development during placement season, and graduating MBAs often take jobs with Associate companies. Similarly, participants in HBS Executive Education Programs regularly come from Associate companies. Moreover, many executives in Associate companies develop long-term friendships with HBS faculty members."

IBM Corporation was by far the most highly valued associate in the program, and was one of the earliest founding members. The relationship began under the guidance of the late professor Theodore Brown, who was a consultant to the corporation and a personal friend of IBM's chairman, Thomas Watson, Jr., until Brown's death in 1973. Brown and a team of HBS professors helped IBM develop the company's first digital computers, the Mark I, and in 1964, the company gave HBS a $5 million, ten-year research grant, which was the first of many large cash and equipment donations made by IBM. By the 1980s, the company's role expanded to the point where it became one of only two computer suppliers, and the only office-machine-equipment supplier, a relationship that was made possible because George B. Beitzel, Harvard MBA '52, was a senior vice-president and director of IBM Corporation, in addition to being a member of the board of directors of the Associates Program. (The school's second computer supplier, Digital Equipment Corporation, which employed more than sixty HBS alumni, was started in 1957 with $70,000 in venture-capital money from the late HBS professor Georges Doriot's company. Doriot joined Digital's board of directors in 1972.)

Beitzel's interest in Harvard Business School went beyond just wanting to make the school one of the company's key customers, although that was a major factor in his decision to pursue close ties. In the long run, he wanted a full-scale information-systems training program for doctoral students and corporate executives that would build a core of highly trained instructors in the field. One of IBM's problems was in finding and hiring enough experts in computer technology because competition for the few qualified graduates from programs that offered degrees was intense. By increasing the supply of instructors, IBM hoped to eventually increase the number of qualified graduates, thus lowering the cost of hiring them. So in 1985, a $2 million joint venture was begun that was expected to produce ten graduates each year by 1989.

IBM also benefited from its ties with the HBS Associates Program in winning large, noncompetitive equipment contracts with the school. In 1985, more than 150 secretarial work stations were remodeled to accommodate $15,000 display writer systems. Earlier, a 1982 IBM-HBS joint study on "the applicability of micro-computers to the school's educational mission," resulted in the sale and lease of 180 personal computers in 1984 to the school's executive-education program. One of the reasons IBM wanted to prototype the use of PCs in the executive program was that it hoped the executives who went through a three-week indoctrination process using IBM PCs would return to their companies afterward and put in large orders for the new equipment, which, in fact, many of them did. Their objective was to make Harvard Business School a sales and training facility for midlevel executives, as well as a model for other business schools and training programs that were thinking of requiring computer training.

But IBM's primary objective in getting PCs into the executive-education curriculum was to establish a captive marketing-research sample of midlevel executives. The company knew that the cost of getting executives to try out new computer equipment, and to give detailed answers to questions about how well they liked and disliked certain features of the machines, would have been either enormously high or impossible, and the results would likely have been inconclusive. No marketing-research company could coerce 180 executives to spend two or three hours answering questionnaires after spending dozens of hours using IBM's new equipment. That target sample, whose responses would really have mattered, would never have consented to submit to that kind of intense questioning.

On the other hand, IBM's executives believed that Harvard Business School professors had a very good chance of gaining cooperation from them, so the decision was made to have one of the school's professors write a questionnaire that was to be mandatorily administered by the executive-education professors. The responses gained from those questionnaires were handed over to IBM for analysis, and did, in fact, prove to be worth a fortune.

From then on, whenever new equipment was introduced, it was to become standard procedure to test it out in the HBS laboratory, a cross-section of America's business executives. More than 99 percent of the surveys taken in this fashion proved to be usable, a much higher percentage than could have been gained through traditional market-research methods. Professors administered them like exams, and the executive students, trained to respond to all questions put to them, answered without thinking twice about who was using the data they provided.

The most concentrated IBM sales effort ever done at the school was to convince Dean John McArthur to make the purchase and use of IBM personal computers mandatory for all MBA students. Never before had a graduate school of business compelled its students to buy PCs, although most schools made computers available to students on an as-needed basis. IBM's push to sell the school and McArthur on the benefits of becoming the first ones to be high-tech was made under the assumption that as HBS went, so went the rest of the academic market. Not only was it one of America's largest business schools, which made it a good account to have under any circumstances, but it was also the most prestigious, which meant the publicity that was bound to come out as a result of this change would give IBM a public relations coup.

The idea was bandied about in discussions as early as 1982, but McArthur at first refused, saying that students could never afford to buy more than $3,000 worth of equipment, and, more important, the school had no software library that was compatible with the case-study method of instruction. What IBM had suggested would mean revamping the entire case system by artificially introducing quantitative analysis into a large percentage of cases that had no numerical bent to them. McArthur was willing to consider moving in the direction of compelling students to buy IBM PCs, but only if IBM was willing to be help in developing new software to accommodate the case system, and in upgrading the HBS staff's computer capabilities.

Money proved to be no obstacle in winning the HBS personal-computer account, and funds were channeled into supporting new computerized cases. At the same time that the software development got under way, the school reached an agreement with IBM for the company to help in rebuilding Anderson House, an office building on campus that was to become the new headquarters for the control department's faculty (who were in charge of teaching information systems). The building rehab project was linked by McArthur to his decision to make PCs part of the MBA curriculum, which meant that if IBM cooperated, the decision would go through; otherwise, HBS would continue to teach MBA students the old-fashioned way. McArthur did not have to ask twice. The $4 million renovation was begun in early 1985, and was completed in the spring of 1986.

Anderson House was to become a model of the office building of the future, filled to capacity with $15,000 word-processing display writers, $5,000 IBM personal computer ATs and XTs, laser printers, and a state-of-the-art network system called local area networking (LAN) in which the building was hard-wired, making it possible for all of Anderson House's PCs to communicate with each other. Eventually, the LAN system was to be expanded throughout the campus so that professors could talk with professors, professors could talk with students, and students could talk with students.

With the stroke of a pen in February 1984, John McArthur made HBS the first business school to go on-line, requiring all incoming MBA students in the fall of 1984 to purchase IBM PCs. More than 750 of the $2,800 units were sold over Labor Day weekend, despite the fact that fewer than fifty cases, out of the thousands in the case system, could be used with the new technology. It soon became clear that for the vast majority of classes, the computers were of limited use. "You're not inclined to expend the time and effort to set up a worksheet for a case when you know it will be of no use the next day," said one student, who discovered that his microcomputer functioned better as a paperweight than as a tool for giving him an advantage in analyzing case data.

Because of the large expense that was incurred in bringing PCs on campus, the chairman of the school's committee on computers sent a memo to faculty encouraging them to invent new uses and to write new programs specifically for the IBM PC. Their response was the equivalent of a giant yawn. Not only was there no incentive for spending hundreds of hours developing new software, there was the usual strong argument against it: The more time spent on academics, the less time there was available to consult. Faced with the choice between writing software, for which they weren't going to be paid, and billing out thousands of dollars for consulting, the faculty unanimously decided in favor of the latter.

In order to motivate faculty, many of whom could not have cared less that the school had indirectly invested millions of dollars in equipment that had limited practical use, the Division of Research established a new software-publishing venture that gave them a piece of the pie. For each $10 package of course material, which included a case study, a diskette, and an instructional note, the author was to receive a royalty fee. This was the first time that a financial incentive had been offered to the faculty for producing anything other than books. The idea was sold to them with a pitch explaining that the market for new HBS case software would not only be other schools', but also corporations' internal training programs. But with a quick calculation, most faculty members figured that it was still not worth investing their time to write software for those small markets, and by 1986 only forty-four cases were sold outside the school on nine different diskettes. The school's best-known and highest-paid professors entirely avoided writing for the new venture; Michael Porter wrote just one software case, while Theodore Levitt, John Kotter, and C. Roland Christensen wrote none.

From a sales-volume point of view, IBM was less concerned about the development of new software, and more concerned about the development of a significant second-hand market for the PCs, much as had developed for used textbooks. Many students, given the choice, would have preferred to sell their little-used machines to incoming first-year students, and recoup part of their initial investment. And first-year students, if given a choice, would have preferred to buy discounted, like-new computers rather than pay retail prices. Many students from the class of 1986 (the first class that had to buy IBM PCs on entry in September 1984) did try hard to locate buyers for their used machines at graduation time, offering discounts of up to 80 percent off the original price paid, but without success.

More than one entrepreneurial MBA student thought about starting a new business in used IBM PCs by snapping up the deep-discounted computers in June and selling them at a profit in September when the fresh recruits arrived. Also, many of those who lived in the Boston area considered showing up at the HBS dormitories with their used equipment over Labor Day weekend, 1986, and hawking it to the highest bidder.

IBM and Harvard Business School announced that all entering students would be encouraged to buy the all-new IBM PC convertible, a twelve-pound lap-top model selling for $2,700. Unlike the base model PC that the class of 1986 had purchased, the lap-top model, they said, would conceivably be used in classrooms and during examinations, information that was conveyed to new and graduating students, the effect of which was to ward off potential used-computer sales.

In direct contradiction, however, the school's 1986 *Course Development and Research Profile* book, handed out on alumni day to visiting HBS graduates, stated that "PC use in the classroom, it should be noted, is not considered likely in the foreseeable future." New students, of course, never saw the alumni book, and unless they had they would have been worried about being at a disadvantage by buying anything less than what IBM and HBS recommended. Imagine one's consternation at trying to lug a used PC to an examination, while everyone else had sleek, PC convertible lap-tops. No sense in risking one's professional future by buying obsolete technology, they thought, so most opted to buy the new convertibles.

State-of-the-art equipment being what it is, there is a strong possibility that, two years hence, the class of 1988 will find itself in the same predicament as the class of 1986, holding on to used IBM equipment that is no longer recommended by Harvard Business School. Disposing of it, at anything other than its salvage value, will be nearly impossible, although functionally it will have been as good as the newer models. But the school has good reasons for protecting its relationship with IBM, a kinship that is strengthened each year that $3 million of new computers and printers are sold to MBA students, especially since the rest of the campus has yet to be hard-wired.

PART III

RESEARCH
AND
DEVELOPMENT

• • •

CHAPTER 12

The Global-Strategy Imitators

• • •

While Michael Porter became Harvard's most prominent strategic thinker, he was by no means alone in trying to establish a reputation in the field of global strategy. After Porter, others soon followed in unsuccessful attempts to duplicate his accomplishments. The most prominent of these imitators was the unlikely team of professors George Lodge and Bruce Scott.

GEORGE CABOT LODGE II

George Cabot Lodge II, who could trace his lineage back more than three centuries to the early history of America,   185 whose father, great-grandfather, and great-great-grand-father served in the United States Senate, and who grew up expecting to trace their footsteps, was a man destined to fail.

Lodge was born in 1927, the son of Henry Cabot Lodge, who, in 1936, was elected to the United States Senate from Massachusetts. The elder Lodge had groomed his son for a political career and, for a while, it looked as though he might succeed in that direction. At the age of seventeen, George followed his father into the army, the elder Lodge resigning from the Senate to enlist, and two years later entered Harvard University. Graduating in 1950, George, in the model of his father, spent four years as a Boston newspaper reporter.

Henry Cabot Lodge, meanwhile, lost his Senate seat to John F. Kennedy in the election of 1952, and was appointed by President Eisenhower to the post of United States ambassador to the United Nations, where he remained until 1960, when he teamed with Richard Nixon in an unsuccessful campaign against the Kennedy-Johnson ticket.

Henry Cabot Lodge, who had always been ambitious for his son, devised what he considered to be a sound, long-range strategy for getting George elected to public office. The plan called for sending his son into government service in the Eisenhower administration and in the Republican administration that would follow. He could then use that as a springboard to an elected position in the Senate. The State Department was seen as too elitist, but the Department of Labor fit perfectly. There, as the champion of blue-collar rights, the Boston Brahmin George Lodge would earn his political stripes. If ever the charge was made that he was out of touch with the working class, pointing to a tour of duty in the Department of Labor would surely silence the critics.

In 1954, Henry had George appointed as the Labor Department's director of information, from where, in 1958, he was promoted to the post of assistant secretary of labor for international affairs. Then, unexpectedly, with his father's defeat to John Kennedy and Lyndon Johnson, George was thrust into the public limelight by his father. Henry Cabot Lodge had considered returning to the Senate but he rejected the idea because it seemed like a step backward and an anticlimax to a distinguished career and, besides, another loss would have been humiliating. George, however, was ready to pick up where Henry had left off. A seat was due to open in 1962, and Henry and George would win it, together, on the issues of labor and unemployment, which George was now well versed in.

Henry called Dean Stanley Teele at Harvard Business School and asked if some office space at the school might be made available where his son could work on a book about trade unions and plan his Senate campaign. Teele, a friend and admirer of Lodge's, offered George the full run of the business school's facilities, and suggested to Henry that his son might have the opportunity to lecture in the labor relations department.

Edward Kennedy, the president's brother, who had the Kennedy name and the Kennedy charisma, easily handled the younger Lodge in the Senate election of 1962. The contest was never really in doubt, as the state of Massachusetts had been solidly behind the Kennedy family for a decade. The defeat was not George's, however; the loss was felt most poignantly by the father. Massachusetts, for the third time, had chosen a Kennedy over a Lodge, as Henry Cabot Lodge had hoped to see his family's name restored in an illustrious political victory.

But if his father was distraught over the defeat, George, at least, was not. Looking back over the campaign he realized that he preferred the purely academic work he did at Harvard Business School to the glad-handing life of a politician. Meeting Khrushchev and attending Washington parties had been fun and interesting, but it was part of his father's life. An academic career, safe and rewarding, became his new goal.

While George found security at Harvard Business School

in 1963, Henry looked for ways to keep active in government, finally deciding to establish the Atlantic Institute
in Paris, which would sponsor international political conferences. Lodge, however, longed for active government
service, and in July 1963, when President Kennedy's ambassador to South Vietman, Frederick E. Nolting, Jr., resigned his post, Kennedy offered the job to Lodge. The
vacancy might have gone to a Democrat, but Kennedy
chose Lodge for two reasons. First, if the situation in South
Vietnam proved calamitous he preferred not to have a
Democratic ambassador associated with the results. And
second, Kennedy was above all gracious in victory. He
had defeated Lodge twice; his brother had defeated Lodge's
son. He now felt that the magnanimous gesture of appointing Lodge would smooth over any lingering bitter-
ness between the Kennedys and the Lodges, two great
political families.

For Lodge, the ambassadorship did, in fact, climax his
career, something he had unsuccessfully tried to do
through his son. With George's hasty retreat from politics, he knew that history would have to remember Henry
Cabot Lodge for what he himself accomplished and not,
as in the case of his contemporary Joseph P. Kennedy, for
what his sons did. The inevitable comparisons between
Edward Kennedy and George Lodge would always come
up, and others would always speculate on what might
have been had the vote been reversed, but Henry Cabot
Lodge never looked back. In time the wounds healed, the
disappointment turned to pride, and the ambitions burned
brightly for the next generation.

At Harvard Business School, George Lodge picked up
after the election where he left off, joining the faculty in
1963 as an assistant professor. Labor relations had always been a moderately interesting subject to him, and
now he had the chance to spend full time on it without
being distracted. Above all, the work allowed him to get
on with his life and forget the painful attempts to live out
his father's dream.

President John F. Kennedy and George Lodge had been bachelor friends together during Kennedy's early years in the Senate, and Kennedy, who respected George for his gentlemanliness, considered ways to assist him in the same way that he had helped his father. In his official capacity as a member of Harvard's board of overseers, Kennedy asked the business school to establish a new school of management in Nicaragua. It would be the first of its kind there and would be funded by the government, conditional upon George Lodge heading up the project. That Lodge, who did not have an MBA or a doctorate and who had no practical business experience, was to establish a new school of business, did not particularly trouble the new dean, George Baker. Lodge would bring honor, prestige, and money to the school, all of which outweighed any lack of academic qualifications.

The faculty of the business school, however, felt less kindly toward Lodge than did Dean Baker. It was unprecedented that Harvard Business School should give someone so completely unqualified academically such an important role in the establishment of a school of management. Why not appoint someone like Georges Lombard, or Robert Merry, men of obvious talent, to head up the project? If Mr. Lodge would like to go along as an adviser of sorts, that would be fine, they said. But the dean would have none of it. The president of the United States had selected Lodge, for whatever reasons, and Baker, for one, would not be the person to countermand a presidential directive.

For six years, Lodge shuttled between Central America and Soldiers Field. The Central American Institute of Business Administration he organized turned out surprisingly well, and provided the school with an outpost to study Latin American business. Lodge, despite his inauspicious beginning, became an accepted and popular member of the faculty. Friendly, sincere, principled, he embodied the estimable qualities that others on the faculty admired. True, he did not have advanced degrees, and his published output paled next to that of another associate professor, Joseph Bower, who was up for tenure at the same time. But he was a Lodge, and he brought new research dollars and influence to the school, and his father had been very generous, directly and indirectly. Tenure and a full professorship were granted in 1972.

Thereafter, George Lodge settled into the kind of academic regime that others envied. He founded a new course called Business and Ideology, which he taught in the prestigious Advanced Management Program, and he wrote two books, *Environmental Analysis*, in 1974, and *The New American Ideology*, in 1975. Within the field of labor relations he became well known and respected. However, it was not until he teamed up with Professor Bruce Scott that he began getting recognition as a global strategic thinker.

BRUCE SCOTT—STRATEGIST

As a young MBA student at Harvard Business School, Bruce Scott dared to criticize both the case system of teaching and quality of work that went into case studies. His attitude shocked fellow classmates and dismayed his professors, and led many at the school to view him negatively.

Nevertheless, Scott was not without his supporters, the most notable of whom was Professor C. Roland Christensen, who singled Scott out in 1957 as a man to be listened to. Despite the fact that Scott was not a Baker Scholar, Christensen recruited him for the doctoral program and became Scott's mentor.

Throughout his career, Scott had an ability to spot winners even if he himself was not one. In 1962, he met a fellow doctoral student, John H. McArthur, and convinced him that their overlapping research on industrial planning could best be completed in tandem. McArthur balked at first, but when Scott explained that he could get a project funded that would take them both to Paris to study the French economy, the lure was too great. Their five-year study was concluded with a report published in 1969 called "Industrial Planning in France," which, when it came out, was largely ignored. The friendship established with McArthur, however, proved useful later on when the latter became dean.

For a time Scott languished on the faculty as an associate professor. His close relationship with Christensen virtually guaranteed his eventual promotion to full professor, but his record of academic achievement was sparse. Somehow he guessed incorrectly about the course of international business scholarship, believing that the trend was toward identifying the causes of Europe's postwar economic difficulties. Instead, Harvard's interest lay in studying the emerging economies of Asia, an area that Scott had no affinity for. His prospects for becoming successful within HBS did not brighten until he spotted a young doctoral student named John W. Rosenblum who had an ability to make things happen.

By all accounts Rosenblum was brilliant, intuitively knowing the right areas to study, the best organizational methods, and the key strategies to follow. In 1972, working with Rosenblum, Scott successfully restructured a course called Environmental Analysis for Management into the Business, Government and the International Economy (BGIE) course, bringing, on Rosenblum's recommendation, George Lodge and Hugo Uyterhoeven in to help surpervise it. Rosenblum went on to become dean of the University of Virginia's business school. The success of the new course, BGIE, helped Scott secure his tenured professorship in 1973, an even more remarkable accomplishment, since he had not, up to then, taught a single course.

In bringing George Lodge and Bruce Scott together, Rosenblum was a catalyst for forming one of the school's most successful working partnerships. Lodge was everything Scott wasn't: rich, well connected, urbane, Harvard establishment, and socially prominent. Scott, who wore undershirts that were visible at the collar of his shirts, could not have had less in common with Lodge. If Lodge ever invited Scott to sail with his family, or visit his seaside mansion in Beverly, Massachusetts, he never mentioned it to anyone. Socially, they were in different leagues.

Despite their disparity in background and areas of specialization, Scott won Lodge over. The ever-affable Lodge was impressed by Scott's tenacity, and a partnership solidified. In 1982 Scott suggested that they team up to lead one of the research colloquia that HBS was sponsoring during 1983 and 1984 to mark its seventy-fifth anniversary. The purpose of this series of conferences was to present the school's current research to specially invited business and government leaders.

Having seen Michael Porter's meteoric rise to prominence on the basis of work on global competition, Scott wanted his piece of the pie. Industrial competitive models were hardly new, and indeed very little in Porter's popular book *Competitive Strategy,* published in 1980, seemed particularly earthshaking. Scott told friends that Porter had simply packaged himself better than anyone else, and had developed a following based on an assumed recognition of his analytical prowess. But had Porter studied the French economy firsthand for five years? Or had he organized an entirely new area in business scholarship around the topic of international business and government? With a little clever positioning of his own he would duplicate Porter's success.

So Scott brought together a group of distinguished Harvard scholars to speak on the United States' competitiveness in the world economy, the central thesis of which was that the United States was becoming less competitive as a nation.

Dr. Ruben Mettler, chairman and CEO of TRW, Inc., and former chairman of the Business Roundtable, was asked by Lodge to invite influential executives from a dozen companies, including DuPont Company, Ford Motor Company, Hewlett Packard, and RCA, all of whom would lend a presence to the event by being there. The co-hosts, Scott and Lodge, then rounded out the guest list by inviting reporters from *The New York Times* and *The Wall Street Journal* as well as other national business periodicals.

At the sessions, conducted over three days in February 1984, George Lodge played the role of the gracious host and business statesman. He was there, he said, to sound an alarm rather than to suggest specific reforms that would improve America's competitiveness. Finding himself thrust into the uncomfortable role of being an expert on global competition, which he was not, Lodge let Scott handle relations with the press.

Scott rose to the occasion. The moment he had waited for, when the spotlight was upon him and the press clamored for interviews, had come. George Lodge, of course, lent his considerable prestige to the occasion, but it was Scott's show all the way. "The United States must recognize what is happening to its economy . . . and be aware of the likely consequences if we do not change our ways . . ." he told the invited audience. The siren was sounded.

Afterward the Scott-Lodge colloquium was talked about in academic circles, and articles were written about it, but the predicted bust didn't arrive. If anything, the U.S. economy seemed to get stronger, not weaker. Undeterred, Scott convinced Lodge to set up meetings with labor leaders in Washington, and for several weeks they made the rounds together. Howard Samuels, head of the AFL-CIO Industrial Union Department, was receptive, but without any specific policy of legislation to support that would remedy the ills contemplated by the two professors, he was powerless to do anything.

Lodge saw the futility in their quixotic mission first. Not only was it time-consuming to travel around the country making speeches, but it was also frustrating to make pessimistic forecasts in the face of an improving economy. By mid-1984, Lodge was ready to call it quits.

Scott, however, was just warming to the challenge. He believed that they were just beginning to gain momentum, and with any luck would find their prescience rewarded by a dramatic economic downturn. With or without Lodge, he was going ahead.

Having made the decision to stay with the global-strategy project, he approached his close friend Dean John McArthur about having the colloquium findings published as a book by the newly organized Harvard Business School Press. McArthur lobbied with the editors to have it published, and when that was done he hired J. Walter Thompson to promote it. The book, *U.S. Competitiveness in the World Economy* (a series of papers edited by Scott and Lodge), became the second title of the HBS Press. Free copies were sent out to corporate executives, members of Congress, and other government officials.

Without Lodge's vigorous help in promoting the book, Scott was unable to maintain momentum for the project. In October 1984, he invited twenty-five international senior editors and economic columnists to HBS for a day-long briefing on the findings, which Lodge reluctantly co-hosted. But the publicity was short-lived.

The Scott-Lodge balloon was finally punctured by a *Wall Street Journal* article that appeared in December 1984. In it, the paper called Scott "an almost-humorless scholar," who, with Lodge, was "using the prestige and resources of the business school to sell their notion to the nation's opinion-makers." The *Journal* debased the campaign by quoting economist Milton Friedman as saying that their concept of a 'competitive edge' for a country was "meaningless." That, coupled with an offhand barb from Professor Robert Reich of Harvard's Kennedy School of Government, who said that the two HBS professors didn't offer enough specific solutions, and the job was done. When 1985 arrived, Scott and Lodge parted company.

George Lodge never talked about his disapproval of Scott's handling of the two-year media display. He was an amiable professor with no aspirations of becoming the next Michael Porter strategy master, even if Scott did. In his own quiet way, Lodge simply avoided Scott, and the two were rarely seen together thereafter.

Scott's rapid rise to the leading edge of research into global competitive strategies only whetted his appetite for more. He redoubled his efforts and in 1986 organized a new independent research project, with funding provided by Dean McArthur, to examine the manufacturing-oriented mercantilist state in Japan. His mission was to document precisely how Japan and other Asian nations beat the United States in the world marketplace. The world had not heard the last of Bruce Scott.

CHAPTER 13

Portfolio Management

• • •

It was just another story on February 22, 1982, in which *The Wall Street Journal* reported that Heublein, Inc., sued General Cinema Corporation in federal district court for violating securities and exchange laws. Specifically, the complaint charged General Cinema with "manipulative and deceptive practices" and with illegally attempting to gain control of Heublein by failing to properly disclose the extent of its holdings. The suit, however, stopped short of accusing General Cinema of trading on "insider" information about an impending billion-dollar merger between Heublein and R. J. Reynolds Industries, because doing so would have been an admission that the takeover 197 rumors were true. Heublein's official position, right up to the moment the Heublein-Reynolds merger was announced, was that the two companies had never talked, and that there was no truth to the story, first published on January 28, 1982, that a deal was imminent.

General Cinema, for its part, readily disclosed that it had purchased shares between early December 1981 through early February 1982, and that it had acquired for investment purposes 9.7 percent of Heublein's stock, just under the 10 percent level requiring reporting to the Securities and Exchange Commission. Months later, the federal district court in New York found Heublein's suit groundless by ruling that General Cinema had broken no laws, a decision that was upheld on appeal, thereby closing the case.

Richard A. Smith was an unlikely corporate raider, a man who had never before attempted either an unfriendly takeover or the purchase of large blocks of a publicly traded corporation. Indeed, in the four years following the purchase of Heublein's stock, despite his incredible success, he had not made any other uninvited purchases of another company's stock. He was a cautious executive, unaccustomed to making hasty decisions, who quietly went about his business, characteristics that had earned him the reputation of being bland and nondescript.

He grew up in Boston and graduated from Harvard College in 1946, after which he joined his family's business, the Smith management company. His father, Philip Smith, had pioneered the drive-in-movie-theater concept, building the first drive-in in Detroit in 1935 and adding forty-six more before taking the company public in the late 1950s as the General Drive-In Corporation. Richard Smith was the company's troubleshooter running the operations down to the finest detail and making certain that his father's plans were carried out precisely. Philip Smith's idea to build new movie theaters in shopping centers was cut short by his death, but Richard Smith developed the concept and in so doing transformed the company into

General Cinema Corporation. Within seven years General Cinema owned twice as many shopping-center theaters as drive-ins, and the company's treasury was flush with cash.

Diversifying into beverages had been Richard Smith's idea entirely. He had noted that the sugared, carbonated water sold in his cinemas had tremendously large profit margins for the bottling companies that supplied them with soft drinks, and he figured out that he had missed out on one of the most lucrative side businesses available to him. He tried unsuccessfully to buy a Coca-Cola bottling company, finally settling in 1967 on American Beverage Corporation, a Pepsi-Cola bottler with four plants in two states, for $18 million. Through a series of astute acquisitions over the next eight years, General Cinema became America's largest independent bottling company, with revenue from that business soon outpacing the motion-picture-projection business.

While bottling companies were Smith's most successful venture, over the same period there were some notable failures in buying such disparate businesses as bowling alleys, radio and television stations, and furniture manufacturers. Shopping-center cinemas and soft-drink bottling had come to him almost effortlessly, but the more he tried to find new outlets for his company's money, the less it appeared he would be able to duplicate his early successes. So Smith sought advice by turning with increasing regularity to Harvard Business School, first by hiring several of its MBAs in the early 1970s, and in 1975 by hiring the Harvard Business School faculty's best consulting company.

On graduating from Harvard College, Smith had been pressed into service by his father, and any hopes of attending Harvard Business School were permanently shelved. Nevertheless, his regard for the institution was undiminished, and he knew several faculty members, one of whom, Hugo E. R. Uyterhoeven, he admired greatly.

Without exception, Uyterhoeven had the greatest financial acumen of anyone Smith had ever met. Eight years Smith's junior, Uyterhoeven had grown up in the Netherlands and had received two law degrees, one from the University of Ghent and one from the University of Zurich, before he was age twenty-four. In 1955, he was chosen for a Belgian-American Educational Foundation Fellowship and was sent to the MBA program of Harvard Business School, where he remained after graduation, joining the faculty and pursuing a doctorate in business administration.

His skill in financial planning rapidly brought him consulting work with General Electric, Chemical Bank, and Caltex Petroleum Corporation, among several others, and board memberships with Greenwich Management Company, the Income Fund of America, the J. Henry Schroder Banking Corporation, and the Schroder Bank & Trust Company, the last two of which had been offered to him because of his friendship with Bruno Schroder, one of his early students, whose family owned the British investment bank that bore the family name.

By 1970, he was a tenured member of the faculty, and four years later was named to the newly endowed Timken Chair of Business Policy. In 1976, he was promoted once again to be the chairman of the Advanced Management Program, a meteoric rise by HBS standards, which showed the level of accomplishment that he had attained. Like many others on the faculty, he formed his own consulting firm, Hugo Uyterhoeven, Inc., which kept his consulting revenue separate from his teaching revenue.

Along with Robert W. Ackerman, MBA '62, DBA '68, Uyterhoeven visited the suburban-Boston headquarters of General Cinema Corporation in 1976. Ackerman was Harvard Business School's only Senior Research Fellow. When he was not working with Uyterhoeven, he was employed by Preco Corporation in Massachusetts, until 1987, when he officially joined the faculty of HBS.

They had come in expecting to help General Cinema to identify its core businesses and to suggest ways to deal with the enviable problem of what to do with the company's excess cash reserves. Their analysis had, however, validated Smith's earlier strategy, which was to build new businesses, such as soft drinks, off of the main business, motion-picture projection. General Cinema's venture into bottling had been successful because the company had been its own best customer during the early growth years. Bowling alleys and furniture stores, by contrast, could not in any way be tied into the cinema business, and for that reason had been unqualified disasters. The future of the company was in cinema-related areas, decided Uyterhoeven, which boiled the problem down to just choosing one area to enter.

Uyterhoeven suggested opening up the company to some high-powered analysis by using the Advanced Management Program students at his disposal. Ackerman and Uyterhoeven wrote a case study of Smith's diversification situation and presented it on a semiannual basis to classes of AMPs in sessions to which Smith was invited. There he would sit at the back of the auditorium and listen to the strategic thinking of America's best managers, one of whom, without fail, would recommend a two-pronged attack into the manufacture and distribution of popcorn.

Some good ideas, however, did come out of the sessions, including the recommendation that Smith invest in other companies. As a passive investor, he would be in a position to take advantage of the growth in the market without having to bring in new management to run an operating division. In fact, ordinarily the only barrier to entry in the investment business was the lack of a sizable quantity of cash, something Smith had more than enough of. By 1978, he was talked into trying the new approach, and General Cinema bought shares in Columbia Pictures Industries, Inc., 4.2 percent, until it was rebuffed by Columbia, which opposed the purchase. With Columbia one of his chief suppliers, Smith was in no position to argue the point and he immediately abandoned the plan.

HEUBLEIN

While Uyterhoeven had long experience in corporate investing as a board member of several international companies, Smith did not. The idea, while it had some obvious advantages, had tremendous risk associated with it, and risks were something Smith had tried to avoid. The only way he would consider getting into such a volatile business was if Uyterhoeven agreed to join the board of directors of General Cinema and act as an official adviser. That way, if a new investment opportunity did present itself, Hugo, with his brilliant financial skills, would be there to share the burden of passing judgment on the acquisition target. Smith's argument was persuasive, and in 1980 Uyterhoeven joined the twelve-man board that included Smith; Emmanuel Kurland, partner in the Boston law firm of Singer, Stoneman; William L. Brown, president of the First National Bank of Boston; and Abram Collier, former chairman of New England Mutual Life Insurance Company.

His appointment to General Cinema's board coincided with yet another promotion at Harvard, this time to be the business school's senior associate dean for external relations, a job that required him to raise money for HBS from a list of several hundred corporations, the HBS Associates. Dean McArthur appointed him to the job primarily because he already had more contacts with those corporations, through board memberships, consulting, and research work, than any other professor. The initiation process for anyone else would have been drawn out, requiring the new associate dean to be introduced to large numbers of chief executives of the corporations that were invited to become HBS Associates. Instead, from his first day on the job, he already knew more senior executives than his predecessor, who had been the external-relations dean for several years.

What spare time Uyterhoeven did have in 1980 and 1981 was spent consulting primarily with one company, The Stanley Works, Inc., whose board he joined in 1975 on the invitation of Donald W. Davis, Harvard MBA '48. It was there that Uyterhoeven first met Stuart D. Watson, a graduate of Harvard's Advanced Management Program in 1951. Watson was chairman of Heublein, Inc., a wine-and-spirits company that also owned the restaurant chain of Kentucky Fried Chicken, and while Uyterhoeven never did any consulting for Watson or Heublein, they attended ten or more board meetings together annually and were friends. In addition, Uyterhoeven knew another Stanley Works board member, Edward B. Bates, chairman of Connecticut Mutual Life Insurance Company, who had been on Heublein's board since 1973 and who shared pension committee responsibilities with Uyterhoeven.

Exactly why Richard Smith decided to buy shares in Heublein in the first place was never disclosed by General Cinema to either the press or the SEC. Neither was the fact that one of his board members, Hugo Uyterhoeven, shared an interlocking directorship with two members of Heublein's board. Uyterhoeven, for his part, did not see enough of a conflict of interest to excuse himself from board-meeting discussions on the Heublein stock acquisition.

In late January 1982, Smith disclosed to the SEC that General Cinema owned 9.7 percent of Heublein's stock, bought through open-market and private transactions at prices ranging from $30 to $40 per share. The public announcement on February 4 of General Cinema's holdings did little to persuade other investors to join the company, and in fact the stock price edged down to $35 per share on March 1, which was fine with Smith, who was buying all he could get his hands on.

While Smith vehemently maintained that his purchases of Heublein stock were for investment purposes only, Heublein's public position was that the company believed General Cinema, half the size of the $2 billion

Heublein, was considering a hostile takeover.

On March 2, in retaliation, Heublein announced it had just purchased $15 million worth of General Cinema stock, and had filed papers with the SEC seeking permission to take over General Cinema. With Heublein unexpectedly turning around and biting off a chunk of General Cinema, the dangers of playing the corporate acquisition game were made painfully apparent. Smith convened an emergency session of his board to discuss a strategy to extricate the company from the cruel clutches of Heublein, and it was decided that General Cinema would buy back three million of its own shares as rapidly as possible to prevent any possible takeover. At the same time, the board voted to try conciliating with Heublein by arranging a stock swap or repurchase plan. With Uyterhoeven acting as intermediary, chairmen Smith and Watson agreed on March 10 that Heublein would sell General Cinema a million of the shares it had purchased if General Cinema agreed not to buy more than 20 percent of Heublein's stock.

At General Cinema's annual shareholders' meeting on March 12, Smith announced his repurchase of stock from Heublein and the fact that the company had entered into a revolving credit agreement with the First National Bank of Boston to provide up to $300 million, money that might be used to buy back stock and notes to prevent any unfriendly takeovers of General Cinema.

He had been at the brink of disaster, risking his entire company in what he assumed was a risk-free investment. He vowed then never to make the same mistake. If any raiders had seen how easily General Cinema might have been taken over, the precautions taken in the wake of Smith's first, and only, stock play would dissuade even the most diehard of them. In the meantime, General Cinema's investment in Heublein continued on schedule and, having taken the steps to prevent any backlash, by May the company's stake reached four million shares, equal to 18.9 percent of the total stock. The price had also risen to almost $41 per share, and the company's once-bloated cash reserves and credit lines had been drawn down, making further purchases uneconomical.

For a while it looked as if nothing were going to happen, and that the purchases had been made unwisely. But on July 30 Heublein announced it would be bought out by Reynolds at $63 per share, and Smith was not only vindicated, his prescience was lauded by the investment community. He netted $74 million in profits in less than six months.

Many had doubted the wisdom of holding four million shares, especially when in mid-June they were selling for $35, which was less, on average, than what Smith had paid. He had beaten the market on his first try, something he was quick to take credit for, pointing out that he had helped bring revitalized growth to General Cinema with a new investment division that went along with movies and soft drinks.

BENDIX

While Richard Smith played the stock market and won, another Uyterhoeven friend and fellow board member, William Agee, played and lost. Agee, Harvard MBA class of 1963 and chairman of Bendix Corporation (a diversified Michigan-based conglomerate), had invited Uyterhoeven on Bendix's board in 1978 as a $15,000-per-year outside director, adding $850 for each meeting of the six committees he sat on. Agee had been a high-flying boy wonder who had built Bendix into one of America's most successful corporations through a carefully planned acquisition program in the late 1970s that had won him the admiration of the faculty and an Alumni Achievement Award from the school in 1977.

It became a fraternal relationship, with Agee constructing brilliant but risky plans and Uyterhoeven methodically analyzing and approving them as they came across his desk. Agee's cockiness disappeared when they were alone together and he went from being a boy wonder to a student learning at his professor's side. Uyterhoeven was the one who controlled the agenda; he would ask the questions that others were afraid to ask. Emerging from those private meetings, Agee could afford to be a little arrogant. He had jumped his toughest hurdle—convincing Uyterhoeven of the merits of his plans.

As Uyterhoeven was advising Richard Smith in 1981 on ways to invest the $175 million he had at his disposal, he watched Agee fortify his plans for Bendix to sell off some nonproducing assets for cash, the first stage in building a war chest to raid companies. By 1982, Agee's consolidation and divestment program yielded $700 million in cash, money that he used, with Uyterhoeven's guidance and approval, to buy large blocks of RCA Corporation and Martin Marietta.

Having witnessed Smith's success in making $74 million over six months by buying Heublein stock, Agee was itching to get into the takeover game himself. Agee was the stuff of which classic case studies were made; who would remember Smith's timid entry, and exit, in the takeover sweepstakes of 1982 after Agee's planned master stroke?

It was called by some the most ill-advised corporate takeover attempt ever made, a bold raid by Agee on Martin Marietta in August and September 1982. Agee had gotten Uyterhoeven's blessing to bid $1.5 billion for Marietta, an offer that was resoundingly rejected. To counter what it believed to be Bendix's next move to buy more of its stock, Marietta took the advice of its investment banker from Kidder, Peabody, Martin A. Siegel, Harvard MBA '71, who suggested a "Pac-Man defense" in which Marietta would buy Bendix and end the whole game. But since the acquisition would have been difficult for Marietta to pull off alone, Siegel brought in Harry Gray, chairman of United Technologies, to guarantee Marietta's tender offer. On September 11, Marietta's directors gave Agee one last chance to back out of the deal completely: Martin

Marietta and United Technologies would drop their plans to buy Bendix if Agee would cancel his plans to buy Martin Marietta.

By this time, it had become less a matter of what was best for Bendix, and more a show of Agee's resolve. He would not give in, he said. He had met with his board and they had all agreed that Marietta was bluffing.

Marietta was not bluffing, a fact that became apparent to Agee on September 21, when it was too late for him to back out. In what was his only alternative besides succumbing to Marietta and United Technologies, Agee hastily arranged a friendly buyout from Allied Corporation. Events had happened so fast that the deal was made without the prior knowledge of the directors, and when Agee perfunctorily asked his directors to approve the merger, Uyterhoeven and two others on the board used it as an excuse to resign. They knew that Agee had no other choice and that the Bendix ship was sinking. But Agee had taken the coward's way out by jumping in a life raft rather than going down with the ship. That, in Uyterhoeven's eyes, was the unpardonable sin.

Uyterhoeven had supported Agee throughout the years he had been on the board, and throughout the Marietta battle until the final moment. Then, rather than going on record as having championed a losing cause and a weak-willed leader, he opted to resign. In fact, Hugo Uyterhoeven's resignation was purely symbolic, since under any scenario he would have been removed from the newly formed board of directors. It did, however, deflect the barrage of negative publicity that followed the Bendix boondoggle. The press incorrectly viewed the resignation as showing Uyterhoeven's disgust toward the power-hungry Agee. Agee got all the blame; Uyterhoeven was remembered as one of the directors who had the sense to leave.

The real significance of the resignation was not lost on at least one of Uyterhoeven's former classmates, Wesley E. Young, vice-president of Kidder, Peabody & Company, who was the secretary of the MBA class of 1957. In his note to the class on the twenty-fifth reunion held in September 1982, he wrote, "In the month of September, just before the reunion, Hugo made the headlines in the NYT when it was announced that he and [two] other dirs. of the bd. of Bendix rebelled against Bill Agee's quick approval of merging Bendix into Allied Corp. Hugo and the other [two] directors resigned and walked out of the heated meeting. To date, neither Hugo nor the other directors have made any comments for the press. Perhaps for our 30th Reunion, Hugo will make this a case study for our class to discuss."

CARTER HAWLEY HALE STORES, INC.

Based on their reading of General Cinema's strategy, Wall Street investment bankers increasingly dangled some tantalizing bait in front of the company, including Entenmann's (Bakery), William Underwood (packaged foods), and Wometco Enterprises, a cinema chain and bottler of Coca-Cola. The consensus of the General Cinema board was that the acquisition opportunities were overpriced or too risky; nevertheless, they were snapped up by other growth-minded firms.

Instead of buying more companies, Smith began selling unprofitable operations, and using his company's cash to pay off the $220 million in bank debt incurred by purchasing Heublein's and General Cinema's stock. By 1984, the company had become virtually debt free, and was growing at a healthy rate of between 5 percent and 10 percent above the rate of inflation. With such an enviable balance sheet, analysts predicted that it would be a very short while before General Cinema would once again take the plunge into the equities market.

One keenly interested observer of General Cinema's strong financial position was the Stanley Roth, Sr., Professor of Retailing at Harvard Business School, Walter J.

Salmon. As a member of no fewer than seven major corporate boards, it was Salmon's job to stay current on the financial health of companies that had ties with Harvard Business School, the primary reason he had been chosen by so many companies. Friendships were built on the principle that one professor did everything in his power to help another professor's company if the occasion presented itself. They were, like Supreme Court justices, there for life, so one didn't turn one's back on a fellow faculty member. It was one of the unwritten rules, the way gentlemen did business together.

The man in need in April 1984 was not Salmon, but Philip Hawley, chairman of Carter Hawley Hale Stores, Inc., a company on whose board Salmon had been since 1974, and that unexpectedly found itself helpless against a corporate takeover. There was persuasive reason for Salmon to help Carter Hawley Hale and Philip Hawley in their time of need. The company's founding chairman, Edward W. Carter, MBA '37, had given more than $1 million to Harvard Business School to endow a chair in 1979, the first incumbent of which was the august professor of marketing Ted Levitt. Carter and his company had helped the school countless times dating back to the mid-1950s, a tradition carried on by Philip Hawley.

Hawley was born in Portland, Oregon, in 1925 and attended the University of California at Berkeley, where he was elected to Phi Beta Kappa, receiving his BS degree in 1946. Hawley looked the part of a chief executive—large, distinguished, impeccably tailored—with a social presence to match his appearance. He came to the Advanced Management Program at Harvard Business School in 1967, not for further training but because he needed the one credential that would guarantee his nomination to succeed Carter, an HBS degree. But the experience proved to be beneficial not only for his career, but also for his social standing. Like Carter, he saw the advantage of dropping the information in passing conversation that he was a Harvard alumnus, and in 1978 he capitalized on his connection with the school by running for election to Harvard University's board of overseers.

The loyalty Hawley felt toward HBS was not entirely of his own making; indeed, much of it was cultivated by Walter Salmon. While Carter had been the company officer who had invited Salmon to join the board in 1974, it was Salmon, not Carter, who encouraged Hawley to run for a seat on Harvard's prestigious board of overseers. Hawley, the new chairman and chief executive officer, had enormous political power, sitting on boards such as BankAmerica Corporation and Bank of America, Pacific Telephone, and Atlantic Richfield, and he also had budgetary power at Carter Hawley Hale. Salmon knew that the company's continued friendship with HBS depended on Philip Hawley's dedication to the institution; he had therefore suggested the idea to him as a way to draw him closer, knowing full well that the status of the job would appeal to Philip Hawley.

On April 2, 1984, Hawley received a telephone call from Leslie Wexner, chairman of The Limited, Inc., who announced his intention to buy Carter Hawley Hale. If the call had been from virtually anyone else but Wexner, Hawley would not have been so upset; it was as if his worst nightmare had suddenly come true. As Hawley saw it, Wexner had no right to buy his company. The differences between the two men could not have been greater.

Wexner grew up in Columbus, Ohio, the son of a budget-apparel chain manager, and in 1963 borrowed money from an aunt to open a moderately priced women's sportswear shop called The Limited. Early in his career he became the protégé of the shopping-mall developer A. Alfred Taubman, who helped Wexner to locate new stores in prime new shopping-mall space. Taubman spent twenty years building gas stations and K mart stores throughout the United States, and then turned to developing scenic pastureland into gaudy shopping malls. That was what really rankled Hawley when he thought about Wexner: both of them making all that money together.

Taubman's multimillionaire status vaulted him into the major leagues of Detroit's investment community, where he befriended the automobile magnate Henry Ford II and the industrialist Max Fisher. He brought them in as investment partners in 1977 for the purchase of seventy-seven thousand acres of undeveloped land south of Los Angeles, which the partners sold six years later for a profit of $660 million. Wexner and Taubman were equally successful in their ventures together, with Wexner building a retail empire and a personal fortune of $1 billion, and Taubman filling his new shopping malls with Wexner's stores. They were both street-smart and nouveau riche, but while wealth had not changed Wexner, it had sensitized Taubman to class differences. He worked to change his image of being just a shopping-mall developer by spending $114 million in 1983 to buy Sotheby Parke Bernet Group, the British auction house. Taubman's efforts paid off in November 1983, when the Harvard Business School Club of Detroit honored him, with Henry Ford II and Max Fisher, as Business Statesman of the year. Myron Burnes, MBA '50, president of Burnes and Company, made the official presentation of the award with the words, " . . . a builder by trade, a master salesman, an international financier, and organizational genius." Coming as it did from the mouth of the Harvard Business School, the flattery could not have been more gratifying.

Although he had supported Wexner throughout every acquisition made by The Limited, Inc., Taubman's support disappeared in early 1984, when Wexner told him he was going after Carter Hawley Hale. If Wexner wanted to make a run at CHH, Taubman said, he would have to do it alone. He was the new Alfred Taubman, someone who was not about to jeopardize his good relationships with either Philip Hawley, whose stores were a tenant of his, or Harvard Business School, with which Hawley was closely allied and which had seen fit to honor him with the Business Statesman Award. An HBS statesman didn't help to take over another Harvard man's company. Wexner could understand none of this. So Taubman went on record as publicly stating that he and Wexner had parted company when it came to Carter Hawley Hale. "It was the only disagreement we've ever had," he said in 1986.

Philip Hawley could not have cared less whether it was Wexner alone or Wexner with Taubman who was trying to take control of Carter Hawley Hale; his reaction was the same: pure disgust. Wexner had a history of dismantling retail chains for the parts he wanted. Hawley, by contrast, was pure upper-crust, well educated, whose son was at that time attending Harvard's MBA program. He had carefully assembled a prized retail group including such stores as Neiman-Marcus, through clever negotiations, never by buying a larger company and discarding the pieces he didn't want. The thought of Wexner purchasing CHH and taking apart what Philip Hawley had spent his professional life amassing, was just too shocking.

Although Salmon and the other board members could understand Hawley's passionate dislike for Wexner, none felt nearly as strongly as Hawley about the urgency to do something to stop him. Wexner's bid had offered essentially a stock swap to CHH stockholders, CHH's stock for The Limited's stock. If it had been a cash offer, there would have been a great deal more to worry about. Wexner's investment banker, Felix Rohatyn of Lazard Freres, had offered only the equivalent of $600 million for 53 percent of CHH's stock, which, given the lack of major financial backing, would probably not have appealed to most shareholders. Looking at it in a rational way, it would have been unlikely that Wexner could succeed; Hawley, of course, was incapable of being rational when it came to Leslie Wexner.

The minimum amount of money needed to guarantee that The Limited would be incapable of buying Hawley's company was $300 million, which, when combined with the $170 million CHH had on hand to buy back its own shares, and with the shares already in friendly hands, would have given the company more than twenty million of the thirty-one million shares outstanding. Raising $300 million for a company the size of Carter Hawley Hale ($3.6 billion in sales) should not have been a particularly difficult problem for Hawley, but it was. From 1970 to 1979 the company had overextended itself, buying department-store chains with low growth and small profit margins. Selling off those assets for cash would have amply provided the money needed to forestall the crisis, but Hawley believed that his time was too short to complete a sale before the stockholders tendered their shares. The only other alternative, then, was to find a lender willing to extend credit, which BankAmerica Corporation, a company on whose board Hawley sat, did within one week of his request in the form of a $900 million credit line.

BankAmerica's credit lines might well have been used to buy CHH shares, except for the high interest rate it would have been lent out at, and the need to repay it rapidly, which would have necessitated selling assets. The object, as Philip Hawley saw it, was to get the company out of The Limited's grasp with the least damage, not to dismantle CHH to spite Leslie Wexner, so Hawley turned to his board to help locate a "white knight."

In the parlance of Wall Street, a *white knight* is a company that is willing to lend a large sum of money quickly to deflect an attempted takeover, without extracating a huge price for the favor or trying to take over the besieged company itself. Hawley saw that as the best alternative. It would allow for much better credit terms for the company than could be had from a bank, and would not force the company to liquidate its holdings. Having made the decision to find a white knight, on April 9, 1984, Hawley gave his board the charge to locate a likely candidate, with a bonus in an unspecified amount going to the member who could find the right company willing to strike a deal.

Unluckily for Hawley, the board he empowered with his battle cry, while composed of some notable former chairmen of major corporations, had an average age of sixty-five, and six members were more than seventy years old. Of the outside directors, most were retired and had very little influence with their former corporations. Indeed, only three agreed to look actively on Hawley's behalf: Robert Di Giorgio, chairman of Di Giorgio Corporation, Walter Gerken, chairman of Pacific Mutual Life Insurance Company, and Walter Salmon, professor of retailing at Harvard. Di Giorgio, who sat on three boards with Hawley, was a longtime friend, but headed up a small food-processing-and-distribution company that did not have the money or the contacts to raise $300 million in a hurry. Gerken, too, lacked a sufficiently high-powered contact base, and his own company was not in a position to invest at that dollar level. Which left, ironically, only Walter Salmon, who, at fifty-three, was the youngest member of the board, and the only member who had neither worked for nor headed up a major American corporation. Nevertheless, he was easily the best-connected of any of CHH's directors, counting among his friends the directors of more than a hundred corporations, most of them working with him at Harvard Business School.

When Professor Walter Salmon returned to Boston on April 10 following the meeting, he decided to contact General Cinema Corporation, which was headquartered in the affluent suburb of Chestnut Hill, Massachusetts, less than twenty minutes from the campus of HBS. It was a *Fortune* 500 company with a well-publicized problem of having too much cash and not enough investment opportunities, and moreover one of its most prominent board members, Hugo Uyterhoeven, was his colleague and friend for almost thirty years, and worked in Morgan Hall, the building facing Fowler Hall, where Salmon's office was. He called Uyterhoeven and arranged for a lunch meeting at the faculty club the next day, Wednesday, to discuss the Carter Hawley Hale situation.

Speaking as one board member to another, Salmon explained why he wanted Uyterhoeven to ask Richard Smith to intercede in CHH's difficult predicament, noting the company's long history of generosity toward Harvard Business School. Uyterhoeven, never one to let emotion play any role in making a business deal, told Salmon that he could not approach Smith with a proposal to bail out Philip Hawley with $300 million just because his company had close ties to the school. What did Smith care about old school ties? Although Smith's son was, right then, by coincidence, in the same MBA class as Hawley's son, Smith hadn't gone to Harvard Business School, and Uyterhoeven argued that it would have been a weak excuse for doing a deal. If Salmon wanted General Cinema's help, he and Hawley would have to structure a financially strong proposal for Uyterhoeven to take to Smith. And speaking as someone who had known Smith for a decade, Uyterhoeven assured Salmon that Smith would never consider buying "risky" common stock whose price, and rate of return, could fluctuate widely. If anything, the Heublein deal, as profitable as it had been, demonstrated that Smith, by Uyterhoeven's standards, was an extremely cautious chief executive. He had pulled back short of making one of the biggest killings in Wall Street history, and in the year and a half since then had opted to pay off debt rather than using his money to get into new investments. Not that he wouldn't be open to receiving a guaranteed rate of return—he would—and Uyterhoeven was the only person capable of selling him on making such an investment. The job for Walt Salmon was to work out the particulars of a viable proposal with Hawley, which Uyterhoeven had agreed he would then present to Smith with his recommendation, if it looked promising to him.

The deal that Uyterhoeven took to Smith on April 11 was generous by any standards. It called for an annual 10 percent guaranteed rate of return on a new class of preferred stock that was convertible into 39 percent of Carter Hawley's common stock at Smith's discretion, and up to seven seats on Carter Hawley Hale's board of directors. Uyterhoeven had run the numbers and figured out that if Smith used the credit line established with the First National Bank of Boston in the Heublein deal, he would make a guaranteed return of 3 percent on the bank's money with no risk to General Cinema. Even better, because of a giant loophole in the corporate tax laws, the dividends paid by CHH to General Cinema, $30 million each year, would be exempt from taxes as "intercorporate dividends." Uyterhoeven's analysis and recommendation: Hawley was foolishly giving away the store, and Smith would be foolish to pass the offer up.

It was the sort of investment that came along perhaps once in a decade, an absolutely risk-free opportunity offered for no other reason than that one man was willing to do anything to keep another man from buying his company. By the time Smith convened his board and had talked with Hawley about the agreements they would make, he had already decided to see how much extra he could work into the deal. Smith, an avid reader, asked for an option to buy Carter Hawley Hale's 843-store chain of bookstores, Waldenbooks, the second-largest chain in the country. That was fine with Hawley since he used Smith's new condition to bargain his own condition for the agreement. If Smith wanted the option on Waldenbooks, he would have to agree to a seven-year standstill agreement that would prohibit General Cinema from either decreasing or increasing its holdings.

Hawley denied that the figure of seven years had anything to do with his age, which would have been sixty-five when the agreement expired. His company had no mandatory retirement age, he pointed out, while at the same time neglecting to mention that Edward Carter had relinquished the post of chief executive officer to Hawley on his sixty-fifth birthday. Whether he admitted it publicly or not, Hawley knew that in approximately seven years, like Carter, he would no longer be at the helm; the problem of holding the company together would be someone else's. On April 16, Carter Hawley Hale's board in Los Angeles approved the plan that General Cinema's board had accepted in Chestnut Hill hours earlier.

If the deal did little to enhance Hawley's reputation as an astute businessman, it went a long way toward creating the myth of a shrewd investor around Smith, an image he tried to perpetuate when he told *Business Week*, "Within five days of getting a phone call, we closed a $300 million transaction. We're not at the tire-kicker stage anymore." The speed with which the deal had been consummated had, of course, been a result of Hawley's fear of losing out to Wexner, and Uyterhoeven's demand to Salmon that Hawley offer a no-lose investment. Smith seized the opportunity immediately, but Uyterhoeven was the one who set it up and who gave Smith the green light to buy in.

Wexner and Rohatyn were outmaneuvered by Carter Hawley Hale's unusual defense, which, in effect, gave General Cinema a controlling interest in the company at a cost of less than half of what Wexner had offered. The New York Stock Exchange, the Securities and Exchange Commission, and The Limited, Inc., each filed suit against Carter Hawley Hale, charging the company with violating securities laws, but ultimately the efforts were unsuccessful in reversing the antitakeover bargain. Wexner had underestimated the lengths to which Hawley was willing to go to avoid being forced to succumb to him, and had failed to win the support of his powerful ally Alfred Taubman, who could have provided the all-cash offer to stockholders that might have made The Limited's bid successful.

Four months later, Professor Walter Salmon found himself on Carter Hawley Hale's new board of directors with some familiar faces, seven new members from General Cinema's board of directors, including Richard Smith, Hugo Uyterhoeven, and William Brown, the chairman of The First National Bank of Boston, who had more than a passing interest in seeing that Smith's investment was paid off.

By packing Carter Hawley Hale's board with his own

men, Smith was protecting his company's $300 million investment. The company had promised General Cinema a $30 million annual dividend and he wanted to make certain that GCC got it even if assets had to be sold off. And they were. In mid-1986, with projected profits for 1987 expected to dip close to a level that would have meant possibly eliminating the common stock dividend and cutting into the $30 million annual cash payment to General Cinema Corporation, Smith and his fellow board members voted to retain the investment-banking firm of Morgan Stanley to sell Carter Hawley Hale's chain of John Wanamaker department stores for a minimum of $180 million. Smith had already seen Philip Hawley's penchant for being too generous, and he wanted Morgan Stanley, not Hawley, to handle the sale in order to guarantee that the highest possible price would be obtained. Carter Hawley Hale's wild spending habits were over, he declared; Smith, unlike Hawley, would have no qualms about selling the entire company, if necessary, to keep the money coming in, and he had the votes on the board, including professors Salmon and Uyterhoeven, to do just that.

If Hawley had doubts about the wisdom of making the original deal with Smith, he kept them to himself. There was apparently no exit clause for CHH in the standstill agreement with General Cinema. Smith, of course, was open to making a new deal. Carter Hawley Hale could always buy out General Cinema's position for a premium with money raised by selling off the company's crown jewel, Neiman-Marcus, or a combination of lesser assets. The question Hawley would have to face then was whether the cure was worse than the illness.*

When Hawley's son Victor talked with him in April 1985

---

*In late 1986, Wexner made a second unsuccessful attempt to buy CHH, the net result of which was a restructuring of the company. Richard Smith gained control over a new corporate entity that included the assets of Neiman-Marcus and the company's other prestigious department stores.

about joining the company when he graduated from Harvard Business School that June, Philip Hawley advised him not to. There was no long-term future at Carter Hawley Hale after 1991, he said. So Victor Hawley accepted one of his other job offers, to become an account marketing representative in Los Angeles, with IBM Corporation.

CHAPTER 14

Professor Bower's Rising Star

. . .

Harvard Business School recognizes just two kinds of professional success: academic and administrative. The first kind is more common than the second kind, being the key measure for promotion in the institution. But the second kind is more highly prized because it is an important indicator of status and power. Every administrator first earns his academic stripes by winning a tenured spot on the faculty before being allowed to climb the administrative ladder of the school. Often the least academically-oriented opt for the administrative jobs, grateful for the chance to leave behind classes, students, scholarly publications, and working papers. With few exceptions, 221 once a professor is put into administration, he directs his full attention away from teaching and toward consulting, board memberships, and running the school. Joseph Bower was the exception.

One of Lawrence Fouraker's last acts as dean was to appoint Bower to teach in the prestigious Advanced Management Program (AMP). AMPs were serious, hardworking, Type-A personalities who spent all day in classes and all night on the phone running their divisions at a distance. To Bower they were a challenge. One afternoon in the spring of 1985, Bower led his AMP class through a case-study exercise about a Japanese textile company that, guessing that import quotas would be imposed, established a large market share by dumping production on the American market at prices below cost. Bower, setting up a straw man argument, asserted that for certain American industries such as automobile and refrigerator manufacturers, a similar strategy would also make sense.

If Ford or General Motors was to run plants continuously, Bower argued, and if it exported all the excess cars to countries like Australia or West Germany, those countries would eventually impose import quotas that would freeze all market shares at the levels that were established. With those high shares locked in, all foreign competition would be effectively squeezed out, leaving the American manufacturers with a foreign-car monopoly of the country they'd chosen to dump production on. It seemed like a plausible argument in favor of dumping, and the seventy-five executives in the class appeared convinced. Bower waited for someone to take him on in argument, but no one did.

"So you all think it's a good idea, right?" he grinned. "So, Peter, you think it's all right if, say, I'm the chairman of GM, I decide to unload my extra cars on Switzerland?"

"No, I don't think so," said the Swiss banker.

"You mean you won't help me finance the importation?"

"Yes, I would likely help you, but no, I don't think it is good for my country. There is a flaw in the reasoning."

Bower tried to look shocked. "And what is it?"

"If I am in the Swiss government, and I see your country promoting these things, I might decide to help the chocolate industry dump candy bars on the United States."

"Send them to me," quipped Bower.

"Your argument assumes that countries have just one response in cases of dumping, which is to establish quotas. They might find ways to retaliate instead."

"Look, when you're smart you don't have to be right all the time," said Bower with a flashing grin. "You just have to know when to bluff." That was precisely how Joseph Bower won people over—by both being smart and knowing when to bluff.

"I am not Marvin Bower's son," Joe Bower would tell people who drew that erroneous connection, thinking it would be a plausible explanation for his success at HBS. If Marvin Bower was a relative, so the thinking went, then obviously the McKinsey director's generosity would have influenced the administration to promote Joe Bower throughout his career. The coincidence in names was, from Joe Bower's point of view, unfortunate.

On IQ tests, Bower scored well into the "genius" category. He attended the prestigious Bronx High School of Science, and from there to Harvard, where he continued to stand out. He was a *summa cum laude* graduate in 1959, one of a handful of John Harvard Scholars. His interest in economics and banking led him to Harvard Business School's MBA program, where he received his MBA with high distinction as a Baker Scholar in 1961.

John K. Butters, Bower's finance professor, talked him into joining the doctoral program at Harvard when Bower complained that the entry-level banking positions open to him didn't seem challenging enough. Butters, who saw "brilliant" written all over Bower, seized the moment to enlist his student in his research in investment banking.

Almost as quickly, Bower received special permission to waive a series of required courses and skip the traditional year-long case-writing requirement. In fifteen months he completed his thesis, received his doctorate, and was appointed to the faculty in June 1963 at age twenty-three.

Realizing the limitations of working entirely at the business school, Bower accepted an invitation to become a member of Harvard's Institute of Politics in 1966, and he became a faculty member of the Kennedy School of Government in 1969. There Bower befriended Ford Foundation president McGeorge Bundy, who spent much of his time at Harvard looking for projects to fund. Bower, with his keen intelligence and wit, became Bundy's trusted adviser, and when Bundy decided to build a new International Institute of Applied Systems Analysis in Vienna in 1967, he called on Bower to help put the project together. The work added one more jewel to Bower's sparkling résumé, and the tenure committee unanimously elected him to a full professorship in 1972, the year the institute was founded.

As impressive scholastically as Bower was, socially he was even better. His impeccable manners and infallible timing put him on the invitation lists of every Boston society function. Dean Lawrence Fouraker adopted him for his natural fund-raising ability, promoted him to chairman of the general management department, and took him along to every significant alumni fund-raising event. Bower was the unofficial ambassador of goodwill from Harvard Business School's faculty and he did what came naturally to him, which was to be charming and witty, erudite and sophisticated, and fast on the draw.

At a 1978 HBS Business Statesman dinner at the Beverly Wilshire Hotel in Los Angeles, Bower and Fouraker represented the school. Peter Peterson, chairman of Lehman Brothers, who delivered the keynote address, turned to Dean Fouraker on the podium and asked jokingly how many award dinners he attended annually. Bower, sitting in the seat next to Fouraker, retorted, "Just the free ones." That was the reason Fouraker wanted him along.

By 1979, Joseph Bower was ready to become the next dean of Harvard Business School. Fouraker had groomed him, introduced him to the right people, made sure he knew the system, and had told him that when he retired he would recommend him to the university president to succeed him. When Fouraker was rudely displaced from his post, he dragged a surprised Bower with him, and for the first time in his career Bower was a member of the unfavored party.

The experience awakened him to two important lessons: first, that in order to become dean he would have to work inside the official organization rather than outside as an adviser or ambassador; and second, that the real power in the organization came from directing a steady stream of attention inward from outside sources. Dean John McArthur had built his power base internally by working in the administration as an associate dean of MBA affairs, as well as externally by doing outside consulting work and joining several boards of directors.

Bower, who was surprised at Fouraker's dismissal, was even more surprised at McArthur's appointment until he realized that McArthur, in his own way, had been cleverer than he. Derek Bok's decision to remove Fouraker formed a vacuum that could only be filled by someone influential in external corporate circles who also had solid administrative experience. McArthur, unlike Bower, had systematically made himself the only viable successor for the job. Bower, with his extensive network of alumni contacts, Kennedy School contacts, and social contacts, had never built a franchise at Harvard or in the marketplace.

Unlike many of his colleagues in the AMP, Bower neither needed nor wanted midlevel management contacts to help find consulting work. But AMPs could be useful in other ways besides being ready sources of consulting work. They were often conduits to companies' executive levels and were potential channels for a Harvard Business School researcher to get in to do interviews for scholarly research, something Bower decided in 1980 to do. His AMP classes provided him with the easy access he needed to get started.

As professors George Lodge and Bruce Scott began to put together their seventy-fifth anniversary conference on United States competitiveness in the world economy, Joe Bower decided to hop on the competitive-strategy band-wagon. Bower's contribution to the conference was published in 1984 just weeks after the publication of his own book on business and government. Eighteen months later, another book appeared, which was based on his study of the petrochemical industry.

Bower had applied his awesome talents to pure academic research for the first time in his career, and made the job look easy. The general opinion among his colleagues was that Bower, who was intelligent, articulate, and intensely bright, was destined for higher office, either in Washington or in a top position at Harvard. In five years he had put together an impressive list of accomplishments that was unmatched even by aggressive tenure-track associate professors. When the job of senior associate dean for external relations (the second highest at the school) came open in September 1985, John McArthur gave it to Bower.

Talk about filling the position with someone less able, but more pliant, than Bower had circulated throughout the dean's office for several weeks. Bower would clearly challenge McArthur's domination of the school's policies, and would very likely outshine his boss. But other pressures prevailed when McArthur's alumni advisory group, including Marvin Bower and Albert Gordon, all wanted Bower. Gordon was the most blunt in expressing the reasons for selecting him: "If you choose someone else, John, you'll lose the support of the alumni, and if that happens, you're through."

In the months following his appointment, Bower began

to reshape the position of external relations dean. The heretofore ceremonial position—as liaison between alumni, corporations, government, and Harvard Business School— began to take on teeth. The social functions of the job, which mainly required attending meetings of alumni, took up less of his time than had been the case with earlier deans. Bower exuded charisma and made an immediate impact on an alumni meeting just by being there. He didn't need to make impassioned pleas for money; instead he talked about the growth of strategic business-government interaction, or the role of managers in international competition, and his audience watched, listened, and opened their corporate bank accounts to him in tribute to his brilliance.

Even as Bower raised money to fund new programs at Harvard, he was traveling continuously and making new contacts. With Michael Porter, he attended a meeting of the Strategic Management Society in Barcelona, Spain. From there, he visited eight alumni council meetings on both sides of the Atlantic, landing finally in Washington, D.C., where he selected 5 of the business school's 350 alumni in the federal government to meet with. And as Bower made his rounds at the State Department, the Department of Treasury, the Office of Management and Budget, and the U.S. Navy, he listened. He began to understand clearly that Washington was influenced by perception as much as by fact. If Harvard Business School was perceived as the center of practical economic and business research, and could enhance its reputation for applying useful decision-making tools to bear on gritty problems of regulation and allocation, government leaders would turn more often to HBS for guidance and help. When he asked how government officials' perceptions were influenced, the same answer came back five times: The media made the difference.

Bower wondered whether real power actually did rest in the hands of the media, a little-understood entity from the school's point of view. He realized that one of the im-

plicit assumptions in the school's approach to fund-raising, recruiting, and promotion was that the press would
print or report exactly what the school wanted, and that
HBS could control the agenda. Now he challenged that
assumption. What if the media had more control than they
were given credit for? That question, only an untested
hypothesis at that point, might lead to interesting consequences. Perhaps there were cogent reasons for cultivat-
ing good relations with the press. In any case, it was an
issue worth investigating.

In January 1986, Bower hit on the idea of bringing the
press into Harvard Business School for a closer inspec-
tion. Working with the chairman of the editorial board of
the *Harvard Business Review*, he set up four different panel
discussions in March and April 1986 for thirteen journal-
ists from national and international print and broadcast
business media, with each discussion to be carefully
structured and videotaped. On the theme of how the daily
press covered business news, editors and reporters from
The Wall Street Journal, *The New York Times*, the *Economist*, the *MacNeil/Lehrer Newshour*, and nine others, discussed their philosophies of reporting, and techniques of
news gathering, in the basement of Cumnock Hall. Tapes
of the sessions were later played back and analyzed by
Bower in the privacy of his office.

At the same time, a day-long seminar for twenty senior
editors from print and TV was organized by Bower, the
difference in this session being that Bower would personally interact with the participants. He would bring them
onto his territory, place them in a totally controlled environment, and scientifically analyze their thinking. Part
of the plan, of course, was that the trappings of academia
would present a safe backdrop against which the men and
women of the press would instinctively take on the role
of students.

Stephen B. Shepard, editor-in-chief of *Business Week*,
saw in the seminar and panel discussions a unique opportunity to get inside the school to do a full feature ar-

ticle on how the school operated. He commissioned Louis Harris & Associates to survey 488 senior executives to get their opinions on business-management education in general, and Harvard Business School specifically. Then he chose Judith Dobryzinski, associate editor, to attend Joseph Bower's seminar, and he personally attended a panel discussion with Walter Kiechel III of *Fortune* and Laura Landro of *The Wall Street Journal*. Finally, he selected three *Business Week* staff members to cover the school, and management education, in-depth, for a cover story that appeared March 24, 1986.

In the end Bower was well satisfied with the results. Although he did not anticipate that the school, and Dean McArthur, would make the cover of *Business Week*, he had expected a lot of reporters and editors to write about their experiences at Harvard; it was their natural inclination to write about places they had been. The *Business Week* article, which could have been very damaging, focused entirely on MBA students, hardly mentioning executive-education programs, industry and corporate research, or alumni associations. Bower's calculated risk had paid off. If the editors and reporters came away thinking they had gotten an "inside" look at HBS, so much the better. The fact was that he had learned a great deal more about them than they had about Harvard Business School.

PART IV

PERSONAL
WEALTH

• • •

CHAPTER 15

Making It
to the Top

• • •

THE WEALTHIEST PROFESSOR

If there had ever been any doubt whether personal wealth was a factor in considering the appointment of a nonacademic to the faculty of Harvard Business School, it was resolved once and for all in September 1981, when the school appointed William J. Poorvu to become adjunct professor of business administration, the first one in the seventy-three-year history of HBS. Two months earlier, Poorvu had cashed out of the most lucrative television-station sale in the history of broadcasting when Metromedia, Inc., headed by the media tycoon John Kluge, 233

purchased WCVB-TV in Needham, Massachusetts, from
Boston Broadcasters, Inc. (BBI), for $220 million. Poorvu,
BBI's treasurer and largest individual stockholder with
6.57 percent ownership, realized a $14.4 million profit from
the sale, which helped to give him celebrity status on the
campus of Harvard Business School.

The sale made the front pages of Boston's newspapers
and publicized the little-known fact that the wealthiest
person at Harvard Business School was a lowly part-time
lecturer, a revelation that boggled the minds of students,
staff, and faculty. Had he wanted to, Poorvu could have
comfortably retired, but he chose instead to continue to
teach real estate classes to MBA students. For the regular
faculty, his decision to stay and accept a promotion to
adjunct professor lent persuasive evidence to the widely
held opinion that Harvard Business School was a magnet
for the rich and powerful. By admitting him to their club,
it somehow made them feel that they were members of
his club.

Some concluded that, like a lottery winner, he should
have taken the money and run, but they were the ones
who didn't know William Poorvu. Money held no fasci-
nation for him, because he had always had all that he
ever needed to live comfortably on. Fourteen million dollars in cash was a nice realized gain from an investment
of less than $100,000, but he compared his good fortune
with someone who had been smart enough to buy Haloid
Corporation shares a few years before the company became Xerox. It was just a speculative venture anyway for
him, since real estate was his chosen profession.

Going into real estate had made him the black sheep of
his MBA class at Harvard, because developing property
had always been looked upon as somehow illegitimate by
the school, like gambling or smuggling. The desire to see
those perceptions changed, to validate the career decision he had made in 1958, was why he had returned to
Harvard Business School to teach. He would prove that
it could be equally as demanding as management con-

sulting, manufacturing, or investment banking, and that he was just as qualified to operate in the major leagues of dealmaking as his classmates at Dillon Read & Company.

Poorvu grew up in a suburb of Boston, descended from three generations of real estate professionals. His father and grandfather had acquired large parcels of Boston and Cambridge commercial real estate at bargain prices as early as 1909, and had placed them in a trust for the benefit of future generations. There had never been any question from the time he was born that William would one day carry on the management of that portfolio. He studied English literature at Yale and, although he had early aspirations of going into the publishing business, he entered his family's real estate development firm on graduating from Harvard Business School in 1958.

The opportunity to branch into non–real estate ventures opened up to him in August 1962, when the Federal Communications Commission (FCC) publicly invited local Boston citizen groups to apply for the license to operate a VHF television station. The station was then owned by WHDH, Inc., which also owned radio stations and newspapers in Boston, and for twelve years the company had successfully defended itself against charges by the FCC of monopolizing Boston's media market. But a new, antitrust-minded FCC board decided in 1962 to put WHDH's television license up for open bids to the applicants who would demonstrate their commitment to serve the public interest, and a scramble ensued to line up as many prominent Bostonians as possible on newly organized media corporation boards.

As the invited guest of family friends, Poorvu attended an incorporation meeting in September 1962 at the Locke-Ober café in Boston, where thirty people had gathered to found Boston Broadcasters, Inc. Sitting at the meeting as the youngest member, surrounded by men two and three times his age, he quietly listened to the strategy the group worked out to win the license: They would design an innovative schedule that would broadcast more local television than any station in the country, and they would operate the station around the clock as a special service to local communities. Since they were short on experience in running a TV station, they would hire the best managers they could find, and plow all profits back into the station so that they could afford to pay higher salaries. Their real strength before the FCC board, however, would be in the diversity of their group: Leo L. Beranek, a Harvard Business School Advanced Management Program graduate and noted acoustics physicist; Oscar Handlin, Pulitzer Prize winner and professor of history at Harvard; Matthew Brown, special justice of the Boston municipal court; C. Charles Marran, president of Spence Shoe Corporation; Dr. John Knowles, director of the Harvard-affiliated Massachusetts General Hospital; attorney Nathan H. David, former assistant general counsel at the FCC; and William Poorvu, a Harvard MBA real estate developer. The "Founding Fathers," as they were later to be called, raised $200,000 for what was a ten-year legal battle before the FCC.

The group's attorney, Nathan David, who had extensive experience with the FCC, had warned them that the whole process would take years, and would require patience and persistence if the license was to be wrested from its current owner. David donated his professional time to represent BBI in lieu of cash payment for his shares of the company's stock, but the others all put in their own money, $10 for each of the remaining nineteen thousand shares. Poorvu, who was elected corporate treasurer because of his finance training at Harvard Business School, bought the maximum allotment of one thousand.

It was a long shot at best, like betting on a team to win the World Series in the next decade. BBI's competition was formidable, the wealthy and prestigious cream of Boston's social register, including Cabots, Choates, Winslows, Halls, and Hendersons. But BBI had the advantage of brain power; they were scrappy intellectuals who were totally unafraid of becoming embroiled in a messy legal battle, and they were smart enough to put together a package of management and programming innovations that would appeal to the FCC.

Poorvu's contribution to the proposal was to set a cap on the number of shares that could be owned by any individual. Since the FCC wanted local ownership, BBI would permit hundreds of local citizens to own shares, as well as the station's management, reporters, and news anchors. In the final analysis it was this egalitarian ownership structure that convinced the FCC to award BBI the license in an unprecedented decision in 1969. It was, however, only after the U.S. Supreme Court upheld that ruling three years later that BBI was able to take control of the license and begin broadcasting, by which time Poorvu had become the company's largest stockholder. On the night of March 19, 1972, the television transmitter was turned on, and Poorvu's shares instantly became worth $2.5 million.

He later justified his accumulation of shares by saying that the FCC and court rulings could have just as easily gone the other way, and that his $90,000 investment in 8,111 shares could have been worthless. But that was not an entirely accurate depiction of the circumstances; Poorvu had reason to believe early on that Nathan David, because of his prior association with the FCC, knew what was required to get the license. He also noted that David himself was buying shares when he could get them.

During the 1960s and early 1970s, real estate development and land speculation occupied the majority of Poorvu's time as he worked to increase his family's holdings and to make significant additions to the changing skylines of Boston and Cambridge. He joint-ventured a $5 million construction project to build a new six-story office/retail complex a block from Harvard Yard, and gradually moved up into real estate deals worth $30 million and $40 million. His work brought him into contact with architects and planners, some of whom, like himself, had Harvard credentials, and in 1973 he was asked by a faculty member at Harvard's Graduate School of Design to be a guest lecturer, a job he found much to his liking.

He was an intellectual in a business dominated by men who had little formal education. Few great thinkers occupied the ranks of real estate developers. They were men who fretted over plumbing fixtures, cursed suppliers for making late deliveries of building materials, and spent their money lavishly, when they had it, in Las Vegas. Poorvu was different; he was articulate, well educated, and restrained. He was an executive-entrepreneur rather than a garish developer. Developers were an opportunistic group of individuals who, when allowed to build twenty-five thousand square feet of space, would find a way to squeeze in an extra five thousand square feet.

Moving closer professionally to Harvard was an intelligent decision. Not only did it distance him from run-of-the-mill developers, but it also gave him a chance to change the image of the profession of being an exemplary role model. Students looked at him and saw themselves in ten or twenty years, and thought of real estate in the same way they thought of management consulting or corporate work.

Harvard Business School didn't have a real estate course, per se, so Poorvu offered to start one. With the aid of some former classmates who were on the faculty of the business school, he convinced the administration that he was capable of teaching a new course called Real Property Asset Management, a title that carried with it the substantial nature of the topic.

During the 1970s, real estate markets in the United States boomed, attracting a number of New York financial-service companies to enter the field. Students who would never have considered a course in property management suddenly came to Poorvu's course in droves, which surprised everyone but Poorvu. It was thought to be an easy second-year elective, but it enticed many outstanding students, several of whom decided to enter the profession based on that brief exposure. Trammell Crow, a Dallas real estate tycoon, learning of the interest generated by Poorvu's classes, decided that Harvard MBAs were underpriced commodities, and he began to hire several each year as $12,000-per-year* commissioned sales consultants, the entry-level job for prospective developers.

Poorvu discovered other opportunities outside the classrooms of Harvard Business School to work with the Harvard MBA students at his disposal. He started annual projects called Field Studies in Real Property, which were independently arranged, for-credit courses in which three or four members of a class formed a team to prospect in the real estate development market.

The field studies were hands-on training at its best, where students who excelled in Poorvu's theoretical course were permitted to apply their academic skills to buying and managing tangible property in the Boston area. As an incentive to his classes, Poorvu invited in a member of a previous field-study group, like the student who had invested $5,000 of his own money in a warehouse development as part of a project, and in only eighteen months had cashed out his share for $300,000. That session, given early in the course to standing-room-only crowds, motivated his students as nothing else could. He was the guru of a philosophy that extolled the virtues of getting rich quick in real estate, and he found receptive disciples in Harvard MBA students.

While he spent an increasing amount of his spare time writing cases, teaching classes, and supervising student projects, Poorvu was, nevertheless, only a lecturer, who had very little chance of becoming a professor. From Harvard's point of view there was no reason to promote him, since he seemed quite content to work on academic

---

*By 1987, Trammell Crow Companies raised the starting base salary for entry-level Harvard MBAs to $18,000, not including sales commissions.

pursuits for the sheer satisfaction it gave him. The popularity of his courses was, in many ways, a fortuitous circumstance, since it took pressure off other faculty to come up with interesting second-year electives. They could pay Poorvu a researcher's salary of $30,000, and get the work of two full professors out of him.

That condescending attitude toward him changed entirely in 1981, when Metromedia, Inc., purchased BBI's television license and property. Many people in the HBS administration knew that Poorvu owned extensive real estate holdings, including a movie theater and an office building in Harvard Square, and that he managed a family real estate portfolio. But all that was viewed as illiquid. He was a paper millionaire, the worst kind, the ones who are chronically short of cash. But then it became public that he had $14.5 million in hard currency, and his cover was completely blown. Questions began to be raised about potential competition for his services. What if the Sloan school of management at MIT, which was starting a new real estate center, or another prestigious business school, offered him a tenured professorship? It was unlikely that he would accept it, but there was no reason to tempt fate. So a new title was invented, "adjunct professor," which signified his status as a member in good standing of the faculty, but did not antagonize the eighty-five full professors who had come up the academic route.

The sudden windfall of cash from the sale of WCVB-TV had little effect on Poorvu's life-style, since most of it was used to buy more real estate. But even if he was blasé about his new wealth, Harvard Business School was not. After taxes, the net gain on the transaction was $10 million, which was a lot of money by anyone's standards. Having that much of it around, even if it wasn't in HBS accounts, gave a certain sense of security. It would be there if it was needed, and as long as he remained on the faculty, the school could keep an eye on it.

What began as an experiment in hiring Poorvu to teach

a single real estate course, became in 1981 a new track for entrepreneurs to reach the level of professor at the school. Where previously the only way to that top rung had been through a precise, orderly progression through postgraduate work and two junior grades of professor, now there was a new way: from MBA, to entrepreneur, to lecturer, and finally to adjunct professor. Those who were interested need only apply, and there were plenty who did, the most conspicuous of whom was H. Irving Grousbeck. Grousbeck was an MBA, class of 1960, who had co-founded Continental Cable Vision, Inc., in 1964, and who, in 1983, after seventeen years in the company, was looking for new challenges as a teacher at HBS. He was an entrepreneur and a multimillionaire, both of which were required credentials for the job, and he was hired instantly to be a lecturer. If, by 1989, he had successfully acquitted himself in his job of helping teach Professor Stevenson's course in entrepreneurial management, he too would be offered an adjunct professorship.

The ancillary benefits that an entrepreneur-turned-Harvard-Business-School-professor could realize were only just beginning to be apparent to Poorvu in 1986. He had fully expected that offers to work on bigger and more interesting real estate ventures would come his way now that he wore the cloak of Harvard respectability, and they did. He expanded his interests into Texas and Florida real estate markets, where he developed side by side with America's largest developers. His close association with Harvard MBA students also won him the friendship of Trammell Crow, whose company had developed more commercial Texas real estate than any other firm. Crow invited Poorvu to join the board of Trammell Crow Realty Investors, a group that raised several billion dollars for large-scale development projects. From Crow's point of view, the benefits to having a Harvard professor on the board were numerous; not only was Poorvu uniquely qualified to judge the abilities of the MBA students he'd taught, information he would gladly pass along to Trammell Crow, but he was solidly Harvard, a member of the faculty, and therefore substantial.

Inevitably, in 1982, Poorvu was asked by his class secretary, Peter Strauss, to be a class of 1958 reunion co-chairman with Andrew Hall, first vice-president of Drexel Burnham Lambert Group. It was not an unpleasant job, raising $1.3 million from his classmates, but it was obvious to him and others that he was given the honor because of his own well-publicized wealth, and because of the expectation that he would share some of it, rather than because of any ability to solicit money. That's why Andrew Hall was co-chairman; he did that sort of thing for a living.

The money that was raised from that two-year-long effort became the endowment for a Class of 1958 Chair of Business Administration. In making the presentation of the gift in October 1983, the reunion chairmen Hall, Strauss, and Poorvu stipulated on behalf of the class that the chair be filled by someone from outside the business school. They wanted a business executive who would bring real-world experience to the school, rather than yet another academic to add to an already full roster. Ultimately, Dean John McArthur settled on Andrall Pearson, MBA '47, president and chief operating officer of Pepsico, Inc., to fill the class chair.

THE BANKERS' CONSULTANT

If Professor Samuel Hayes III avoided fraternizing with investment bankers, his former teacher in the commercial-banking side of the finance department did not. Charles Williams built a thriving consulting business with every major New York bank, and sat on the boards of more than a dozen corporations.

Williams was born in 1917, the son of a banker in West Virginia who was nearly bankrupted by the Great Depression. Williams helped support his family during that time by working on a construction crew in Romney, West Virginia, doing menial labor, scrubbing plaster off of bricks and carrying water. It was then, surrounded by men of inferior social standing, and degraded into doing back-breaking work, that Williams vowed to never again be poor. His goal was to make enough money to buy himself bankers' suits and bankers' respectability, and he succeeded beyond his expectations.

Sports and scholarship were his tickets out of West Virginia and he applied himself to excelling at every high school sport. He was admitted to Washington and Lee University in Lexington, Virginia, on a full scholarship and graduated in three years with Phi Beta Kappa honors. After traveling to Europe in 1937 on money he had saved for three years, he attended the MBA program at Harvard Business School and received his degree in 1939. Before taking a job with Manufacturers Trust Company in New York, he toured Europe again, where he at once felt comfortable with the prospect of working in the European office of a major bank. His ambition was not realized, however, as war interrupted his plans. Enlisting in the navy in 1941 as an ensign in the Naval Supply Corps School, he returned to Harvard Business School, where the program was held, as a teacher. By 1947, after two tours of active duty, his ambitions of becoming a banker were tempered by his experience with the profession. Academics had certain advantages over the business world. For one thing, it would give him broader experience, and for another, it would allow him to work as a consultant on the side. He joined the business-school faculty upon being decommissioned, and earned his doctorate in 1951.

Williams was a gifted and enthusiastic teacher whose passion for his subject encouraged hundreds of the six thousand MBA students he taught to enter the profession of banking. Thomas Theobald, vice-chairman of Citicorp/Citibank, credited Williams with giving him his start in commercial banking, as did Richard Thomas, president of the First National Bank of Chicago. Other students included Charles Pistor, Jr., chairman and chief executive officer of RepublicBank Dallas, and Richard Jenrette, chairman of Donaldson, Lufkin & Jenrette.

Contacts came easily to Williams, as the field was wide open. In 1965, he decided to direct more of his time to putting on seminars for bankers, and to that end formed Charles M. Williams & Associates, a company that sheltered seminar and consulting income under a separate corporate name. Seminar fees ranged from $5,000 to $20,000, depending on the number of bankers in attendance. His client list was strictly blue-chip: Bank of America, Citibank, Morgan Guaranty, Chase Manhattan, Chemical Bank, New York Trust, The World Bank, Bank of Boston, and dozens of others.

He discovered that his former students, both MBAs and senior managers from executive programs, provided some of the best contacts in the industry. Thomas Theobald, then a rapidly rising executive at Citicorp/Citibank, helped Williams establish a management seminar for some of Citibank's senior executives, and years later Williams repaid the favor by using his personal influence with Lawrence Fouraker, then dean of Harvard Business School and a member of Citicorp/Citibank's board of directors, to get Theobald elected to the board.

Other friendships with former students were beneficial to both Williams and Harvard Business School. C. D. Spangler, Jr., whose father built the C. D. Spangler Construction Company in North Carolina, became chief operating officer of the Bank of North Carolina, where his father, C. D. Spangler, Sr., was the major stockholder. When the Bank of North Carolina experienced problems in the mid-seventies, Williams provided timely advice, and in the process earned Spangler's undying gratitude. Later, when the bank returned to financial health, Spangler donated more than $100,000 to the school's annual fund drives. Williams, who had been a director of Hammermill Paper Company since 1967, was heartened by Spangler's generosity, and recommended him for membership to the board of Hammermill.

Williams retired in June 1986, at age sixty-nine, after thirty-nine years of work at HBS, to devote his full energy to his second career, professional board member. In addition to his membership on Hammermill's board, he also sat on the boards of Sonat Corporation, Merrill Lynch Institutional Fund, U.S. Leasing International, National Life Insurance of Vermont, and Southern Natural Gas Company. Working as a professional director, he earned the equivalent of his annual salary at Harvard, and by the time of his retirement Williams had become very wealthy indeed.

CHAPTER 16

Industrial
Espionage

• • •

Harvard Business School offers just one MBA course in business ethics, a second-year elective called Ethical Aspects of Corporate Policy. In 1987, even after several HBS alumni pleaded guilty to insider trading on Wall Street, the course attracted just sixty students out of the eight hundred who were eligible to sign up. Few professors were willing to discuss whether they believed the school's ethics training was adequate. "Whether it's because the school doesn't want to bring it up, or because people don't want to spend their time talking about it, I don't know," said one second-year student. Indeed, it was a very sensitive subject around HBS.

The ethical standards of Harvard Business School's professors first came into question following publication of a September 1982 *Fortune* article entitled "Industrial Espionage at the Harvard B-School." In it, the magazine documented examples of espionage by teams of first-year MBA students that competed with each other in simulated computer games. The object was for students to come up with corporate strategies to gain market share and increase profits against competition from their classmates' companies. Each team's decisions were programmed into a computer model that factored in variables such as general economic conditions and the competitors' moves, and arrived at decisions on how each company (team) fared against the others.

According to the game rules, each team was to have its own secret password that permitted members to program their decisions into the computer. But halfway through the game in 1982, one of the teams discovered the password of one of its competitors and began to sabotage the competitor's corporate strategy.

Fortune, which had already highlighted Harvard president Derek Bok's admonishing the school three years earlier to put more emphasis on business ethics, ran the bold headline THE BUSINESS SCHOOL DOESN'T SEEM TO HAVE FIGURED OUT WHERE ETHICS FIT IN over the story, which explained how several students complained to the administration that their professors implicitly encouraged espionage activities, and turned a deaf ear to their calls for tighter monitoring and ethics training. "We felt let down," said one. "My question was, if there was nothing on the line here and they did this, what would they do when there was money riding on it?" another MBA student said.

Professor James L. Heskett, associate dean for the MBA program, said he was unperturbed by the story, which stated that the MBA students had taken a harder proethics stance than the faculty. "Most of the faculty wouldn't have raised an eyebrow at the way the instructor handled it," he said. (The instructor assessed damages against the team that was caught.) "They would have seen an educational opportunity and taken it." According to Heskett, there was no official faculty position on business ethics, and he added that what came up was a real-world problem that each student would have to deal with when he or she became a member of the business community.

That was precisely the wrong public response for him to make at that point, because it came on the heels of a second message from President Derek Bok to Dean McArthur to demonstrate some support for his 1979 report. The *Fortune* article seemed to prove that nothing was being done at HBS about ethics, and that the school McArthur took over from Lawrence Fouraker had made no progress in the two and a half years since the Bok report. McArthur realized that he was on a collision course with the president, so he did the one thing that he felt would keep their relationship on solid footing: He asked Professor Heskett to step down in favor of Professor Thomas Piper as the associate dean in charge of the MBA program.

James Heskett wasn't disturbed by the prospect of leaving the job of associate dean behind him, a thankless position that wasn't worth the aggravation it had caused him. He was looking ahead to doing more consulting anyway, and three years in administration was about all he wanted to take. As a self-made man, he had learned to rely on himself, and his goal was to return to a profitable business career.

He grew up near Cedar Falls, Iowa, where he played the saxophone in his high school band and was talented enough to join a jazz band afterward that toured the Midwest. By saving money that he earned as a musician, he was able to support himself through Iowa State Teachers College, after which his plans to start in business were put on hold by his being conscripted. A friend in the army who shared Heskett's interest in business convinced him to apply to and attend the Stanford business school, where he stayed after graduation to get a Ph.D.

in 1960. In 1965, he was already a tenured associate professor at Ohio State when he was invited to visit Harvard, and by 1969 he was promoted to the rank of full professor at Harvard Business School.

After his rapid fall from grace in 1982, Heskett returned to the campus of Harvard Business School in late 1984 a new man. In the interim, the ethics issue had blown over, and he had all but been forgotten as the person who had unwisely stepped in the middle of the fire and gotten burned. John McArthur made good on his promise to him to pave the way for a comfortable return to academic life, and waved through his budget request to film a documentary on the Italian knitwear company Benetton that winter for two weeks in Treviso, Italy. McArthur even approved the unusual request of allowing Heskett's wife to accompany him as co-producer on the film. The fifteen-minute film was completed and edited in mid-1985, and members of the Benetton family were invited to Harvard Business School to watch the case taught and film shown to MBA classes.

Upon his return to full-time research in 1985, Heskett experienced a professional rebirth as he left the field of logistics behind and branched out into the more expansive area of studying service companies, which, broadly defined, included Benetton. It was a strategic move designed to improve his private consulting business, and he attempted to make a name for himself by taking on such well-known public figures as Lee Iacocca, chairman of Chrysler Corporation, in a spirited debate over the service industry. Responding to Iacocca's remark that America "can't afford to become a nation of video arcades, drive-in banks, and McDonald's hamburger stands," Heskett wrote in his new book, *Managing in the Service Economy*, "This attitude suggests a lack of understanding of the significance of the service economy and of the nature of the market for its services." Unfortunately for him, the debate never got going, because Iacocca refused to pick up the challenge to defend himself.

His primary agenda in changing his research interests from business logistics to the service industry was to capitalize on a new stock index he had invented called "The Cambridge Service Index," which plotted the market behavior of thirty service firms listed on the New York Stock Exchange. He called it the new "measure of the productivity of America," and quickly stated at the same time that he had no personal stake in any of the thirty companies he had selected. It was to be a new kind of Dow-Jones index, except that his was better, invented apparently for no other reason than that he wanted to draw attention to the importance of service-industry companies to the American economy. In fact, he was a small investor in the stock market with ambitions of becoming a bigger investor by being among the first to identify and capitalize upon trends in the service-industry sector.

Heskett's interest in the stock market led him to discover a rapidly growing electronic-information-system company called CompuServe, which was a division of H&R Block, Inc., an income-tax preparation company. In early 1985, CompuServe was the leader of a handful of firms that were entering the new market to provide on-line electronic trading capabilities for owners and personal computers. Through a dedicated brokerage firm, CompuServe customers were to have an ability to buy and sell securities directly, get minute-by-minute stock quotes, index prices, and analysts' reports, and speculate in commodities and options, all without having to talk with a broker. As Heskett saw it, computerized investing networks such as CompuServe's were the wave of the future in financial services, and an area he believed he could rapidly become a leading expert in, making money both as a consultant and as a speculator. Also, he hoped that CompuServe would be the first to pick up his "Cambridge Service Index," if he offered the company the right incentive. So he contacted CompuServe's chairman, Jeffrey M. Wilkins, to gain his reaction to having a case written about his company.

The thirty-nine-year-old Wilkins didn't really want another case written about CompuServe. The Stanford business school, which had published fewer than four hundred full-length case studies in its history, had done two major studies of CompuServe in the late 1970s, just before the company was bought out by H&R Block. Wilkins sent copies of the two Stanford cases to Heskett, who never read them and sent them back saying that his Harvard case series would be measurably superior to Stanford's, without justifying his reasons for believing that to be so. It never occurred to Wilkins that Heskett might have anything other than a scholarly interest in his company, which finally led him to allow the Harvard professor to do a Harvard case and have access to his staff and to the company's confidential industry reports.

Shortly after Jeffrey Wilkins invited James Heskett to CompuServe headquarters in Columbus, Ohio, serious disagreements arose between Wilkins and H&R Block chairman Henry Bloch, apparently over Wilkins's performance as the chairman and chief executive of the company. Their dispute centered around Wilkins's demand to Bloch that he be allowed to buy shares in CompuServe, which he and his father founded in 1969 with $1.15 million in venture-capital money, but then sold in 1980 to Bloch for $23 million and a seat on H&R Block's board of directors. Wilkins was angered by Henry Bloch's refusal to listen to his proposals to change the ownership structure, and their dispute spilled over into heated boardroom debates that extended over several months.

Henry Bloch decided that to end the matter he would have to fire Wilkins from CompuServe, but not before he had retained two independent management-consulting firms to study the division and recommend Wilkins's termination. Their job had been to give evidence to the other H&R Block board members that Wilkins had become disruptive to the organization, with the result that earnings would soon suffer and morale would slump. Bloch's plan was to come up with concrete evidence so overwhelming that the board, with one exception, would vote to remove Wilkins, without having to blame it on a personality clash between the two chairmen. Over Wilkins's strong protest, two consulting teams converged on his company with letters of authorization from Henry Bloch, and both wrote unequivocal reports stating that Wilkins had to go.

On Friday, April 26, 1985, Bloch fired Wilkins as chairman of CompuServe and immediately appointed a successor. Wilkins, who had sensed the impending actions of Henry Bloch, had called together several of his top executives to plan a strategy to deal with the aftermath of his forced leaving. They had decided that if they, the most valuable executives of the company, all followed Wilkins out the door, then Bloch would be pressured into coming around to give the concessions that Wilkins wanted. In any case, Wilkins intended to keep his seat on the board of directors of H&R Block. But when the firing occurred, only one of Wilkins's top lieutenants left with him, while the others vowed to stay on and fight the system from within.

During the next two days, Wilkins met with executives of Banc One of Columbus, Ohio, who agreed to help finance a takeover bid by Wilkins of CompuServe, and on Monday, April 29, Wilkins sent the board of H&R Block a $72.5 million offer for the division. Henry Bloch, of course, was completely unwilling to consider the offer, or any offer, from Jeffrey Wilkins, a man whom he had grown to dislike enormously. H&R Block's directors rejected the offer on May 8, but gratefully accepted Wilkins's resignation from their board.

After Wilkins's stormy exit, Professor Heskett's status at CompuServe was in limbo, and several people there expected that he would be the next person to be invited to leave by chairman Henry Bloch. Their assumption was that since he was there on the invitation of Wilkins, presumably they were friendly toward one another, and Bloch was not someone who wanted friends of Wilkins's around. Much to their surprise, however, a month later Bloch not only gave his approval for the CompuServe case series to be written, but he also approved a paid management-training seminar, to be conducted by Heskett that summer for the executives of CompuServe.

In the intervening period, Professor Heskett ably positioned himself as an ally to both sides. Jeffrey Wilkins, who was just starting to build a new competing company directly down the street from his former employer, agreed to assist Heskett for the benefit of the HBS case study. Henry Bloch, for his part, lent the full assistance of CompuServe's new management team. Indeed, each man knew of the other's support, and the result of this cooperation between the rivals was a richly detailed CompuServe case series.

Neither Bloch nor Wilkins got any direct benefits for telling his story and opening his files to the Harvard professor. James Heskett, however, walking the fine line between them as an "impartial observer," became a clear winner. Based on his success at teaching the seven-part series to the top management that summer, he was invited back to CompuServe to give regular paid training seminars.

CHAPTER 17

Company
Manners

• • •

While C. Roland Christensen did more than anyone at Harvard Business School to influence the development and production of cases, it was John A. Quelch who raised Christensen's methods to new heights. Quelch was a man who seemed always to be in motion—teaching, consulting, meeting with students, talking with colleagues. Despite a full-time schedule at Harvard, he consulted extensively, and earned a considerable amount from this work.

Quelch grew up in a working-class suburb of London and attended public schools, where he was an outstanding student. His top score on Oxford's admission test gained him entry to Oxford's Exeter College on a partial scholarship. Years later, whenever complacency or self-satisfaction set in, he would recall the sacrifices he made to attend Oxford, and the financial strain he had endured. It was that spur, to lift himself out of bad financial straits, that convinced him to apply to Wharton in 1972 to study for an MBA. The idea of going to America, and leaving behind his unsatisfactory living circumstances in London, set him to work even harder. Luck played no part in his successful academic career, he often said. He had simply hustled his way to a position of security.

In his second year at Wharton came several job offers, including one from Procter & Gamble for a product-management position in Venezuela, but an influential marketing professor convinced him that his long-range prospects would improve if he pursued a doctorate before going into industry. Remaining a student for three or four more years disheartened him, until he learned that he could consult while working for his degree. So he applied to Harvard Business School, the top school in the country, and did part-time work for the Marketing Science Institute.

For three years, he labored mightily to impress the school's faculty with his industry, but failed to get appointed to the business school's faculty. In an emotionally wrenching meeting with his mentor, Professor Stephen Greyser, Quelch was informed that the marketing department had found him a job teaching on the faculty of the University of Western Ontario that was his, if he wanted it. If he accepted, he would be assured that Harvard would not forget him when a job came open. But it was still the low point of his career.

Two years later Professor Ted Levitt did call to offer him a job, which he accepted, but by then his attitude toward Harvard had changed. He decided that it was foolish to build a single career plan based on that school alone, and that it was safer to build a base of consulting

contacts in case his academic career did not work out.
Even if all did go according to plan, and if he was offered
a tenured job at Harvard, he would by then be able to
have both the professorship and his own consulting firm.

No one worked harder than Quelch. He traveled to Cincinnati, New York, Los Angeles, and Minneapolis all within
a single week. He worked in airports, on planes, in taxis,
sometimes for twenty hours straight.

In choosing a researcher to work under him, Quelch
looked for contacts alone. The more corporate contacts
an associate brought with him, the easier was the job of
gaining access to companies. In his second-floor office of
Fowler Hall, sitting behind a large desk piled high with
complimentary product samples from Procter & Gamble,
Quelch took pains each semester to interview all 170 of
his MBA students from two sections, and every manager
in his executive-education sections. In MBA students he
was looking for connections, those whose families owned
manufacturing companies, or who had several years of
experience at a consumer-products company. The interviews were done under the pretext of getting to know his
classes better, but those who fit the profile were offered
one-year research jobs under him. Most saw it as a dead
end and politely turned him down. It was a formality,
anyway, since he rarely expected any of them to actually
accept. Once offered a job, he hoped, they would naturally be more inclined to share their contacts with him.
A good crop of MBA students could yield five solid leads,
of which three resulted in cases, and two in consulting work.

Quelch's most lucrative work was done with a major
consumer-products company, where he spent more time
than anywhere, except for Harvard. For several years, he
was solely responsible for the executive-management
training in that firm's consumer-products division, where
he used Harvard case materials to lead staff-training sessions. The contact had been worth more than $150,000
per year and was the single most important factor in his

being able to build a new house in Lincoln, Massachusetts. Unfortunately for Quelch, the senior executive who had hired him to work in the training program was purged from the company in a management shakeup in early 1984, and the program was eliminated.

"Dan Pates,"* a Harvard MBA graduate with two years of work experience at the company Quelch was forced out of, and family connections at the company's executive level, suddenly shot to the top of his student contact list. Not only was Pates well connected, but he was sharp, articulate, and could write well. In a full-court press lasting three months, Quelch recruited Pates to spend a year as his research associate. Pates had never felt enthusiastic about doing research, but Quelch sold him on the benefits: all expenses paid, exposure to numerous business situations, and an easy Harvard credential on his résumé. Even if the salary of $35,000 was below what Baker Scholars got, he could augment it by doing an occasional consulting report for him. With Pates's help, Quelch's company connection was reestablished, and the faucet began to pour money again.

THE "COMPANY CONTACT REGISTER"

For companies that were willing to pay the price, there were sound reasons for hiring Harvard Business School professors, none of which had anything to do with analytical skills or brain power. Because the school used the case system of teaching and research, most faculty members had contacts with a least a dozen companies, and for some that number exceeded fifty, which meant that these professors were in a unique position to broker information. Even when one professor did not have direct knowledge about a specific company or industry, it was easy enough to find a colleague at HBS who did. The confidential "Company Contact Register" circulated

* Name changed on request.

throughout the school, the information for which was collected and tabulated by the school's research division.

The "Company Contact Register" worked in two separate ways. First, when someone wanted to avoid accidentally stepping onto another's territory, using the register was the safest method for making certain that no one else was in the corporation at that time, although it was not foolproof because not everyone was willing to divulge his contacts. Some companies, like IBM and Hewlett-Packard, had four or more professors inside at once, which meant that anyone who wanted to initiate new research or consulting was obliged to contact each professor before he proceeded.

The primary function of the register, however, was to facilitate the exchange of intercorporate information. If someone at HBS was working for a competitor, there was no mechanism by which a company could check, and no one dared insult the integrity of a professor by asking. The register did not circulate outside the school.

Few companies ever turned down requests from professors to do research. To them, it was unimaginable that the sensitive information they gave to HBS for free, in the name of academic research, was being sold to their nearest competitors for large sums of money, although that was sometimes the case. The fact was that some faculty considered brokering information to be part of the job. They bristled at suggestions that what they did was clearly unethical, even if it was not illegal. Ethics was something that was taught, not practiced, and that pertained to a narrow segment of the business population, not to them. "MBAs find ethics Mickey Mouse," said Dean John McArthur. So, too, did some of the faculty.

SHARK REPELLENT

The months of March and April 1986 were good ones for Walter J. Salmon, the Stanley Roth, Sr., Professor of Retailing at Harvard Business School. Another fine academic year was drawing rapidly to a close, bringing with it the promise of a busy and productive summer. This would then be followed in the fall by a much-coveted teaching assignment in the Advanced Management Program. It has been the long-awaited promotion he was expecting, the move at age fifty-six from teaching MBA students and two-week summer seminars in retailing to working with serious business executives from around the world. That was the way to finish out a career; he would be there until 1995, whereupon he would become a professor emeritus and a professional board member.

Already he had planted the seeds for his eventual second career by joining the boards of Carter Hawley Hale, Zayre Corporation, Holiday Inns, Inc., Stride-Rite, Inc., and others. Indeed, since being selected to occupy the new Stanley Roth, Sr., Chair of Retailing in 1980, he had devoted an increasing amount of time to corporate rather than academic work.

The first hint that something was wrong came in early-May 1986, when Salmon noticed that John Quelch, the associate professor of marketing whose office was across the hall from his on the second floor of Fowler Hall, began keeping his door closed more frequently than he had ever done before. Previously, the door had only been closed when Quelch was in conference with someone; even when he was talking on the telephone, the door was wide open. Now he made it a habit to close the door as soon as he walked in the room. It was a small point, perhaps insignificant, but it had not been Quelch's style. Quelch was an extroverted Englishman whose voice had been known to carry three or four floors when he became angered. But lately he hadn't been himself; he was calm and quiet.

Quelch's demeanor had started to change several months earlier at about the same time that Salmon told him to write teaching notes for cases on Stride-Rite, Inc., a Cambridge-based shoe manufacturer whose board Salmon had joined in 1972, and about which Salmon had written three case studies from 1978 to 1981. Quelch, who taught the consumer-marketing course each year to two sections of MBA students, had used the case more than anyone else, and was therefore the logical person to write the teaching note, a ten- to fifteen-page description of how the case should be taught, what the correct approach to analyzing the situations should be, and the key points that were to be brought out in the class discussion.

In many ways the teaching note was similar to the executive summary in a management-consulting report since it gave a thumbnail analysis of the key issues relevant to management of the corporation being studied, and recommended solutions to remedy whatever problems were identified. In writing a teaching note, professors often went beyond the limited scope of the case to analyze industry data and trends, as well as to examine private information from inside corporate reports and competitors' data, and sometimes talked with corporate executives to see how they viewed the case problems. Professors often made a pretense of stating that case studies were complete unto themselves and that no additional research was necessary to analyze a case. In writing a teaching note, rarely did anyone rely solely on the written case as the basis for the "official" analysis. Insights gleaned from classroom, library, and field research became part of the note, a document that was occasionally passed along to senior executives of the company that had permitted HBS access to write a case. Salmon, who knew Quelch's abilities as a very well-paid and well-traveled business consultant, wanted the benefit of his analysis not only for future generations of professors who would teach the Stride-Rite cases, but also for his own use as a member of Stride-Rite's board of directors. As an associate professor whose candidacy for full professor would be before the tenure committee in 1988, Quelch was in no position to argue with Salmon's request, for to do so would have meant instant academic suicide. Salmon was his boss, something he never forgot, so he accepted the assignment with the proper amount of courteousness, promising to do a splendid job of the teaching notes for what was obviously a landmark case series in consumer marketing.

As it turned out, having to do background research on Stride-Rite came along at a propitious moment, since, shortly after he began work on the assignment, Quelch was approached to join the board of directors of the American subsidiary of Reebok International Ltd., a British manufacturer of running shoes. Reebok, which was riding the crest of a new American fad in upscale, soft-leather aerobic shoes, had watched sales of its athletic footwear skyrocket from $1.3 million in 1981 to $307 million in 1985. The company was looking to expand into other sportswear, much as Nike had, by entering into agreements with licensees who would produce Reebok clothing bearing the company's distinctive logo, a British flag. Paul Fireman, president and chief executive of Reebok, had concluded that Quelch would be a good addition to the board; not only was he a Britisher who had consumer-marketing training at Harvard Business School, but he was also knowledgeable about licensing agreements, having written articles on the subject for the *Harvard Business Review*. Fireman offered him the job, and Quelch accepted without giving it much further thought. It was due recognition of his marketing skills that Reebok, a company rapidly becoming the nation's top athletic-shoe manufacturer, should want him as a director, and it seemed to be a lucky coincidence that at the same time he was busy studying the footwear industry as part of Walter Salmon's directive to write teaching notes for the Stride-Rite cases. He had a very real sense about how the industry was changing and what the new trends and opportunities would be, ideas that were solidified when he met with the board for the first time in early 1986 in Avon, Massachusetts.

In March, Fireman convened the board to discuss plans for the company to expand into other market segments beyond the adult women's aerobic-shoe sector. The consensus of the board was that children's athletic shoes would be the next market to experience rapid growth, a consequence of the growing number of children and teen-agers in the United States. It was decided that Reebok should enter the market as quickly as possible; if there was any delay, the window of opportunity might close when others jumped in ahead and gained an insurmountable lead in market share. The speed with which they needed to act ruled out the possibility of Reebok building its own manufacturing facilities, since tooling and staffing would require three to five years, an unacceptably long preproduction time.

As it was, the company had already lost millions of dollars in potential sales by being unable to deliver enough shoes to retail shops in 1983 and 1984, and had been forced to rely on new Asian manufacturers to meet the demand. The new Asian manufacturing plants, many of which had lower quality-control standards than was acceptable, had turned out hundreds of thousands of pairs of shoes that looked sturdy but didn't hold up under heavy use. Women whom Reebok had encouraged into the market in the first place began looking for other manufacturers for their second pair of aerobic shoes, a marketing analysis that brought home the need to manufacture a superior product to begin with, rather than risk losing brand loyalty and trying to catch up with the market once the products caught on. The company had very nearly missed the wave of aerobic-shoe mania in 1984 because of its limited production facilities, and it was this they wanted to avoid in bringing out a new line of children's shoes. This time they would do the intelligent thing; they would buy an established children's shoe manufacturer rather than try to develop production expertise and capacity in-house. Stride-Rite seemed like a good candidate for acquisition, and the board meeting adjourned with the chairman, Fireman, agreeing to talk with the company's investment-banking firm about making an unsolicited offer.

The quandary created for Quelch was in gauging the degree of his responsibility to Professor Salmon concerning the takeover offer. He had already decided that he would remain on Reebok's board, since it would have served no higher purpose to abandon such a fine opportunity to direct the growth of a successful British company. But he was justifiably concerned about the effect such a takeover would have on his relationship with his boss.

Stride-Rite was takeover-proof, a fact that was obvious even before Reebok made its offer to Stride-Rite's board in June 1986. The company had adopted, long before, methods to ward off unwanted suitors. There would be no prolonged proxy battles or attempts to seize control of the company by buying large blocks of shares. It would have been futile anyway, since Stride-Rite held the balance of control in friendly hands, and such actions would have been both counterproductive and expensive.

Stride-Rite's board rejected Reebok's offer. The company was not looking to be taken over, and the board would not entertain any offers, even Reebok's, which was $7 per share higher than what the stock was then trading for.

Reebok, unaccustomed to dealing in the world of corporate deal-making, had not come up with a counter proposal. The offer was hastily withdrawn, and the determination was made to explore other expansion opportunities. It was the gentlemanly thing to do, a decision that met with the approval of every member of the board.

Epilogue

• • •

Those who care about the course of business scholarship in this country agree, I believe, that keeping Harvard Business School strong is in all our best interests. Since 1908 the school has led the way in bringing vital new ideas to the marketplace; its philosophy and outlook on society have indirectly affected us all. That it is the top business school in the country remains an indisputable fact.

Harvard Business School holds a special place of trust and respect in the world of business. It is more than just a school. For millions of people worldwide it is a symbol of the best that American business scholarship has to offer. Whether justifiably or not, we hold its professors and administrators to a higher standard than we do their counterparts at other schools.

As Harvard Business School drives forward into the 1990s, I see five areas where greater attention ought to be focused. First, and most important, the school must make more than token efforts to remedy the overwhelming male domination at the institution.

Second, the teaching of entrepreneurship ought to be given greater emphasis in the classroom and in research than it currently receives. On this same point, George Gilder wrote in his book *The Spirit of Enterprise,* "Business schools . . . tend to turn out cynical manipulators of existing values rather than entrepreneurial creators of value. Leading professors at Harvard Business School, preoccupied by the calculable maximization of self-interest, show a pathetic incapacity to comprehend the essence of entrepreneurship."

Third, the case system needs to be managed better and monitored more closely, perhaps by an independent agency within the university. Whether it is admitted or not, abuses of the system are commonplace and result in negligible research activities and the squandering of millions of dollars.

Fourth, outside business consulting and directorships ought to be strictly limited so that they do not interfere with the school's business. Difficulties arise when professors become consultants first and scholars second. Along this same line, complete and up-to-date lists of outside interests ought to be publicly available to anyone who requests them. Companies contacted for research ought to be able to determine for themselves whether the confidential information they give HBS professors is well placed.

Finally, if Harvard Business School is to retain its place of preeminence, it must make the teaching of MBA students its top priority. The declining interest by professors in the MBA program has led students there to see the school as a two-year obstacle course, the winners of which get high-paying jobs.

COMPANY CONTACT REGISTER
BY FACULTY

Note: The following are excerpts from the "Company Contact Register." The complete register, which is updated monthly, is more than a hundred pages long and does not show the director (D) designation. The professors who appear in this list were chosen either because they are included in this book or because they are well known in the business community.

Faculty/Company	Location	Date Registered
Andrews, Kenneth		
Duriron, Inc.	Dayton, OH	10/82
Xerox Corp.	Stamford, CT	2/84
Bower, Joseph		
ATO Chemique	Paris, France	12/83
British Petroleum	London, England	12/83
Digital Equipment	Maynard, MA	10/79
Dow Chemical	Midland, MI	12/83
General Motors	Washington, D.C.	2/82
Marks & Spencer	London, England	12/74
Montedison	Italy	12/83
Prime Computer	Framingham, MA	12/81
Brown, Milton		
Allied Stores Corp.	New York, NY	6/68
Bank of America	San Francisco, CA	10/85
Dunkin' Donuts	Randolph, MA	8/76
Merchants Bank	Indianapolis, IN	10/85
Christensen, C. Roland		
*(D) Arthur D. Little	Cambridge, MA	10/84
(D) Bank of New England	Boston, MA	9/69
(D) Cabot Corp.	Boston, MA	9/69
Nike	Portland, OR	5/82
(D) Cooper Industries	Houston, TX	†
(D) N.E. Merchants Bank	Boston, MA	
Goldberg, Ray		
Advanced Genetics	Greenwich, CT	9/82
Archer Daniels	Decatur, IL	11/81

* (D) = Director

† Where no date is listed, author has gotten information from annual reports.

Faculty/Company	Location	Date Registered
China Ministry	Beijing, China	11/81
Coca-Cola	Atlanta, GA	10/84
General Cinema Bev.	Chestnut Hill, MA	11/81
General Mills FDN	Minneapolis, MN	5/84
Heublein, Inc.	Hartford, CT	9/69
Nestle Co.	White Plains, NY	11/73
Pepsico, Inc.	Purchase, NY	10/84
RCA Industries	Hillsdale, MI	11/76
Stop & Shop Co.	Boston, MA	10/81
Levitt, Theodore		
(D) AM International	Chicago, IL	10/84
American Express	New York, NY	5/81
(D) Consolidated Nat.		
Gas	Pittsburgh, PA	5/82
(D) GCA Corp.	Bedford, MA	11/73
(D) Gintel Fund, Inc.	Greenwich, CT	5/81
Rothschild, Inc.	New York, NY	10/85
(D) Saatschi & Saatschi	London, England	1/83
Lodge, George C.		
Merrill Lynch	New York, NY	11/85
McArthur, John H.		
(D) Chase Manhattan	New York, NY	
(D) Rohm & Haas	Philadelphia, PA	
(D) People Express	Newark, NJ	
Pearson, Andrall		
(D) Pepsico	Purchase, NY	
(D) May Dept. Stores	New York, NY	
(D) Hasbro, Inc.	Greenwich, CT	11/85
Piper, Thomas		
(D) Bay Banks	Boston, MA	10/81
(D) Genrad	Waltham, MA	5/84
(D) Marriott Corp.	Washington, D.C.	10/81
Porter, Michael		
Arthur Anderson	Chicago, IL	10/83
Aspen Ski Corp	Aspen, CO	10/83
Canon, Inc.	Tokyo, Japan	9/82
Hyundai Co.	Seoul, Korea	10/84
NEC Corp.	Tokyo, Japan	10/85
Sulzer Brothers	Winterthur, Switzerland	10/83
Tatung Co.	Taipei, Taiwan	10/84

Faculty/Company	Location	Date Registered
Quelch, John		
General Foods	White Plains, NY	10/84
General Mills	Minneapolis, MN	10/85
General Motors AC	Detroit, MI	10/84
(D) Reebok International	Chicago, IL	10/85
United Airlines	Avon, MA	1/86
Salmon, Walter J.		
(D) Carter Hawley Hale	Los Angeles, CA	
(D) Zayre Corp.	Framingham, MA	
(D) Holiday Inns	Memphis, TN	
(D) Quaker Oats	Chicago, IL	
(D) Stride-Rite	Cambridge, MA	
Salter, Malcolm		
Chrysler Motors	Detroit, MI	10/81
Ford Motor Co.	Detroit, MI	10/81
General Motors	Detroit, MI	10/81
United Auto Workers	Detroit, MI	10/81
Volkswagen, AG	Wolfsburg, West Germany	11/84
Moet-Hennessy	Paris, France	11/84
Stevenson, Howard H.		
Hillerich & Bradsby	Louisville, KY	8/84

Glossary of Selected Terms

• • •

Below are a few of the more common words, expressions, and abbreviations used at Harvard Business School.

The Business Game: A first-year MBA students' computer exercise in which teams of students manage competing (simulated) corporations in a game of strategy.

The Coop: Short for the Harvard Cooperative Society, a Harvard-run department store in Harvard Square. The Coop also maintains a smaller department store on the campus of the business school, where students from all programs buy their books.

ISMPs: ISMPs are students from the International Senior Managers Program, which is designed to give top executives from other countries an eight-week course in HBS management techniques.

JD/MBA Program: Harvard Business School and Harvard Law School offer a joint degree program that allows candidates admitted separately to both institutions to complete the two degree programs in a total of four years rather than in the customary five. JD/MBA candidates tend to be outstanding students.

OPMs: OPMs are students enrolled in a nine-week program for Owners and Presidents of smaller businesses (called Owner/President Management Program), which takes place in three three-week units spread out over several years. Other, shorter programs (besides the PMD, ISMP, and OPM) are offered for specialized executives in such areas as information services, agribusiness, and retailing, among others. Because they typically last less than two weeks, these programs do not have the same esprit de corps as the longer programs.

Organizational Behavior: Organizational Behavior, or "O.B.," as it is sometimes known, is the study of human behavior in organizations. At Harvard Business School, O.B. is a required course in the first-year MBA program.

PMDs: We have already run into MBAs, DBAs, and AMPs, but there are hundreds of other students who take courses in programs offered by the school. The second-largest program for executive training is the Program for Management Development (PMD), which was started in 1960 for "exceptionally promising younger managers." It is a twelve-week course that is similar in content to that offered to AMPs. The AMPs, however, are more likely to be taught by senior faculty.

Power and Influence: A very popular second-year MBA elective course that was taught for many years by professors John Kotter and Jack Gabarro. A book based on the course was published by Kotter.

Sections: Each incoming class of 780 MBA students is divided into nine different sections (*A* through *I*) of roughly 86 students each. Sections, which are determined prior to the first day of class, follow the same mandatory program of eleven first-year courses. The students meet together for a total of thirteen classes weekly, each of which is eighty minutes in length. Because they spend a great deal of time with each other, both in and out of class, section mates often develop strong friendships that continue after graduation.

Notes

• • •

This book is based on the author's personal experiences as a staff member of the Harvard Business School, and on discussions with faculty, staff, and administrative officials both during and after his tenure at HBS. The following is a list of the published sources that corroborate or amplify material used in the book, and of events at which the author was present.

Prologue
The Competitive Advantage

Page 12   Porter quote: "Harvard Professor and NFL Trial," *The New York Times*, May 28, 1986, p. 21.

Monitor Company statistics: Ibid., p. 21.

Chapter 1
The Organization

Page 17 Two token links: Melvin Copeland, *And Mark an Era* (Boston: Little, Brown and Company, 1958), p. 74.

18 Income figures: *Harvard University Fact Book,* June 30, 1985.

20 Lorsch quote: Author was present at AMP class in 1985.

21 Baker Scholar salaries: Job postings, Cole Room, Baker Library.

22 Case studies: *MBA Admission Catalog 1987,* p. 7.

23 Pearson quote: Author was present at MBA class in 1985.

28 "Substantive contribution" tenure criteria: Affadavit, *Jackson* v. *Harvard University,* U.S. District Court, Boston.

32–3 Gabarro quote: Author was present at DBA class session of "Teaching by the Case Method," fall 1984, conducted by Gabarro.

33 AMP statistics: *The Business of the Harvard Business School* (public relations material). Also: *HBS Bulletin,* February 1983, pp. 23–27.

Chapter 2
The Strategy Master

Page 35 Porter episode: Author was in Morgan Hall at the time, October 1984.

36–37 Background on Porter: *Course Development & Research Profile 1984,* pp. 104–5 and *CD & RP 1985,* pp. 112–13. Also, Walter Kiechel III, "Three Ways to Win," *Fortune,* October 19, 1981, p. 39; "Industry Competition Analyzed," *The New York Times,* January 2, 1981, p. D1.

44 Information gathering & data base: "Explorations: A Report from the HBS Division of Research," *HBS Bulletin,* January 1980, p. 4.

Chapter 3
The Success of a Strategy

Page 48 Jerusalem Institute: *HBS Bulletin,* November/December 1977, pp. 10–14.

49 Fouraker/Bok feud: Richard Norton Smith, *The*

Harvard Century (New York: Simon & Schuster, 1986), pp. 325–26.

52–54   Background on Derek Bok: Ibid., Chapter 8; *Harvard Magazine,* September/October 1986, pp. 203–7; "Bok to the Future," *Boston Magazine,* September 1986, pp. 138 ff.

55   Full text of the president's report: *Harvard Magazine,* May/June 1979, pp. 73–84.

55   Strategic misrepresentation: *The Wall Street Journal,* January 19, 1979, p. 1.

56   Full text of Fouraker letter: *HBS Bulletin,* March 1979, p. 2.

57   Bok quotes: *The New York Times,* April 30, 1979, p. 1.
Bok quote: *Fortune,* June 18, 1979, p. 54.

58   Heskett quote: "Harvard: a Real-Life Case Study," *The New York Times,* May 6, 1979, p. D1.
Stacking the task force with McKinsey men: *HBS Bulletin,* January/February 1980, p. 5. Also: *The New York Times,* January 28, 1980, p. D1.

59–61   Background on Marvin Bower: *HBS Bulletin,* February 1985, pp. 61 ff.; *HBS Bulletin,* September 1970, pp. 13–14; *HBS Bulletin,* July 1967, pp. 19–21.

61   Background on McKinsey: "McKinsey & Co. Learns Some Lessons of Its Own," *Business Week,* June 23, 1986, p. 108.
Footnote quotation: Ibid., p. 112.

63   Director of Communications quote: *The New York Times,* March 5, 1984, p. D1.

Chapter 4
Leave It to the Dean

Page 66   McArthur background: *The New York Times,* October 17, 1979, p. D1; *HBS Bulletin,* March/April 1973, p. 22; *HBS Bulletin,* November/December 1979, pp. 5–6; Susan Anderson, "Business Dean Sets New Harvard Style," *The New York Times,* October 6, 1980, p. D1.

67   McArthur hat story: Told by McArthur to meeting of researchers in July 1984 and on numerous other occasions.

69 Donation statistics: *Harvard Business School Individual Contributors, 1984–85.*

70–71 Awards information: *HBS Course Development & Research Profile 1984, 1985, 1986.*

72 Bower/Gordon Award: *HBS Bulletin,* April 1982, pp. 34–35.

Chapter 5
An Introduction to Power and Influence

Page 77 Dean's private accounts: *HBS Bulletin,* September 1981, p. 12.

78 Statistics on cases: *Directory of Harvard Business School Cases and Related Course Materials 1985–86.*

79 Shapiro quotes: Benson Shapiro, "Case Studies for Harvard Business School," (1-576-026) May 1982, copyright © 1975 President and Fellows of Harvard College.

Buzzell quote: "Alas, Poor Harvard," *New England Monthly,* May 1985, p. 76.

Endowed chairs statistics: *The Wall Street Journal,* November 11, 1986, p. 1.

80 ff. Daewoo/Chairman Kim visit: Author was present.

83 Goldstar/P. W. Suh visit: Author was present.

84 Employment statistics: *Harvard University Fact Book,* June 30, 1986.

Chapter 6
Personages of the Faculty

Page 87 Background on Stephen H. Fuller: *HBS Course Development & Research Profile 1986,* p. 13.

88 Henrietta Larson: *HBS Bulletin,* January 1961, p. 14.

88–89 Background on Regina Herzlinger and Robert Anthony: *HBS CD&RP 1986,* pp. 96–97; *HBS Bulletin,* June 1986, pp. 14–15; *HBS Bulletin,* February 1983, p. 72.

90 Jackson case: *Boston Magazine,* May 1985, p. 22; U.S. District Court for Massachusetts, Civil Action No: 84-4101-G.

Committee of 200: "HBS Hosts the Committee of 200," *HBS Bulletin,* June 1984, p. 28.

91–93 Rosabeth Moss Kanter: *Boston Globe,* December 20, 1985, p. 93; *U.S. News & World Report*, December 2, 1985, pp. 59–60; *Working Woman*, September 1986, pp. 60 ff.

93 McNair: F. J. Roethlisberger, *The Elusive Phenomena* (Boston: Division of Research, GSB, 1977), pp. 263, 282–84; *HBS Bulletin*, winter 1957.

93–94 Levitt quote: *HBS Bulletin*, December 1983, p. 96.

94 Background on Levitt: *Harvard Business Review*, July/August 1956, p. 7; *HBR*, September/October 1958.
Levitt quote: *HBR*, July/August 1956, p. 7.

95 Levitt quote: *HBS Bulletin*, December 1983, p. 96.
"Marketing Myopia" sales figures: *HBS Bulletin*, December 1983, p. 9.

96 Levitt quote: *HBS Bulletin*, October 1985, p. 7.
Background on Hayes: *HBS Bulletin*, June 1963, p. 8; *HBS Bulletin*, April 1985, p. 22.

99 Whitehead/Goldman, Sachs exchange: "A Fair Exchange," *HBS Bulletin*, April 1985, p. 40.
Background on Christensen: *HBS Course Development Research Profile 1984*, p. 60; *HBS CD&RP 1985*, p. 64; *HBS Bulletin*, June 1984, pp. 4–7.

Chapter 7
Communications and Public Relations

Page 104–5 Memorandum to HBS faculty and staff; from Tom Piper, September 6, 1985.

106 *Business* magazine: "HBS Attracts Interest of National and International Publications," *HBS Bulletin*, June 1986, p. 20.

108 Concentrations of alumni: *HBS Directory of Former Students, 1985–86.*

109–10 Background on Howard Stevenson: *HBS Bulletin*, February 1982, pp. 37–39; *HBS Course Development & Research Profile 1985*, p. 128.

110–11 Background on Lawrence Fouraker: *HBS Bulletin*, January 1970, p. 24.

112–14 Background on Fayez Sarofim & Arthur Rock: "Arthur Rock: The Best Long-Ball Hitter Around," *Time*, January 23, 1984, p. 55; *HBS Bulletin*, December 1981, pp. 26–27.

113 Cooper Industries information: Cooper Industries Proxy Statement 1982.

114 Naming the chair: *HBS Bulletin*, December 1981, p. 27.

115 Stevenson's entrepreneurship work: *HBS Bulletin*, June 1983, pp. 50–51; *HBS Bulletin*, April 1984, pp. 46–48.
Entrepreneurship findings: "Entrepreneurship: A Process of Creating Value," *HBS Bulletin*, February 1984, pp. 48–56.

116 Stevenson quote: "Wharton," *The New York Times Business World*, June 8, 1986, p. 104.

Chapter 8
Welcome to HBS, Professor Pearson

Page 117 Author was present at class sessions led by Pearson on April/May 1985.

119 Background on Andrall Pearson: *HBS Bulletin*, February 1985, pp. 69–73; Pepsico annual report, 1984.

120 Background on Donald Kendall: *Nation's Business*, May 1981, pp. 67 ff.

122 Pearson's salary statistics: Pepsico, Inc. proxy statements, 1968–1983.

123 NYC Harvard Club dinner: *HBS Bulletin*, July/August 1978, p. 14; *HBS Bulletin*, September/October 1979, pp. 78–79; *HBS Bulletin*, July/August 1980, pp. 91–92.

124 Background on Sculley: "Why Sculley Gave Up the Pepsi Challenge," *Business Week*, April 25, 1983, p. 28; *Fortune*, July 9, 1984, p. 183.

127 Pearson quote: *HBS Bulletin*, February 1985, p. 31.
Pearson's directorships: Pepsico, Inc., proxy statements, 1968–1983.

Chapter 9
The Industrial Bank of Japan Chair of Food Service

Page 131–33 Background on Kaneo Nakamura: *HBS Course Development & Research Profile 1985*, pp. 46–50.

134 IBJ & HBS developments: *HBS Bulletin*, October 1984, pp. 6 ff.

135 Background on endowed chairs: *HBS Bulletin*, September/October 1977, pp. 9–13.

Background on Tom Piper: *HBS Bulletin*, October 1984, pp. 6–7.

136 Marriott case study: *Marriott Corp.* (9-282-042).

137 Piper directorships: Marriott Corp., proxy statement, 1983.

Chapter 10
The Master Plan

Page 141 History of campus buildings: Melvin Copeland, *and Mark an Era* (Boston: Little, Brown, 1958), pp. 70–145.

143 Background on Moshe Safdie: *The Wall Street Journal*, August 28, 1985, p. 21.
Background on Coliseum Project: *The New York Times*, August 18, 1985, p. 25.

144 The master plan: *HBS Course Development and Research Profile 1986*, p. 23.
Baker Library parking lot: "New Campus Master Plan Developed," *HBS Bulletin*, June 1986, p. 28.

146 Background on Goldman, Sachs: Beth McGoldrick, "Inside the Goldman Sachs Culture," *Institutional Investor*, January 1984, pp. 53–67.

147 HBS-Goldman ties: *HBS Bulletin*, April 1985, p. 47.

147–48 Background on Sidney J. Weinberg: Alden Whitman, "Sidney J. Weinberg Dies at 77: 'Mr. Wall Street of Finance,'" *The New York Times*, July 26, 1968, p. 1; *HBS Bulletin*, September/October 1967, p. 15.

149 Whitehead/Weinberg alliance: Irwin Ross, "How Goldman Sachs Grew and Grew," *Fortune*, July 9, 1984, pp. 155 ff.

150 Whitehead faculty exchange: Deborah Blagg, "A Fair Exchange," *HBS Bulletin*, April 1985, p. 40.

151 Background on Richard Menschel and the class of 1959 gift: *HBS Bulletin*, October 1984, p. 66; *HBS Bulletin*, December 1984, p. 30.

153–54 Background on Bert W. Twaalfhoven: "Class of '54 Endows New Chair in Entrepreneurship," *HBS Bulletin*, April 1985, p. 11; *HBS Bulletin*, August 1983, Notes, p. 32.

Chapter 11
Doing Business with Harvard Business School

Page 167   Sumitomo/McKinsey consulting work: Nicholas D. Kristof, "Japanese Maverick Expands," *The New York Times*, August 7, 1986, p. D1.

167–168   Background on Matsushita: *HBS Bulletin*, February 1983, pp. 109–16.

169   Matsushita chair: "Matsushita Donates Chair," *HBS Bulletin*, December 1981, p. 8.
McKinsey/Bower–Harvard Business School relationship: "A Conceptual Architect," *HBS Bulletin*, July/August 1967, pp. 19–21.

171   Bain & Co. bonus system: "Harvard Tells a Recruiter What Just Won't Wash," *The New York Times*, September 21, 1980, p. C21.

172   Exploding fellowship program: *HBS Bulletin*, February 1985, pp. 59–64.

173   First Bower fellowship program: *HBS Bulletin*, November/December 1968, pp. 34–35.

174   Enlarged fellowship program: HBS News and Information Office press release, July 9, 1986.

175   Information on Associates: *HBS Bulletin*, September/October 1976, pp. 18–19.
Background on IBM/HBS relationship: Nancy O. Perry, "Managing the IS Power," *HBS Bulletin*, February 1986, pp. 40–47; Eddy Goldberg, "Harvard, IBM train MIS faculty," *Computerworld*, December 9, 1985, p. 2; "IBM's Watson Receives Business Statesman Award," *HBS Bulletin*, May/June 1964, p. 17.

176   Sales of equipment: "Anderson House: A Technological Renovation," *HBS Bulletin*, February 1986, p. 30.

177   PCs in the curriculum: James W. Kilman, Jr., "Taking Computers Personally," *HBS Bulletin*, October 1982, p. 15 (reprint of *Boston Globe* article).

178   Mandatory use of PCs: Garry Emmons, "Getting Personal," *HBS Bulletin*, December 1985, pp. 61–67.

179   Student quote: Ibid., p. 64.

180   Software program: Pamela Kruh, "HBS Publishes Case Software," *HBS Bulletin*, April 1985, p. 34.

181   Announcement of lap-top PCs: "New MBAs Will Use IBM Lap-top PCs," *HBS Bulletin*, August 1986, p. 13.

Use of lap-tops quote: *HBS Course Development & Research Profile 1986*, p. 21.

Chapter 12
The Global-Strategy Imitators

Page 186   Background on George Lodge: *HBS Bulletin*, July/August 1972, p. 28; *HBS Bulletin*, April 1982, pp. 177–85; *HBS Course Development & Research Profile 1985*, pp. 89–91; *HBS Bulletin*, April 1984, pp. 5–6.

186–87   Background on Henry Cabot Lodge: William J. Miller, *Henry Cabot Lodge: A Biography* (New York: James H. Heinemann, Inc., 1967); Karl Schriftgiesser, *The Gentleman from Massachusetts* (Boston: Little, Brown, 1944); H. C. Lodge, *The Storm Has Many Eyes* (New York: W. W. Norton, Inc., 1973).

188   Lodge's appointment to South Vietnam: David Halberstam, *The Best and the Brightest* (New York: Random House, 1972), p. 260.

189   George Lodge's experimental appointment: *HBS Bulletin*, April 1982, p. 179.

190   Background on Bruce Scott: *HBS Bulletin*, April 1982, pp. 99–105.

192   Scott-Lodge alliance: *Harvard Magazine*, November/December 1983, pp. 44–49; "Authors," *HBS Bulletin*, December 1984, p. 20.

193   Press briefings: *HBS Bulletin*, December 1984, p. 21.

194   Puncturing the campaign balloon: David Wessel, "Harvard Professors Market Their Belief That U.S. Is Losing Its Competitiveness," *The Wall Street Journal*, December 12, 1984, p. 24.

Chapter 13
Portfolio Management

Page 197   Background on General Cinema/Heublein lawsuit: A. Michael and I. Shaked, *Takeover Madness* (New York: John Wiley & Sons, 1986), pp.

32–38; *Boston Globe*, February 4, 1982, p. 23; *The Wall Street Journal*, February 22, 1982, p. 3.

198 Background on Richard A. Smith: "Like Father, Like Son," *Forbes*, April 15, 1968, p. 71; Paul B. Brown, "Technology Isn't Everything," *Forbes*, October 12, 1981, p. 55; *Business Week*, May 20, 1972, p. 31.

200 Background on Hugo Uyterhoeven: *HBS Bulletin*, May/June 1974, p. 14.

Background on Robert W. Ackerman: *HBS Bulletin*, December 1986, p. 16.

203 Interlocking directorships: See proxy statements for Heublein, Stanley Works, and General Cinema Corporation, 1982.

205–7 Background on Bendix: Michael and Shaked, pp. 13–30; Mary Cunningham, *Powerplay* (New York: Simon & Schuster, 1984); Peter Hartz, *Merger* (New York: Wm. Morrow & Co., 1985); Allan Sloan, *Three Plus One Equals Billions* (New York: Arbor House, 1983).

208 Classmate quote: *HBS Bulletin*, February 1983, Notes, p. 20.

General Cinema after Heublein: "Dick Smith's Midas Touch at General Cinema," *Business Week*, October 22, 1984, p. 70.

209 *Carter Hawley Hale* v. *The Limited: The New York Times*, April 4, 1984, p. D1; *The New York Times*, April 11, 1984, p. D1; *The New York Times*, April 17, 1984, p. D1.

Background on Philip Hawley: *HBS Bulletin*, September/October 1978, p. 8.

210 Background on Leslie Wexner: William Meyer, "Rag-Trade Revolutionary," *The New York Times*, June 8, 1986, pp. 41 ff.; "Parlaying Rags into Vast Riches," *Newsweek*, December 30, 1985, p. 30.

211 Background on Alfred Taubman: *Time*, June 27, 1983, p. 51; *The Wall Street Journal*, September 18, 1985, pp. 1 ff.

212 Taubman quote: *The New York Times Magazine*, June 8, 1986, p. 122.

213–14 Carter Hawley Hale board: CHH annual report and proxy, 1983–84.

215 Risk-free investment: *Business Week*, October 22,

1984, p. 74; "Carter Acts to Foil Bid by Limited," *The New York Times*, April 17, 1984, p. D1; "Varied Cast in Carter Hawley Struggle," *Boston Globe*, May 6, 1984, p. 85.

217 Smith quote: *Business Week*, October 22, 1984, p. 70.

218 CHH after the agreement: Roger Neal, "Phil Hawley's Last Chance," *Forbes*, January 28, 1985, p. 44.

Chapter 14
Professor Bower's Rising Star

Page 222–23 Classroom scene: Author was present in spring 1985.

223 ff. Background on Joseph Bower: *HBS Bulletin*, December 1985, p. 13; *HBS Bulletin*, October 1983, p. 63; *HBS Course Development & Research Profile 1986*, pp. 68–70; *HBS Bulletin*, December 1986, p. 14; *Contemporary Authors*, ed. Hal May, Volume 112 (Detroit, Michigan: Gale Research Co., 1985), p. 72.

228 Relations with the media: *HBS Bulletin*, December 1985, p. 18; "HBS Meets the Press," *HBS Bulletin*, June 1986, p. 86.

Chapter 15
Making It to the Top

Page 234–35 Background on Poorvu: *HBS Bulletin*, October 1983, p. 108; Monica Collins, "The Biggest TV Deal in History," Boston *Herald American*, July 23, 1981, p. 1; Jack Thomas, "The Sprouting of 45 Millionaires," *Boston Globe*, July 26, 1981, p. 1; Sterling Quinlan, *The Hundred Million Dollar Lunch* (Chicago: J. Philip O'Hara, Inc., 1974), pp. 135–99.

236 Background on BBI: "Back to the Court with WHDH-TV Case," *Broadcasting*, June 23, 1969, p. 39; "Multiple Ownerships Now Up for Grabs," *Broadcasting*, January 27, 1969, p. 25; "Metromedia," *Broadcasting*, July 27, 1981, p. 27.

237 Additional background on Poorvu: *HBS Course Development & Research Profile 1986*, pp. 118 ff.

239 Footnote: "Crow Bait," *The Wall Street Journal*, October 24, 1986, p. 31.

240   Background on real estate management course: *HBS Bulletin*, February 1984, pp. 81–92.

241   Background on Irving Grousbeck: "The Case for Entrepreneurship," *HBS Bulletin*, October 1985, p. 119.

242   Class of 1958 reunion: " '58 Looks at the Basics," *HBS Bulletin*, October 1983, pp. 72 ff.; *HBS Bulletin*, December 1983, p. 27.
      Background on Charles M. Williams: John March, "A Calculated Walk Down Wall Street," *HBS Bulletin*, December 1981, pp. 41 ff.; "Charles M. Williams Fund Announced," *HBS Bulletin*, April 1986.

245   Consulting/board memberships: See proxy statements (1960–1986), Sonat, U.S. Leasing International, Fort Dearborn, Merrill Lynch Institutional Fund, Hammermill Paper, Keystone Custodian Services, San Francisco Real Estate Investors.

Chapter 16
Industrial Espionage

Page 247   Ethics at HBS: Thomas Palmer, "Harvard MBAs Shrug Off the Scandal," *Boston Globe*, February 22, 1987, p. A9; David Nyhan, "B-School Not Bullish on Veritas," *Boston Sunday Globe*, February 22, 1987, p. A5.

248   *Fortune* article: Thomas Moore, "Industrial Espionage at the Harvard B-School," *Fortune*, September 6, 1982, pp. 70 ff.

249   Background on James Heskett: *HBS Course Development & Research Profile 1986*, pp. 100 ff.; *Contemporary Authors*, ed. Ann Evory and Linda Metager, New Revision Series, Volume 8 (Detroit, Michigan: Gale Research Co., 1983), pp. 245–46.

250   Videotaped case: See *Directory of HBS Cases and Related Course Materials, 1986–87*, p. 576.
      Book quote: J. L. Heskett, *Managing in the Service Economy* (Boston: HBS Press, 1986), p. 187.

251   Background on CompuServe: Carol Trune Thiel, "Using Computers to Connect with People," *Infosystems*, April 1984, p. 78.

252   Wilkins/Bloch dispute: David O. Tyson, "Block

Rejects Bid for CompuServe," *American Banker*, May 10, 1985, p. 2; Jonathan P. Hicks, "Offer to Buy Back H&R Block Unit," *The New York Times*, April 30, 1985, p. D5; " 'We're Not Selling,' says Henry Bloch," *Business Week*, May 13, 1985, p. 36; Norman Nicholson, "Scramble on the Screen," *Barron's*, April 29, 1985, p. 16.

Chapter 17
Company Manners

Page 255–56 Background on Quelch: *HBS Bulletin*, December 1984, pp. 10–12; *HBS Course Development & Research Profile 1986*, pp. 120 ff.; *HBS Bulletin*, October 1985, p. 32; *HBS Bulletin*, December 1983, p. 16.

259 McArthur quote: Susan Heller Anderson, "Business Dean Sets New Harvard Style," *The New York Times*, October 6, 1980, p. D2.

260 Background on Walter J. Salmon: "Roth Endowment Will Support Doctoral Program," *HBS Bulletin*, June 1984, p. 21; *HBS Bulletin*, June 1984, p. 43; Stride-Rite Corporation proxy statements, 1972–86.

262 Background on Reebok: Linda Watkins, "Reebok: Keeping a Name Hot Required More Than Aerobics," *The Wall Street Journal*, August 21, 1986, p. 32; *Women's Wear Daily*, May 20, 1985, p. 10; *Footwear News*, January 28, 1985, p. 40.

264 Quelch at Reebok: Reebok International, annual reports and proxy statements, 1985–86.

266 Gilder quotation: George Gilder, *The Spirit of Enterprise* (New York: Simon & Schuster, 1984), p. 147.

Acknowledgments

· · ·

I wish to thank several people whose help, support, and guidance were essential to the writing of this book:

Esther Newberg at International Creative Management; at William Morrow, Sherry Arden, Adrian Zackheim, Mary Ellen Curley, Amy Edelman, Thomas A. Bisdale, and Richard H. Sugarman.

I wish to thank those photographers who did allow me to purchase the rights to their work despite understandable misgivings.

Because of the sensitive positions held by many of the sources of this book, I will not acknowledge them individually. They know who they are, and I thank them.

My typist, Bettina Braun, always did first-rate work on short notice.

In addition, I would like to thank the following people, who, though they did not assist with this book, have helped in other ways: Sol Gittleman, Christine Vitins, Ulla Fontaine, A. O. Smith, Deval Patrick, Valerie Sonnier, Elli Crocker-Morse, and Dale DeLetis.

And finally, I would like to thank especially my family, for constant encouragement and support.

All errors of fact or judgment are exclusively my own.

J. PAUL MARK
Brookline, MA
June 1987

Index

• • •